Instructions for using AR

LET AUGMENTED REALITY CHANGE HOW YOU READ A BOOK

With your smartphone, iPad or tablet you can use the **Hasmark AR** app to invoke the augmented reality experience to literally read outside the book.

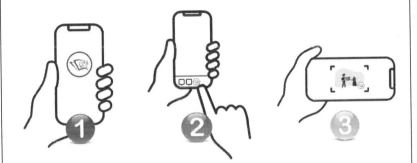

1. Download the **Hasmark app** from the **Apple App Store** or **Google Play**

2. Open and select the (vue) option

3. Point your lens at the full image with the and enjoy the augmented reality experience.

Go ahead and try it right now with the Hasmark Publishing International logo.

WITHOUT any
WARNING
CASUALTIES OF A CARIBBEAN VACATION

"Stefanie's story is filled with courage, adversity, and inspiration. Everyone would benefit from spending time with her on her unforgettable journey."

—**Amy Purdy,**
New York Times Best-Selling Author of
On my Own Two Feet, Motivational Speaker,
and Paralympic Athlete

"Wow! Such an unbelievable real-life story of what this beautiful, young lady had to endure after a dream vacation turned horrific. Stefanie tells her story with amazing raw honesty and grace, detailing the nightmare but more importantly her recovery. It is a riveting, emotional story that will leave you feeling nothing but truly inspired by her insurmountable strength and will to keep moving forward. It is an important must-read as Stefanie reminds us all that life can change in the matter of a second, but we must remain focused on how we react and move forward."

—Roseann Sdoia Materia,
Boston Marathon Survivor,
Author of *Perfect Strangers,* and
Motivational Speaker

WITHOUT *any*
WARNING

STEFANIE SCHAFFER

Hasmark
PUBLISHING
INTERNATIONAL

Editor: Harshita Sharma harshita@hasmarkpublishing.com
Cover Design: Anne Karklins anne@hasmarkpublishing.com
Book Design: Amit Dey amit@hasmarkpublishing.com

ISBN 13: 978-1-77482-131-2
ISBN 10: 1774821311

DEDICATION

This is for you, Mom! Because there would be no story worth sharing if it had not been for you. No words will ever be an adequate thank-you for all that you do, but this book will be as close as I can ever come.

And also, this is written for all of us, the ten passengers aboard that boat that day, whose lives were permanently changed in differing ways. My life today is a gift, granted only as a result from you all remaining strong, courageous, and uniquely brave beside me in those moments. So, I tell this story, the one we will never forget, for us.

CONTENTS

~ BEFORE ~

*I*t's Superbowl Sunday, usually a sort of holiday in our home, but in New England, if the Patriots aren't playing, does it even count? Okay, I know that it does, but my football knowledge consists only of knowing the words "Tom Brady" and "Touchdown!" But it's given us an excuse to get together, and the game plays quietly in the background as we all talk with the enthusiasm that comes when it's been too long since you've seen one another.

Since moving back home to Vermont, I've found that I, more often than not, spend my time with my mom and her friends, and I quietly laugh as I look around this scene that's grown so familiar. Twenty-two years old myself, sitting with my mom and Sheila, who's come to visit with her son and her husband, John. With glasses of red wine in hand, we three women chat as if we're all the same age. It's strangely comfortable.

A year ago, I would have been running out of the house to find the busiest bar nearby. Looking to spend the night with other twenty-something-year-olds, as I'd move too fast and spill my gin and tonics, clumsily maneuvering my way around the crowded bodies before me. This, this table with cheese and crackers, a lone glass of expensive wine to last the night, and talk of one another's lives, is quieter and slower, but more peaceful.

"How about Mexico?" The sound of my mom's question pulls me from my thoughts and back into the conversation.

It's been a long Vermont winter. One that was typical in its never-ending way. So, the decision we've just made, for this group of us to all go on vacation together, was an easy one to make. But now, the decision has been followed with a more difficult question to answer and a friendly, low-energy debate has ensued. The question is simple: Where should we go?

We debated traveling to Peru and hiking the famous Machu Pichu trail. We'd been captivated by the idea, thrilled by the challenge, and eager for the satisfaction of success. We'd even begun researching and planning every detail. But this research is where the plans took a turn. Photos of terrifyingly large spiders had appeared in online searches, and the possibility of one morning waking up beside one of these creatures had been enough for us to quickly toss the idea aside.

We discussed keeping the plans casual and visiting John and Sheila's lake house. But the location was still in a northern state, and the temptation of a destination with white-sand beaches was too much to resist. That idea, too, was forgotten.

A trip to Mexico though, feels like a chance to have the best of both options. It offers its own hiking trails—nowhere near as challenging as that infamous Peruvian trail—presents historical sites to visit like the Mayan ruins, and is sure in its promise of gorgeous beaches, drinks of tequila by the oceanside, and dips within the ocean waters as the sun shines from above with the intensity we crave. I begin to share my agreement.

"Look at this," Brooke, my little sister, says, joining the conversation.

Turning toward her, I see her with her hand held high and her iPhone on display. On its screen is a stereotypical image of vacation: a woman standing knee-deep in the ocean, her skin tanned and her smile wide. It takes a minute to notice the oddity within the frame—a pig swimming beside her.

"It's called Swimming Pig Island, in some place called Exuma, Bahamas."

Of course, I know of Nassau, Bahamas, but I've never heard of this place before. Somehow it feels more foreign and desolate, perhaps even more dangerous, given its attraction, than any other Bahamian location might feel. I smile and look back to my phone, ready to begin another new search. But the sound of conversation picks up around me, with an obvious touch of enthusiasm that's been missing, and I realize that the rest of the group seems far more hooked on this idea than I am.

"Let's go!" I hear someone declare.

Mom and Sheila are clearly intrigued, as I see them with a laptop propped before them. Possible flights to the Bahamian island are visible on its screen. I have to agree: my sister found a good photo. And I know that any vacation with an island destination should be seen as a dream. But for some unknown reason, a sense of dread consumes me as I watch these plans begin to come together.

I'm not someone who ever disagrees with a decision; instead, I am the kind of person who is always content to go along with the plans made by others. But this time, something is different. This time, the unfamiliar rejection is adamant and intense.

It tells me we must find somewhere else to go.

CHAPTER 1

The sun sneaks through my blinds, waking me up early this morning. Instinctively, I roll over, hoping to hold on to a few more precious moments of sleep. Something tells me I should be getting up, but I can't remember what it is. As I grab my phone from its charger, my tired eyes blink quickly, adjusting as I focus on the bright screen. I see the date and remember what today is. It's the day I should've been packed and ready to head to Boston's Logan Airport with the rest of my family. We have a dream vacation planned, and yet I've been procrastinating getting ready, having too much fun in this new home to ever be ready to leave. Groaning, I stand up, preparing to begin my least favorite task—packing—and I look around my tiny room, wondering what it is about this place that has me so hesitant to leave.

The floor is dusty from the recent move, with only a small patch of open space leaving a pathway to the door. The rest of the bedroom floor is taken up by the mere two items of furniture I have. My mattress lies tucked in the left corner, made up with silky blue sheets and a downy white comforter but directly on the hardwood flooring. The bed frame would have been much too challenging to bring up the narrow staircase leading to our apartment. A large wooden bureau takes up the opposite corner, and far too much space, but is necessary since the room has no closet or built-in storage for clothing or shoes. A single desktop mirror sits haphazardly next to my hair straightener and makeup bag, unzipped and overflowing from the night before, and the tapestry and string of lights pinned on the wall are the only clues that the room is actually inhabited.

This room is far different from any other room I have ever called my own, which are usually nicely decorated and overfilled with belongings, and yet this is where I have found myself the happiest, the most content with life, with no desire for anything to change.

Maybe my room should be more organized. Maybe my clothes should be taken out of the duffel bags I'd used to carry them upstairs, and I suppose a bed frame would help to pull the room together. But each day, I choose instead to go out on some type of adventure, exploring the hidden gems of the city with my new roommates, rather than spending the day decorating or organizing.

I'm now living in Burlington, Vermont, an eclectic little city about two hours away from my hometown. It's calm and safe, but also vibrant. It's energetic and youthful, with the well-respected college nearby and a renowned medical center as well that entices graduates to stay in place. I've moved here not only for the change in scenery, and not only because my longtime friends have welcomed me as their fourth roommate, but because this is where I am positioned to begin my final internship at the medical center. This is where my life outside of college is set to begin.

I've moved in recently and am in that transitional phase in which responsibilities and work shifts haven't yet begun and have taken advantage of this time, checking off the boxes on most of our summer to-do list. We've gone to the local beaches to lie out in the chilly Vermont summer sunshine, finding a rocky ledge large and flat enough for each of us to spread our towels out, as we play music through speakers and sip our drinks from the cans beside us. We've gone to wine tastings at the local winery, always buying a bottle to take home, and ending the days with planning where we would go on our first hikes and runs. As the evening sky arrives, music blasts through each room and we get ready once more, this time to return to the lively downtown streets filled with unique restaurants, bars, and an occasional food truck in the later hours.

It isn't this house that makes leaving here difficult. It's the life I see being created here that makes me stop to ask why I'm leaving. Will life still be this good when I return? It feels as though leaving will pop this bubble and life will go back to a duller reality.

But a one-week getaway couldn't really change anything, could it? Besides, not only am I about to spend my days on an island, in a rental home that looked as though it was picked from the pages of a travel magazine, but I'm being blessed with stress-free time to spend with my family and our friends. It's something that I know I don't want to miss out on or be left out of.

A text from my sister appears on my phone, asking if I'm on my way home. The message gets me moving a little faster, and as I see the tank tops and bathing suits piling in my bag, I finally begin to feel the excitement that I've been waiting for.

Realizing how late I really am, I don't stop to say goodbye to my roommates. As I swing open the door, bags in hand, I pause for only a second and yell a quick goodbye.

"Bye guys! See you in a week!" my voice rings through the air.

The door hangs open as I run down the stairs, and I hear the chorus of their goodbyes repeating back to me. Then the door slams shut.

I rush down the steps coming off the airplane with a spring in my step and the same excitement you might see in a college student at the start of spring break, forgetting about the tedious task ahead of going through customs. The airport is already filling with the heat of the sun, and the space gets stuffier with each new person who enters. I watch as the expression on each of our faces changes from excitement to frustration at the slow pace of things. It's as if we can all read each other's minds as we impatiently push closer inch by inch, daydreaming of the pools of water, sandy beaches, and fruity drinks that lie ahead.

Once we've proven ourselves to be simply innocent tourists, only here for a few stress-free days, we walk with our checked passports and approved belongings in hand through the open doors, taking our first steps into the vacation.

Sheila, my mom Stacey, and I sip cool beers, leaning against a tall picnic-style table and savoring the taste. Brooke—my thirteen-year-old sister—and Haiden sit just a few feet away, conversing in hushed tones, and John and my stepfather, Paul, are off getting two rental cars to take to the house where we'll be staying. We could've stayed with them while they did this, but a quiet bar was right next to the car rental area, already open in these early hours of the day, and it seemed the better choice to us. We'd stuck them with the tedious job and quickly snuck away.

The island is admittedly different from the image I had in my head, and I laugh as Paul pulls up in a beat-up minivan with the bumper hanging so low that it nearly scrapes against the ground, and John follows behind in another. It seems that this car was actually the best one to choose, as the lot is lined with nearly identical cars in nearly identical condition. But we pile in anyway, eager to stow our belongings and cool off at the beach.

Following the directions given to us by the car rental staff, someone who knew the location of the home we were heading for, our two cars drive off, following each other closely. The road twists and turns, and with nothing else around, it feels as though we might be lost. As the road transitions to an uphill climb, we realize that our battered cars are actually crawling up a steep driveway, and then before us appears the impressive beach house we'll be calling home for the next week. We rush into the house and drop our bags in a room, claiming it for our own and acting as though we'll be able to stay here forever.

It's a dream house, with a long wooden back deck overlooking the ocean, so close you feel as though if you reached out, your fingertips just might skim the water. The kitchen has an open floor plan, the back wall consisting only of floor-to-ceiling windows with long breezy curtains draped at each end, swaying slightly as the breeze makes a subtle entrance. The grill, outside lounge chairs, and palm trees around us give the place an air of ease and relaxation, and the brilliant sun shining through the windows fills the house with warmth and light, seeming to beg us to run outside. And so, we do just that.

These first few days have been perfect in their simplicity. It's as if we've found some private island, such a well-kept secret that we were never meant to discover its location. And if it wasn't so beautiful, the emptiness might be eerie.

We spend our days on the beaches, walking for miles along the sand, feeling the sand beneath our feet and the warm water on our toes, and we never meet another soul. Our only companion seems to be a stray dog who darts out from his hiding post among the rocks, rambunctiously jumps about in the waves, and then without a look back, sprints off, leaving us alone once again.

The water is so pleasantly warm that we walk within the waves without pause or hesitation. We stand and chat, and the mellow waves rock us only slightly. We dip and dive beneath the surface, and swim deeper each day. The only sounds to be heard are our own and the soothing crashing of waves against sand. It's peaceful and breathtaking. It's relaxing and simple, everything we could have dreamed it to be and more.

We've rented kayaks at a local hotel, taking them out into the ocean, just far enough to find the smallest island we'd ever seen. After tucking our kayaks into the sand, we'd jumped into the waves with flippers on our feet and masks with snorkels over our faces. Swimming laps around the island with our faces underwater, we watched the waving underwater plants and the brightly colored fish that look striking with their contrasting shades. Bursting back above the surface, our eyes full of wonder, we look at one another, thankful for these moments.

At nighttime, with our skin washed down and slightly crisped from the sun, we often drive into town, visiting the local restaurants where we dine on freshly caught fish and tropical drinks with umbrellas standing tall above the rims, and we seem to be the only tourists in sight, surrounded by locals alone. I've already had the night when a few too many margaritas were consumed, and Sheila and I returned to the house challenging everyone to a rowdy card game, our voices louder than when we'd left, full of bravado, both of us fueled by the buzz within our brains.

And when the moon replaces the sun, the dark sky reflects on the water. It creates a beautiful mirror image we simply can't miss gazing at. We walk back out the door and down the hill. Brushing our toes against the water's edge, and ignoring all the advice and warnings we've ever heard never to swim in the ocean in the darkness of night, we can't seem to resist, and prepare to dive in. We're still wearing our bathing suits under our long baggy t-shirts. We toss our shirts on the sand and lunge into the waves. The moon shines down on us as we float on our backs in the deep ocean water.

I had worried that we might grow bored here once I'd seen how secluded the house was and how quiet the beaches were, but we've managed to fill every moment of these past few days with excitement, and tomorrow, I know, will be the best one yet. Tomorrow will be almost the whole reason we've come to this island.

Tomorrow we go to that strange but intriguing destination known as Swimming Pig Island. In our typical and nearly always over-the-top need to research and plan before each vacation, we'd seen this tour on every "Must Do While Vacationing in Exuma" list and decided that clearly, this was something we *must do.*

We'd driven around the island after we'd arrived, stopping at two separate tour companies, both offering this same tour that our families were looking for. We chose what appeared to be the more professional and safer company of the two—Four C's Water Adventures. It looked to us to be the closest to something we'd find at home in the United States. From our visit, we could see that the dock wasn't rickety, the building was impressive, and the boats seemed newer.

The company had brochures and websites with reviews to pour over and scrutinize. We'd seen the same advertisements at the car rental company, back at our beach rental home tucked away in a drawer, and pinned on the fridge, and we'd seen this same business name on countless websites with five-star ratings often appearing beside it. We noticed the premier busses parked out front, that we understood to be for hotel pick-up and drop-off on the island. We recalled with satisfying assurance that the company was even advertised on the Bahamian official tourism website, proving to us that this company was the one to choose.

Having seen enough recommendations to reassure us, we booked the tour without much discussion right then and there. Tomorrow morning, we are set to go.

CHAPTER 2

Swinging my legs off the edge of the twin-sized bed, I let my toes embrace the already-warmed wooden floors beneath me, courtesy of the Bahamian sun that seeps through the window. I extend my arms above my head and my back curls into a deep stretch, awakening my body for the day to come. As I make my way out of this room and into the kitchen, I'm expecting to see everyone still half-asleep, maybe easily sipping their coffees, but instead a scene of bustling activity greets me.

Mom and Sheila are packing for the day, tossing each other items and stowing them in bags. Sunscreen sits open beside them, evidence that they've already applied their layers. The front door flies open and gently swings closed over and over. The cars are being packed, last-minute runs to the grocery store are being made, and everyone's showered with their bathing suits already on.

Silently, I step my way backwards, moving quickly and hoping no one's noticed my ratty sleep tank or my messy hair—both proof that I've just woken up. Gently shutting the bedroom door, making hardly any noise, I sprint toward the bathroom and strip down to jump into the shower.

After turning off the water and wrapping my hair and body in two towels, I walk back into the bedroom with water still dripping from my toes, leaving a trail of footprints behind me. Holding my towel tight with one hand, I rummage through my suitcase with the other, absentmindedly grabbing hold of any swimsuit materials that I feel and tossing them on to the bed. Thankfully, this is the only decision I have left to make. Which suit am I going to wear today?

The decision is between a brand-new and still perfectly white bathing suit, the top styled to resemble a simple tank top, and a bright yellow bikini with a strapless top and tiny bottoms to match. I call Brooke over for help with the decision. Normally, I would throw one on without thought. But Brooke and I have already decided to be one another's amateur photographers today, hoping to capture the memories this excursion will create. We decide the all-white suit will look incredible against the backdrop of crystal-clear waters and bright-blue skies, so I throw it on and rush toward the door, offering some half-heartfelt apologies for making everyone wait.

We load into the two cars, my family and I in one, and John and Sheila and Kyle and Haiden in the other. The loading dock isn't too far away, and we hope we remember how we got there the last time.

We pull in to an empty parking lot. Rolling my eyes, I think about the calm morning we could have had if we hadn't felt the need to arrive so absurdly early. It's not even eight a.m., but the sun already beats with such intensity that it seems to melt its way through the worn-down roof of the car. I sink lower in my seat, hoping to avoid the direct assault of the rays. The tugging against my scalp alerts me to the presence of Brooke's hands working their way through my still-wet hair, weaving the strands into intricate braids, so tight that the lingering sting tells me they'll surely last the day ahead.

Eventually, we catch a glimpse of activity, and those who have arrived behind us seem to get ready to begin, so we open the doors and stumble out of the car, already fatigued and groggy from the heat. We meet up with the rest of our group in the middle of the lot before walking down to the dock, but I hang back, just an inch or so, standing outside of the circle we form. So close to the rest of them that no one seems to notice the distance that to me feels so obvious. I'd been hesitant about this trip, feeling like the awkward one of the group. Usually, I'd pair up with my sister, but she has Haiden with her today. I turn and see my mom and Paul happily holding hands, and I don't want to intrude. I let the group lead the way and follow behind.

At the dock, two boats are lined up in the water—one for the half-day tour and one for the full-day tour, I hear someone behind me explain. I head to the first boat and watch, as everyone boards and chooses a seat. Brooke and Haiden head toward the middle of the boat, and Sheila, John, and Kyle head right to the very last row at the stern. All of them are sitting underneath the tall canopy that blocks the sun. My mom and Paul sit in the first row on the left side of the boat.

I decide that I want to stay in the sunshine, determined to return home to Vermont the deepest shade of bronze I can achieve, but still I hesitate for a moment, unsure. A pang of loneliness hits me, as I realize I'll be spending today sitting alone. I sit down in the front row, directly across from my mom and Paul, in the same first row, but on the right side of the boat. *Maybe once we're farther out on the water, we can all get up and socialize,* I tell myself, trying to ignore the slight sting I feel as I sit alone on this bench made for two.

There are only ten passengers, of whom our group are eight. A couple sits behind me, a man and woman, likely husband and wife. They sit in comfort together, at ease, with his arm thrown over her shoulder, as if the act is second nature. The woman and I make quick eye contact, she smiles. I smile back.

The captain seems to me to be as eager to get the day started as I am, and the boat takes off without much delay, giving my mind a distraction from this seating arrangement. I turn around as the captain begins to shout with excitement, explaining where we will go first.

"It's gonna be a fun day!" I hear him yell after some rushed and basic instruction. Then the boat begins forward.

There's something about the unknown of the ocean and the vastness of it all that gives today a whole new thrill. I scan the never-ending waters surrounding us in every direction and feel a slight chill crawl across my skin despite the sun above.

I listen to the carefree voice of the captain behind me but keep my eyes on the view ahead. Then his voice disappears, drowned out by the noise of the engine propelling us forward with an unexpected speed. We soar into the air, crossing a stretch of space before we slam against the water once more. We continue in this way, seeming to hop and jump and leap our way across, rather than gliding smoothly, as I wish that we would.

My fingers instinctively find their way to the edge of my seat, wrapping around the curved edge, knowing that I must hold on or one of these times that we land, the impact will toss me to the floor. *Don't you dare fall off this seat,* I silently tell myself, picturing the mortifying image of myself sprawled across the deck of the boat. I hold on as tightly as I can, fighting to remain seated while pretending I haven't a worry at all.

I sneak a peek around me, checking to see if anyone else seems concerned about the speed, but everyone seems calm. (Though later some of them will tell me that those expressions had only been masks hiding the reality that their nerves had been just as high and they had been as terrified as I'd been). *Relax Stef. Just enjoy this,* I repeat in my mind, trying to slow my racing heart, trying not to ruin this moment.

We lurch back into the air, feeling almost as if we're trying to jump over something. Long strands of hair have come loose from my braids, the braids that had been so tight I'd been sure they'd last the day, and whip my face and cover my eyes. Reaching up with one hand, I hold the strands behind my ear, letting me see clearly again, while keeping a firm grasp on the seat with the other, still too afraid to release my grasp.

Relax Stef, I repeat back to myself. *He's been hired to be the captain of this boat. He must do this all the time. He must know what he is doing, or he wouldn't stand at the wheel today.*

As those words repeat through my mind, I angle my face upward, toward the sun, soaking in the moment. My surroundings are so beautiful that for a moment I forget about my nerves. I forget about my stress and feel a consuming sense of serenity.

We fly into the air once more, going higher than ever before. We crash into the water, and this time the water doesn't welcome us. As if the ocean has evaporated, sucked up by some drought and replaced with concrete, we land upon an unforgiving surface.

A cracking noise, like the shot of a rifle, splits the air. Many in our group will recall this sound with a chilling certainty, but I will never remember hearing it. Though physically I am still present aboard this boat, in another sense, I am already too far gone. The boat has just exploded beneath us.

My surroundings are dark.

Relax Stef, I try to tell myself once more.

As though she were in a movie scene playing in slow-motion for added effect, my mom's petite frame is thrown into the air. At the mercy of the wind, she has no control over where and when and how she will land. She's carried away, whipped around and behind the boat.

It all happens in only a second, but her eyes take in many of the details around her. She notices the black pieces that soar alongside her, so close they nearly chip against her flesh. She can't tell what they might be, but it looks to be pieces of metal, like lethal shrapnel.

She knows now—she hasn't been thrown from the boat as she feared she would be. We weren't just going too fast. Something far worse has happened. She splashes into the water that remains an unforgiving surface. Her lung collapses upon the landing. Likely, this is the moment her ribs cracked.

She sinks beneath the shallow water, losing sight of which is the surface, which is the water, and which way she must go to find air.

There's a watercolor design above her. Rays of sunlight spread through the water, extending toward her, telling her which way to go. She reaches for the light, and stands, gasping for air. But it's hard to swallow. Her chest makes an ugly, painful sound.

Before her is an unforgettable scene. A boat burns atop the ocean waters, smoke billowing from its frame, turning both the water and the sky an ink-black shade.

"Help! I can't swim!" a woman screams. Mom realizes that she's not alone in the water.

Making her way toward the voice, she sees that it comes from the woman who'd sat just behind me. The woman who had smiled that kind smile, the woman I'd hoped to get to know today. Her name is Maleka.

Back aboard the boat, Brooke regains consciousness. Her eyes open to the sight of the deck of the boat beneath her. She wonders why she's no longer in her seat. She pushes upright, slowly moving into a kneeling position, her palms pressed against the deck. Her ears ring with piercing intensity. A deeply red substance oozes toward her.

She wonders to herself, *Am I awake? Is this a dream? Why can't I wake up?*

Smoke has made the air thick, and as her eyes move upwards, she spots Paul, her stepdad, standing before her. Thick red blood gushes from his skull. It spreads down his back and splatters on the deck. She looks back down at her hands. The substance trickling toward her has reached her palms. She can see it dyeing her skin, she can feel the viscosity of it, she can smell it.

Oh my God, this is real. I'm already awake.

"Jump!" She hears someone yell.

She stands and without thought throws herself from the boat's side. The redness on her hands is washed away, as though it was never there.

Mom wades through shallow water toward the voice, moaning with every inch she moves. The noises she makes are not in her control; the pain is great, her breaths come labored and slow, but all of this, she cannot yet focus on.

She reaches Maleka, and the woman grabs on to her shoulders with such strength that it frightens her, worried they might both go under the water. Though the water is shallow enough to stand in, to wade through, this woman before her seems physically unable to do these things.

"I can't feel my feet!" Maleka shouts in uncontrolled panic.

Then, she calms. She pauses. She looks my mom directly in the eyes and speaks now with controlled emotion: "Tell my husband I love him. Okay?"

"We're going to be okay. We're going to be fine," Mom answers her, as she holds her up above the water. She's hoping she's right, but she fixes the other woman's words in her memory, just in case.

She catches her first glimpse of Paul, her husband. She sees Brooke, her youngest daughter. She finds Sheila and John and Haiden and Kyle. As she checks them each off the list, alarm begins to grip her. There's one person missing. She's wearing a bright white bathing suit. She should be easy to find.

"Where is Stefanie?" she shrieks, her voice cutting through the air.

Paul hears her scream. Kyle hears her, too. And now, she isn't alone with her urgency. They begin to search.

I'm laying perfectly still. A deep panic has grabbed hold of my body, pinning me in place.

I need to move, I need to run, but I can't seem to do anything at all.

My eyes flash back and forth, trying to understand my surroundings.

I scream, expecting to hear a blood-curdling noise escape me, but I'm not sure if I've made any sound.

The air is filled with horrific shrieks and cries. The passengers of the boat behind us beg to be taken away from the horrors on display.

Their shouts make it clear that they are sure our boat is going to explode again, and if it does, they may be engulfed in our carnage. What no one yet knows is that I am trapped on the deck of this boat, pinned in place by terror and injury, and also by the pile of metal debris that has fallen on top of me. I am hidden from view, and those around me have already jumped from the boat and into the waves, under the assumption that I had done the same. Should the boat explode again, it will be me alone who will go up with it.

The captain of the other boat, seemingly ignoring his passengers' cries, holds his position. Two of the many that stand beside him, a Bahamian pair, who appeared to be a young boy and a middle-aged man, react unlike their fellow passengers. They leap off the boat's side. Moving with determination, they push through the water that seems to fight against them, as if in some desperate effort to slow their movements. They're in search of a stranger, facing unimaginable danger for me, a person they have never known. Step-by-step, they come closer.

The man lifts the young boy up and on to the deck. Moving with speed, possibly fueled by both adrenaline and uncertainty about how much longer this boat will last, the boy begins his search. Before him, he sees a pile of debris, and he heaves each piece away. This is where he finds me—awake, conscious, mangled, broken.

John and Sheila arrive at the boat's edge, standing beside the Bahamian man, each of them with life vests in hand. They work carefully together now, as they lift my limp body up and over the boat's side. But I'm only dead weight, and my body slumps into an awkward shape, with my legs and head high in the air at opposite ends, and my torso hanging low. They've lifted me over the side, and I lay flat against the water, as they begin to float me away from this boat and toward the one behind us.

"My back," I moan.

My arms flail beside me, searching for something to grasp on to. Something to help me sit myself upright, to alleviate the tremendous pressure and piercing pain within my spine, but my palms find nothing beneath them, only water that slips through my fingertips. My eyes grow wide. I can't understand where I am. I can't understand why I can't sit up. Everyone stands tall above me in the shallow water, holding me flat, focused on not letting me sit upright. Don't they understand? My back hurts!

Looking up and into their eyes, I keep my voice steady, calm even, with this question: "What's happening to me?"

Sheila responds. I see her lips move. But I can't hear her.

"My back," I moan once more, drawing out the length of that one-syllable word. Forcing the pained, tormented sound of my voice to hang in the air.

Those around me now hear my broken voice crying out for a familiar sense of comfort: "Where's my mom? Please, I want my mom!" I wail, drawing out the words once more.

As we arrive at the other boat, John prepares to help lift me over the side, but as he grabs hold of my legs, a wave of nausea hits him. A grotesque thought occurs: he doesn't know what he's holding. My legs rest in his palms, but he feels nothing recognizable—no bone, no muscle, nothing firm or identifiable. There's nothing left.

Once I'm laid on the safe surface of this new boat's deck, Paul and John immediately get to work. A physician is aboard, and quickly gives John and Paul instructions. They tie tourniquets around my legs. I feel them tighten. This time, I hear my screams.

John grabs any supplies he can find and leaps back into the water, arriving at a third boat that's just arrived. This boat, owned by a different tour company, was some distance away when the sound of an explosion tore through the air. The captain rushed to our aid.

He's picked up the wounded, my mom and Maleka, and the children, Brooke and Haiden.

John jumps aboard, working to help Maleka. He ties one tourniquet around her leg, not knowing he has used the last remaining supplies. He knows he should add a second. His eyes scan both boats with a focused determination. He can't find anything. There's nothing left that he can turn into a tourniquet—no rope, no more life vests, no first aid kit, nothing at all.

All that's left to do is speed back to shore and get to a hospital. As the two boats idle next to each other, the combined noise of their engines is loud, nearly deafening. In synchronized timing, both boats gun their engines to rush to shore, but their roar is nothing compared with the sound that pierces the air. It doesn't sound human, and yet it is.

The engines are loud, but my screams are louder.

My body seems to have caught fire. The bright colors of my surroundings blend into a blur of white, a strange taste fills my mouth, and my eyes feel as if they have rolled back into the depths of my skull. It's as though I'm possessed, with my mouth hanging open and a wailing screech escaping my disfigured frame, which remains eerily still as I erupt in sound.

"Stop the boat!" someone cries out.

As we'd sped forward, the diving platform's ladder, which sits just in front of me, had been too low in the water. With each inch we moved, the ladder chopped through the water, spraying salty ocean water onto my skin. Each droplet sank into the gashes in my flesh, making my freshly torn and fiery hot skin seem to have a million tiny razors sawing within them.

The ladder is lifted, and we move more slowly, and now, at last, the shore is in sight.

Dread fills Brooke as she sits on the shore, watching a group of people floating her sister's too-still body toward her, dyeing the once clear water a deep red. She knows, with certainty, that her big sister is dead.

My mom's screams snap Brooke back to reality. She hadn't meant to scream. The sight of her daughter, arms and legs torn apart, bones visible above the cracked-open flesh, has made her lose all control. She hadn't meant to scream, but she can't make it stop.

Relief floods though Brooke as she realizes that I am still alive. She rushes over to our mom with an instinct we had never known she had and takes control. Patiently and confidently, she rubs my mom's shoulders.

"Mom, we have to be strong now, okay? We have to get through this," she says, before jumping into the back of the pickup truck in which I've been placed. She's determined to help me survive.

She won't die. I won't let her; her new thoughts repeat in her mind.

"I love you, Stef.... I love you so much," these words repeat from her to me, never ending.

She feeds me sips of water, resists my attempts to sit upright, and begs me to keep my eyes open.

"Don't fall asleep, Stef... Have some water... Keep your eyes open."

I'm too far gone to hear her words. She's right before me and yet she's a thousand miles away. I've gone deaf, blind, senseless, but somehow I'm still awake. Nothing can reach me.

The weight on my chest seems to keep growing heavier, as if I'm covered in wet cement. I'm growing weaker. I'm so tired. An unfamiliar feeling tugs on me now, trying to coax me into unconsciousness. Whispering in my ear how sweet sleep will feel.

Just close your eyes, just for a minute, I hear it saying. As if I've just swallowed a handful of medications, each one making me increasingly drowsy. The feeling is so strong, but something tells me that I can't listen. It hits me now, this odd realization—I think I'm dying.

CHAPTER 3

*I*n a hospital in Ft. Lauderdale, Florida, a press conference gathers. Reporters sit with their recording devices, pads of paper, and long lists of questions. Two doctors sit at a long table, on a platform slightly above these reporters, dressed in their white coats. They're releasing as much information as they can, as much information as they have, while much still remains unknown. The press conference is recorded, documented, and even live-streamed to viewers.

This is a shortened version of the conference:

Dr. Parra, my trauma surgeon, begins with a straightforward introduction.

"She arrived unstable and was found to be in multiple shock stages—she was in hemorrhagic shock, she was in septic shock, and spinal shock. We initiated management, so we took her to the operating room initially, to control her ongoing hemorrhage; we placed two chest tubes, we did a laparotomy, we had to pack her pelvis and had to stop the bleeding from her pelvis, and we completed care of her lower extremities. She had devastating injuries to her lower extremities."

A reporter jumps in: "So as a result of the damage we're hearing that her lower extremities were amputated?"

"Yes, she received at the Bahamas a guillotine [amputation], which is a preemptive management of trauma," Dr. Parra replies. "This is a trauma that you see usually in war zone areas, like Afghanistan."

"We did a more formal amputation, below-the-knee amputations on both her extremities, to control the sepsis, and also the hemorrhage of that source."

Another reporter continues the conversation: "So right now, what is her status?"

"She is critically ill," Dr. Parra says. "She is undergoing right now, in the Intensive Care Unit, damage control resuscitation. She underwent five hours of damage control surgery with me, and currently we are correcting the deficits in her blood volume and her coagulation parameters."

Reporter: "Is she in a coma? On a respirator?"

Dr. Parra: "She is. Due to the explosion, the initial injuries, and most devastating injuries, were to her extremities, but she also suffered injuries to her pelvis, abdomen, chest, and she also suffered a brain injury.

"We stopped the bleeding as best we could; we believe we now have that under control. Unfortunately, due to the massive blood loss she suffered, currently what we're trying to do is correct the clotting parameters of her blood system.

"She arrived in a comatose mode, and we induced that mode to continue her care."

Reporter: "What's her prognosis, doctor?"

Dr. Parra: "It's guarded. She is in critical state… her condition is critical.

"The family has been informed, and we're doing everything in our power to help her through this devastating injury she's suffered. I spoke with both parents, both the mom and dad, and being a parent myself, it's a devastating worst-case scenario that can happen to any parent. Be it a one-year-old, two-year-old, or twenty-two-year-old, it's the worst nightmare a parent can go through. I told them that we're doing everything, not only me, but all my co-workers, all the staff—everyone is working as hard as we can to help her get through this. But they're fully aware; I was very honest with them about her condition. Every twenty-four hours, it becomes more hopeful."

The focus now shifts to the doctor beside him, Dr. Roberts, Chief of Neurosurgery at Broward Health Medical Center.

Dr. Roberts: "She does have a brain injury and also an unstable spine injury, which will need to be surgically stabilized, but obviously her abdominal injuries and things certainly need to be corrected before we can proceed with that.

"Her brain injury, it's not an operable injury, but it's something that can be treated medically. Essentially this is a bruise on the brain."

Reporter: "Are you concerned about paralysis?"

Dr. Roberts: "I am."

Now a question to them both: "I know it's early to ask this, but as her medical professionals, do you think that she will survive this?"

Dr. Parra: "It's too early to know. The number of injuries she's suffered is nothing secondary to a war zone, so, as with any of our soldiers abroad who have suffered these injuries, it's too early to say. But centers like ours are trained … we're trained to do this, and we're doing everything possible."

~~~

Unconscious and oblivious to the world around me, I've been handed over to the care and responsibility of others. My room is filled with machines, leaving room for only one visitor at a time.

Cameras stand over my bed, ensuring no sign or signal goes unnoticed. Tubes are inserted into my neck, stomach, groin, and arms. Wound VAC (vacuum-assisted closure) systems with their long hollow tubes are on each of the massive open wounds on my legs. Traction weights are screwed into my skin and pull against my femur. Thick casts cover my arms. A ventilator has been forcefully inserted into my throat with cushioned pads attached to plastic tightly gripping each cheek.

Every human function must now be done by machinery. I am comatose, with a 50 percent chance of waking again.

My body is shattered and torn to pieces, yet my face remains recognizable. My dirty-blonde hair is pulled into a braid to the side of my head. My face is tanned from the early days of that vacation. My eyebrows are freshly waxed, drawing compliments from those trying to lighten the mood, despite the left corner of my eyebrow having been freshly singed off.

But my cheeks are swollen, having filled with fluid my now unresponsive kidneys can't filter away, and my eyes look puffy, as if I've cried for days on end. A single bruise covers the corner of my right eye stretching across my eyelashes, and a soft line of fading red lies diagonally across my forehead. One eye is just barely open, as if I am sneaking a peak at the world around me. Yet I do not see. I do not hear. The world goes on, and I remain, just barely hanging on.

My face is washed; my hair moves from braid to ponytail, anything to keep it out of the way. My body is cleansed, and my bandages changed. My stretcher moves from operating room to recovery and back again as each of many intensive surgical procedures is completed. My body endures long incisions and countless stitches and staples, and still I remain, just barely hanging on.

My family takes turns coming in to see me. They talk to me. They remind me of life and stories and memories. Their words go unheard.

Activity bustles in my room, shifts change, visitors come and go, and I know nothing of it.

Mornings turn into evenings and days turn into weeks, and still I remain, still just barely hanging on.

My mom is also a patient at this Florida hospital. Not in this Trauma Intensive Care Unit where I lie, but in the Trauma unit a few floors and hallways away. A unit in which, in most cases, the patients don't get to leave their rooms or wander about, as they are all still in serious condition. My mom is the same in this way, requiring intensive inpatient care. Her legs are encased in heavy black boots, so stiff that any precise movement has become impossible. A chest tube hangs below her, and her broken ribs try to confine her to bed—using a wheelchair is painful and a slow and daunting process. But she knows, and everyone around her knows, that despite all of this, she must get up. She must get out of her room.

The nurses and doctors, assistants and aides, the front-desk attendants and the Starbucks baristas, and everyone in between, knows of our story. They care for my mom and they know of her daughter who remains in critical condition, in a balance between life and the unknown, unsure on which side she will eventually land, in a hospital room just a short distance away. The extra effort is always made to get my mom to that ICU room.

They slowly remove her from bed, carefully, so as not to detach any tubes or bump any wounds. They dress her and clean her and prepare her for this excursion. As they arrive at my room, it's only particular movements that will allow her large wheelchair, far too oversized for my mother's barely five-foot-tall frame, into this room. Her chair is angled toward me, but the bed where I lie is high, too high for someone sitting in a wheelchair. She reaches forward to feel closer. She grabs my hand, and she sings to me, as she did when I was a little girl. The song that has become a distant but beloved memory between us: "You Are My Sunshine."

As she holds my hand and sings these words, she expects no reaction. My eyes remain closed, as she knew they would. This is hard for her, spending so much time in this room, not wanting to be apart, yet unable to speak or embrace or see any familiarity. During one of these visits, after so many others, she continues softly singing, still gripping my hand, and a small drop of water gently escapes one of my eyes, continuing down my cheek. She recalls how she quickly looked around, until finding a nurse behind her.

"Are her eyes watering, or is she crying?"

Another drop now escapes the other eye, continuing down the other cheek. The nurse looks at my mom and answers, "I think those are tears. I think she's crying."

The words of this song are the words she sang to me every morning when I was young. When she'd catch her first glimpse of my blonde ringlets bouncing as I ran down the stairs, my small hands rubbing my still-drowsy eyes. *You brighten each day, you are my sunshine,* she's told me a thousand times.

She'd told me each story so clearly that the words made me feel like a small girl all over again. Stories of the memories she held but I had been too young to remember—I now feel as though I've lived them over and over, as her words wrapped around me, bringing me back in time to a place I am thankful to know.

Her tales have told me of the mornings she'd woken me up as a child, when my hair had been its curliest and its color had not yet darkened and was still a silvery-white. The mornings my head rested on the pillow, but my face couldn't yet be seen, as my hair had tangled during my deep sleep. She'd push away the curls until my face revealed itself, and as she pushed away each strand, she sang to me these words.

Soon there will be a new tale for her to share. Neither of us knows this yet, but many weeks later, I will be awake once again, and she will tell me this new story. She'll tell me how she sang those words to the girl she hoped would wake for the day to come. My hair now darker, and my ringlets replaced by a knotted braid, messy from the weeks spent lying against the same pillow. Though there was no hair to clear from my face and my head rested on a new and unfamiliar bed, she'd sat by my side, again singing those same words.

You are my sunshine, my only sunshine.

You make me happy when skies are grey.

You'll never know dear, how much I love you.

Please don't take my sunshine away.

This time, a new emphasis on that last line, as she sang this song with a sound of pleading in her voice. Unable to imagine not being able to ever have another morning together, without another time of seeing my still-drowsy face or one last time for me to hear these verses. Knowing her life would feel too painfully dark without her sunshine to brighten the way.

When that day comes when she shares with me this newest story wrapped within the words of this familiar song, her words will not come as a surprise. I'll be looking down, slightly embarrassed, and without planning a response I will hear myself reply, "I know you did."

No noise or image or action had broken through my sedated unconsciousness. Yet somehow the words of that song made their way through. Her soft voice and whispered words had been loud enough to find me.

My answer will take the both of us by surprise. I'll even begin to question myself, wondering if I had ever really heard her, or if

I simply wanted to believe that I had. But I won't be able to shake the certainty that I had always felt the words within me. That I had known there was a world out there that I needed to get back to.

Maybe those tears she spotted had been the first of many, crying for the pain I knew I had suffered, and the pain I knew was about to come. Perhaps my brain had been more aware in that time of rest than it would be again when I finally awoke, when denial and rationalization and disbelief entered the equation. Perhaps silence and stillness and being trapped within a brand-new self had been my clearest time of all.

I'll never be entirely sure of what happened during that time away from the world. Yet I'll remain sure about this one moment, sure that I had heard her words. Believing with certainty that in a time when nothing was familiar any longer, not even my own self, that those well-known verses that had been instilled in me so long ago, had broken through all barriers, so that just for a moment, I felt clarity.

Just for a moment, I shed two single tears, for the loss of the girl I once was. Just for a moment, I felt pain and longing to return.

CHAPTER 4

*I*n the deep hours of the night, the nurse on duty looks up and sees two brown eyes looking back at her. These eyes don't flicker but instead remain holding a steady, confident gaze. As if there had never been a question in my mind that this moment would come.

The nurse thinks back to all the moments she'd heard the shaky, emotional voice of my mom pleading with an unfamiliar world that suddenly seemed so cruel. "I just want to see her big brown eyes again," she'd always say.

She smiles. It's nice to finally see them.

Then she rushes to my bedside. As she quickly checks every machine and vital sign, ensuring that all is okay, her soft voice begins to speak to me.

I mouth one word to her now, attempting to reply. I'm unable to speak, but clearly trying to communicate. She watches intently, deciphering what it is that I wish to say after this time away, wondering what will be my very first thoughts.

"Mom?" I try to whisper.

We might all believe that awakening from a coma is a picture-perfect moment. That it's a quick and easy transition filled only with emotion, love, and gratitude. It's easier to assume that there's one specific moment in time when the eyes of the patient open wide, she looks around the room, and her first words are some prophetic and wistful phrase, creating a moment that can be remembered from that day on. But in reality, it's time-consuming, and far uglier than any of us would like to believe.

For me, there was no exact moment on one day alone that we could label as the time that I awoke from this month-long coma. Instead, there were many attempts made to regain consciousness. That moment, in the middle of the night with my nurse by my side, was only the first of many more to come.

When I do wake up, there will be machines with bits inserted into my body, tubes wrapped round me, all my strength and every human ability ripped away from me. There will be the medications making everything seem unreal and nightmarish. There will be strangers surrounding me, examining me, staring at me. I'll be alone and terrified and have no way to speak or feel comfort. Those will be the worst moments of my life.

The sedation and medications lie upon me like the thickest of blankets. As my eyes try to open, the physical effort that each attempt toward freedom requires is visibly obvious. My eyelids push away at the weights that sit upon them, flickering and moving so slowly. Many times, they will open, but more often than not, the effort needed will prove to be too great and they will simply remain closed. It's a cruel event for those around me to watch, as this attempt to return to myself is frustrated by the medications that I clearly wish to get out from underneath. As if I have no right to return to the body that is supposed to be mine.

This time though, as my eyes open, they will not need to shut once again. I am awake. I remember being asked only one question, though I'm sure they've said much more.

"Do you know where you are?"

I scan frantically around me, taking in these strangers, this room, and all that makes no sense.

"Vermont," I attempt to answer.

It's the only answer I can think of. There's a part of me, a part that I can't understand, that feels an urgent desire that this answer be correct, that I do know where I am. Because if I don't know the answer to this simple question, then what would this say about me? I watch as the two people beside me make quick eye contact, silently communicating. I wonder what they're saying. I wonder if I was right. But something feels different, and entirely unsettling.

Even though I am awake, I am only a shadow of myself, a person stuck in a drugged stupor. My mind has constructed new days, new realities, and they are all far from the truth. This might seem a kind gesture, or even a protective gesture, except the scenarios my mind has constructed are ones you might watch on any episode of the popular TV show *American Horror Story* or read of in some thrilling horror novel. It is not kind. It is not protective. It is only cruel.

I am convinced of my own truth, that I am not in a hospital, that I have been captured, given up by my family, and trapped within this laboratory like some animal to be used for testing. As I look around me, it's a story that makes absolute sense because my surroundings are the perfect background: my room is far too white, far too sterile, and far too brightly lit. The metal fixtures are not comforting and the fluorescent lights shining upon me seem to reveal every microscopic detail.

All that I can see before me is one heavy wooden door, and as I look through the doorway, I see a hallway that not only matches the room in its sterile appearance but seems to be empty and silent so much of the time. It's as if I'm the only one here, wherever this place is. When a man or woman walks by, always wearing scrubs, I try to shout to them, believing that if they knew that I was in here, they would surely release me. But as I go to scream, no sound comes out, and that's when I discover this awful truth: *They've taken my voice from me.*

Many moments from these earliest days will never form into memory, and for that, I will one day be thankful, but from these actions I've acquired a new nickname: the nurses have begun to call me Houdini. Only they know that they are trying to help me, while I think that they are trying to keep me here forever as their permanent lab rat, and so, I attempt to evade all of their treatment attempts. I can hardly move, I'm held down by casts and medications and incisions and wounds, and yet I have grown to be slyer than ever before.

The bedrails beside me have come to be my greatest tool. I can place the cast that surrounds my arm underneath a single rail and with a shrug of my shoulder, the cast begins to push away. When I repeat this many times over, combined with the slightest of shimmying movements, that cast comes free. While I feel only relief at having my wrists and arms released from their entrapment, everyone else sees my fragile and broken bones lying exposed and unconfined. They quickly replace my casts, and in my mind, the act is a confirmation of their plans to never allow me to leave.

When the nurses put what is only a feeding tube down my nose and into my stomach, I reject this invasion, and hand-over-hand, I pull that piece of equipment all the way out. This is a process that for any sane, any sober, person would not only be uncomfortable but also painful. As the nurses turn around, after placing that tube one more time, they see an all too familiar site. I stare them directly in the eyes, an obnoxious grin on my face, and I lift the rubber hose into the air, above my slumped figure, and over my head. This is when I turn that feeding tube into the grossest form of a lasso, and I whip it around my head in a circular motion, never breaking eye contact with the tired nurses before me.

During this practiced performance of mine with the lassos and escapades is often when a nurse by the name of Alison steps toward me. She's young with long blonde hair made longer by extensions that blend so naturally. When she's on her shift, she makes her dark blue scrubs the perfect outfit with her hair tightly pulled back, and often a pair of characteristic glasses framing her bright blue eyes. But she will also come in to visit on her time off, and this is when she wears her floor-length skirts and tight tank tops, and to me, looks to be some beautiful angel. When I'm frantic, she calms me down. When I'm alone, something I clearly despise as I slam my broken arms against the bed railings as a call for attention, she sits beside me and I begin to breathe again.

When I am pushing my casts away or whipping a feeding tube round my head, or when Alison sits beside me, these are the moments that the terrors no longer find me. It's when I'm still, when there is only silence, that I begin to drown in terror. It happens when visiting hours have ended, when I am alone, that the hallucinations and the distorted sense of reality sink my heart into a feeling that at any moment I am going to die, and no one will have arrived to save me.

My worst form of PTSD will arise from nothing real, but to me, it will be an attack and a victimization far better remembered and far clearer than the actual horror I have already survived. I am hallucinating, with a clarity that creates fictional characters so extravagantly detailed and personable that the vision will be truer than even my own self.

I talk to the walls beside me. I attempt to barter with my dialysis nurse as I think that she is a store clerk refusing to sell me a twelve-pack of Bud Light, and there is a man who hunts me down with his sharply edged scalpels and tools. It is this character who I will remember not only in this unreal time, and not only within this hallucination, but for years to come. When I am healed and far healthier than I am now, this man will haunt my thoughts and my days, and I'll need to remind myself, *He was only a hallucination; he was not real; this never happened to you.*

He's tall with dark brown hair and sickly pale skin. He's a professional, and he is respected by the women who work for him, though they clearly wish to not have to follow his commands that are filled with brutish direction.

Today, he has found me himself.

I've walked into a large open area, and it's where I will be working. He's directing a movie, and I am needed to be an extra in his film, the type who isn't seen or heard and only stands in the distant background. As I arrive, I find myself undergoing his unusual inspection process. *I'm just an extra,* I think to myself, wondering why he needs to inspect me, too. There's a woman who works with him, and she's checking to ensure that I pass his tests.

She's finished up, and now we only need his approval to let me go and then she'll move on to the next person behind me. But I watch, he marches toward me with an intensity to his steps. He stands before me and begins to shout so violently that spit flies through the air. I'm distracted as I watch his anger, wondering what I have done to earn it, so I hadn't noticed as they put me on a cool, narrow metal table and handcuffed my arms to the sides. I pull at my wrists, trying to break free, but the metal chains are too strong.

He looks toward the woman beside me and instructs her to begin. *What is she beginning?* My mind races, though from the look in his eyes, I know that it cannot be good. *I'm so sorry,* she says to me slowly, clearly not wishing to do what it is she has been instructed to do. *Wait!* I shout. *Please, no,* I beg. She reaches toward the tray beside her, carefully selecting the metal tool with the thinnest edge. She has to continue, because that man with the dark hair and the pale skin stands before us watching, seeming to enjoy the moment.

My heart drums so loudly I'm sure she must be able to hear it. I look to either side of me, searching for an exit, searching for a way to break free. Her arm moves closer to me, but I turn my head away, and suddenly, I see my sister! She's standing to my left, looking in at me, watching me, and I know she will help me. *Help!* I shout to her, but she shakes her head sadly and walks away. Everyone is leaving me here. Everyone is forcing this to happen to me. What have I done to deserve this?! This woman's hand and that silver tool shines in the fluorescent light. She's only an inch away. She's going to cut me open.

The man with dark hair and pale skin still stands watching. As she leans closer, now hovering above my skin, her hand begins to disappear into the air, like some video game character disappearing bit by bit. Then she's gone. The metal table beneath me changes to the familiar bed with its ordinary bed rails. The room is empty. It's been only me in here this entire time.

I look down, my heart beating against my ribs with such force it feels as though at any moment it might break free from my chest. Frantically, I look around my room, wondering now, *If that wasn't real, then is this room even real?* The confusion is heartbreaking.

There's only one similarity between what I see now and what I saw within my mind. My arms are in fact still handcuffed to this bed. Though it's not metal handcuffs or a metal table, and there is no woman beside me with any scalpel, I still cannot break free from these restraints attached to my bed rails. As I study these odd contraptions against my skin, my mom makes her way toward me.

What I don't know is that it's early in the morning, visiting hours have just begun, and I have remained awake all night long without gaining a moment of sleep, and have only tortured myself with the emptiness around me and the horrors within my mind. Mom takes one look at my panic-soaked eyes, studies the contraptions against my skin, and sighs sadly. She's seen me like this before, with my arms pinned on each side, so she knows what she needs to do. She finds a nurse to release me by promising her she won't allow me to remove my casts anymore, and then once I am free, she sits beside me.

"It's going to be okay," she tells me.

My eyes stare back at her, wondering how she could possibly think it's going to be okay, wondering why she's left me here, and needing to know what it is that's happening to me.

"Your friends will be here in just a few days," she continues, her voice as soothing as she can make it.

This breaks through my panicking mind. *My friends.* I repeat the words within my mind. The contemplation of these words feels like stepping back into another person and another lifetime that I'd forgotten, as if the words have called my subconscious back to my body. Flashcards begin to play through my mind, and I begin to wonder who it is that will be here soon. I stare at my mom beside me, and my heartbeat begins to slow.

This is what's real, I tell myself, over and over again. *Hang on to this,* I remind myself, hoping this will keep that imagined man from finding me again.

CHAPTER 5

*P*rinted-out images of my closest friends are taped across every inch of my hospital room's walls, but to see them now, standing here, makes me feel alive for the first time. Their presence takes my mind off the pain, the confusion, and it takes me out of this unfamiliar environment and back to a place of comfort.

Deep down, I know that I am not the same as when they last saw me. Yet somehow, with them by my side, I feel as though nothing has changed, as if maybe they can't even see my two arms held in their casts or the tubes coming from my body. Maybe they haven't noticed that I'm in the hospital, or that I look so different.

I struggle to show strength so that they can see me just as they have always known me. I can't sit up, but I try. I try to make jokes about what I know I must look like, but I can't speak well enough for that. I want them to hear my thoughts, to hear my real voice, the voice that I hear in my mind that isn't rough and shaky, nor limited and weak. I want them to know that I'm okay, that it's still me in here.

I'm trying my best to communicate with them. I make expressions on my face, roll my eyes, and mouth my words. Then I anxiously wait, hoping they've understood. The room fills with their laughter. I knew they knew me well enough for this. A look with my eyes, and they know what I'm thinking. Long strings of sentences mouthed to the crowd, and Duffy translates to the rest of them. I never would've guessed she'd be the one to figure out my silent correspondence, but again, she's taken me by surprise, as she always seems to do.

Duffy is tall and skinny, with bleach-blonde hair and big brown eyes. She goes by her last name, which has a ring to it, matching her bubbly personality, and she's been my best friend for many years. Of course, with college, and years apart, we've gone extended periods of time without seeing each other, and sometimes not even sending a text. But nothing ever changes between us. It's simply a friendship that is meant to survive, enduring since the earliest grades of middle school and through both the expected challenges of life and those moments you wonder why you were ever burdened with.

We'd gone to the same small middle school together and played on all of the same sports teams. But we'd grown far closer in high school. She's one year younger than I, so when she was a freshman and began dealing with the typical drama and cruelty that a high school girl often has to endure, we had found each other. Instantly, she felt like family—a sister to me and to my siblings, another daughter to my parents.

She's kept me laughing every day, but we have also helped each other through the toughest of times—the times no one should ever have to know, as her life has also not always been one of ease but one with painful phases. There have been many moments of seeing each other at our lowest. So I feel no embarrassment or shame as she sees me in this hospital bed now. We've laughed through the hard times together before, and I know that we will once more.

Mom, Paul, Tiger, and Tati listen to Duffy's translations of my silent words.

"Her head itches, she wants a Diet Coke, and she says you all suck at reading lips," Duffy explains to the room.

I nod in agreement. Tati laughs and walks over to the bed to scratch my head. I smile at her gratefully, feeling only comfort and no shame as her fingers work their way across my itching scalp.

"My soulmate," I call Tati. We'd met in college, when in our sophomore years, we made a decision that surprised everyone who knew both of us: to rush for a sorority. We'd both already established our own groups of friends, but we had both made a decision to try something new, something beyond our comfort zone. After going through the weeks of getting to know each organization, we wound up choosing the same sorority, where we met each other. Our friendship began with the somewhat forced get-togethers, filled with unrevealing and guarded conversation, but we quickly became the best of friends, eventually knowing every secret, every detail of the other, and talking without pause or fear of judgment.

She's little, just barely over five feet tall, but she is striking, with her thick black hair, soft facial features, and a large tattoo of an impressive lion covering her thigh. She's 100 percent Colombian and speaks fluent Spanish. She's different from any friend I ever had while growing up in Vermont, but I wish I had always had her by my side. She lets me be me, but still pushes me to be better, stronger, more confident, without her even trying.

I'd say I'm most surprised to see Tiger here, though I'm thankful she is. I'd met her in my sorority, as well. She was a few years above me, and when I'd met her, I thought she'd forget my name as soon as she left the room. I was too quiet and too shy, while she's outgoing and bold as can be. But she'd noticed something about me that I hadn't yet noticed myself, and the two of us became a pair.

Like Duffy, she goes by her last name, and just as with Duffy, it just makes sense. I often joked with her, telling her how lucky she is to have a last name that fits her so well: Tiger. She has this magnetic quality of being able to turn any painfully ordinary event into a moment you'd never want to miss. She draws you in, until you find yourself craving her company, always wanting to be around her. Her perfectly straight and pearly white teeth look right out of a dental commercial. Her dirty-blonde hair is often perfectly curled into loose beachy waves, and her makeup only makes her impressive features more obvious. Her loud, confident voice, and contagious laugh make her even easier to love.

I look at my friends before me, in awe and gratitude. They haven't been here long, so I can't understand why my mom and Paul are already asking them to leave the room. I want to object, but my friends each turn to me with matching looks in their eyes.

"We'll be right back," they say in unison.

"Okay," I say, pushing the single word out, wondering what those looks were silently trying to convey.

Before the door has a chance to close behind them, new intruders come in as replacements. Two doctors now join the room and stand at the end of my bed. The room feels crowded.

The first introduces themself as a psychiatrist, and the other, a surgeon.

They start to remind me of that vacation that everyone seems to always talk about, and look at me expectantly, obviously awaiting some reaction, but I feel nothing. But as they continue talking, more than anyone around me ever has before, new memories begin to flash before my eyes. They're vague memories, and it's physically challenging to call them to mind, as if my brain is hard at work, searching the depths of some dark and bottomless canyon.

While they speak, I no longer see the bland hospital walls. I see me and my sister lying on the beach. I see the water, which is the loveliest shade of blue. A new memory spins into view, transitioning into the nighttime, and I see an image of myself, floating on my back in the warmest water, underneath the moon. As if someone had pressed fast-forward again, another image appears before my eyes and comes to a screeching halt. I see my feet, and my cheap flip-flops clinging between my toes. I'm stepping onto a boat that sways atop the waves. I sit down, in the front row, and we're speeding forward.

I can feel the breeze against my face, so strong it tosses my hair before my eyes. I can feel the warmth of the sun, and I remember turning my face upward to the sky.

But then, as if the movie's run out of film, the screen goes dark and the memories refuse to continue to play. I know that this can't be the end, yet when I try to call anything else to mind, I am blocked by an unbreakable force. It's as if my brain holds the memories and has tossed away the key, keeping them hidden from me.

I refocus on the doctors before me. What they tell me now takes my breath away, makes me study their faces to gauge whether they're speaking the truth. They tell me those memories are missing, that they come to a sudden end, for one reason. They say that the boat had exploded. Then they continue: "We were able to save your life, but your legs, they couldn't be saved," the one who is the surgeon says.

My eyes instinctually flash to my mom. If they're lying, she would tell me, right?

Expecting to see my mom rise in protest, I see her instead with tears in her eyes. She reaches her hand out, gently touching my shoulder.

"I'm so sorry, but you've lost both of your legs," this stranger concludes.

"I have to ask you: Do you understand what this means?" the psychiatrist asks.

I nod my head yes, but this doesn't make sense. I can feel my legs underneath this blanket. I've seen the bandages wrapped round each limb. I know they were hurt, but I didn't *lose* them. Why are they making me listen to these words when they aren't even true? But there's a deep feeling of loss that sits on my chest with such a heavy weight that it's impossible to ignore. A few tears slide down my face and a mixture of sorrow and confusion whirls around my mind.

"Are there any questions you'd like to ask us?" the psychiatrist asks.

I ask if my friends can come back in.

They each hesitate, surprised by my changing the conversation. Then mom nods her head yes, and the doctors turn to leave. My mom and Paul walk out of the door, crossing paths with my friends who walk in at the same time. The two groups give each other strange looks, and I can't help but wonder what conversation could they be having that they're leaving me out of.

The room returns to the way it was before. I mouth long strings of words to Duffy, she translates for the rest of them, and a grin has returned to my face. The room is filled with laughter. Those words, that shocking news—already forgotten, pushed away by the wall of denial my mind had quickly erected.

Beyond those doors, my mom is not smiling. She's certainly not laughing. She is in reality, a place that I am not ready to yet be.

"You might have to tell her this news many more times. Her brain is protecting her," the doctors explain.

She wants to break down, to fall to the floor, as the burden of this responsibility lands with a crushing intensity upon her. But she knows she has to remain strong, and she knows that she will need to tell me this truth once more, though it will break her heart all over again.

CHAPTER 6

*A*s the door closed behind my friends, their visits now at an end, something disappeared in me, as well. I feel detached and disconnected from the world, as though outside the walls of this room, life goes on, but in here, life and time are both at a standstill. I haven't left this room, gotten out of bed, or even seen the sunshine through a window, in all this time. I just lie here, waiting for each moment to pass. It's like I'm alive, but at the same time, I'm not.

It helps me, I suppose, to hold on to this detachment. It's easier. Especially now, as I deal with far more than the obvious injuries alone, but also with new complications of infection and illness, which seem to suck the remaining life from my withered body.

The first complication is one we hadn't known to expect. Never-ending nausea now brings relentless vomiting—a side effect made far more dangerous by the hollow tube still in place within my throat, which I need to help me to breathe. With too many possible causes for the nausea—the injury to my brain, a side effect of some medication, kidney failure, dialysis—there's no sure way to treat it. So I'm left to endure the heaving motions of my body that continue until I'm crumbling in fatigue. I choke. I sweat. I beg for a moment of relief. But still it continues. So I keep myself muted, disconnected, disappearing from the world, while remaining present.

Then there's the newest infection: pneumonia has settled within my lungs. We'd known to expect this. I've been immobile for too long for this infection not to take its opportunity to strike. Though we knew it would one day arrive, we remained unprepared. In our minds, it was only an infection, something so small compared to all I've already survived. We couldn't have been more wrong. We couldn't have known how cruel this would prove to be. There's no mind creative enough to imagine the noises that escape my chest. There's no way to prepare for the terror as you watch your breaths come so slowly, and with such obvious effort—the act of breathing now a chore rather than a natural reflex.

Sometimes, pneumonia does far more than make my breathing sounds loud and horrific. Sometimes, those breaths transition from challenging to nearly impossible, with only short puffs of an audible inhale breaking into the too-long silence. When this happens, Mom and I lock eyes, and launch into a practiced routine. The call button is pressed, and as we wait, the paranoid thoughts of *What happens if they take too long to get here? What if I die while I'm waiting?* parade through my mind.

A nurse walks in with equipment held in gloved hands, and I feel the first glimmer of hope as I imagine that first gulp of air. But this sense of hope comes alongside the overwhelming fear, and dread, as I know what must happen now during a process that seems so inhumane.

The reason my breaths are now nearly impossible is that my tracheostomy tube has grown thick with infection. A long suction tube will be threaded down my throat to clear a pathway for air. I stare at the ceiling. I place my palms flat against the mattress, hoping that they will remain where I have positioned them. Then I open my mouth wide, and the process begins. I try to stay silent. I try to force myself to remain still. And those in the room beside me try to force themselves to look on in a protective observance, but they can't help it as their faces turn away. It's too difficult to watch.

My face begins to grow a bright purple, and my hands have lifted in the air, against my instructions, and they flail in desperation, struggling to convey that it has been too long since I have taken a breath. Sounds of choking and gasping and sputtering fill the air. My eyes begin to roll, and my head grows dizzy.

Then they pull the tube away. The moment is over. My face returns to its normal shade, and my body relaxes. As the nurse walks away, I mumble a thank-you, though we both know that soon I'll be pressing the call bell again to have the same routine done yet again.

The thought of continuing this process that makes my head grow dizzy, my face turn purplish-blue, and my eyes bulge in their sockets makes me want to scream and cry into the pillow beneath me.

Why am I here? Why is this happening to me?

I lie in this dark room, a thick wooden door sealing me in, wondering how I got to be here, and how my life got to be this way—living with harsh and echoing noises escaping my chest, my head sinking into buckets held before me, and every drop of energy having already been spent by the body that's fighting so desperately to survive. But all the explanations that I have been given about what has happened to me and why I am here have been forgotten. The information that makes my world make sense has been pushed away from my memory.

The stories of that vacation aren't held within my mind. The story of what happened aboard that boat isn't held within my mind. The lists of my injuries are also forgotten. So, as the nurses sneak in through that wooden door each night, and they sink needles into my flesh, I groan aloud and wonder silently why they do these things.

When that one nurse whose shadow I've come to recognize arrives, I prepare for the several attempts that will strike against my skin and burn as though a small flame has been applied. I'll wait as each pin-prick moves to a different location in that desperate search for a vein. Eventually, I will moan until it's clear that I'm being tormented. Each time, I know how and when and where it will end, and I am never surprised as I feel the successful sinking into the back of my hand, and I return to lying with my eyes wide open—too hurt, too confused, too damaged to relax into sleep.

Why am I here? Why is this happening to me?

Mom's friends Kathleen and Janna have flown to Florida and now sit in this room beside me. Since I don't sleep anymore, my mom doesn't either. But now, I watch as she swallows a sleeping aid given to her by the nurse earlier today and slips into the peacefulness of sleep, a gift made possible only by knowing that someone other than she will be watching my bedside tonight. Kathleen has offered to take the first shift.

Watching my mom fall quickly asleep, the process looks so natural, so easy, that it almost seems odd. With nothing to distract me now, no noise other than my breaths, there is nothing stopping the anxious thoughts that stampede through my mind each night and have already arrived once more. I search through the last memories I have, trying to find the missing piece that is the answer to the question of why I am here. But I find nothing, remembering only a quiet, peaceful life in Vermont.

How did I get here? What has happened to me?

I think back to that story that my family once told me. The story they'd made my friends leave the room for. The story they always seemed to talk about. But I can't remember the details. I can hardly remember what it is that they had to say.

My mind begins to race with thoughts that are out of control, so intense they make me want to stand and run from this bed, fueling me with some forgotten energy and a physical need to find the answers. I look over to Kathleen, who sits beside me beneath a blanket to keep away the air-conditioned chill. Her eyes pop open as if she could sense that I'd turned her way.

"What do you need?" she asks.

I gesture to my phone, which sits on the windowsill. Quietly she walks toward it, her steps making no sound as she does her best not to disturb the sleeping figure of my mom. As she goes to hand it to me, I stop her.

"Type in my name and search it," I instruct. "I want to know what happened to me."

Her face drops. She feels a surge of many emotions. First, relief at the sound of my voice, the set of clear direction of familiar tasks, as this proves the functioning of my brain. She'd been worried about that, after hearing of those ominous markings on those scans. She also feels fear, anxiety, and uncertainty. She knows the injuries I'm living with, as everyone else does, but somehow, I still haven't grasped my reality. Can she really be the one to tell me? Can she do this while mom has finally found sleep?

She nervously unlocks my phone and begins to follow my directions. It doesn't take long, and after only the first four letters of my name have been typed into the search engine, previously searched items appear in the search bar. My brow furrows in confusion. She continues, typing my full name: S-T-E-F-A-N-I-E S-C-H-A-F-F-E-R. With the tap of a finger, the search begins.

Pages of article titles appear on the screen, one after the other, in perfectly straight lines like brochures of information all somehow related to me, like classified documents I've just been granted access to. I read the titles one by one:

"Vermont Woman Who Lost Legs in Bahamas Tour Boat Explosion."

"Student Loses Both Legs in a Fatal Boat Explosion."

"22-Year-Old Has Legs Amputated."

I direct Kathleen to click on the first article at the top of the page. My body shakes as I take in each word. There are pictures of my face alongside the black and white words, proving that this is me they're discussing. There's personal information and quotations from family and friends. All showing me that everyone has already known all this. Everyone has been talking about this, discussing this, and I have been the only one who has not known.

I stop reading and look up at Kathleen once more. Speaking in raspy and rushed words, I rattle off questions that have formed in this moment. They are questions that, perhaps, my subconscious has known to ask for some time, but I haven't been able to form the words until now:

"Why did I do that? Why did I get on that boat?"

"Why did anyone save me?"

"Why didn't they just leave me there?"

"Couldn't they tell that I would have been better off dead?"

Every inch of my being shakes as thoughts run wild through my mind. Kathleen reaches forward, grabbing my hand, and pulling me away from my thoughts.

"I don't know, honey. I don't know why this happened to you. I just know that you are fighting the hardest fight there is."

Kathleen settles back into the stiff armchair and pulls the blanket across her legs once more. For the first time in many weeks, my eyelids feel heavy. Fatigued by the information I have read, exhausted from all I have learned of my own life, I feel my body, at long last, begin to melt into sleep. My subconscious, relieved at this discovery of all missing information, guides me now into the peaceful darkness.

As my eyes open to the morning hours, I first see the figure of my mom sitting across from me. She looks rested today. Her eyes look brighter and her voice sounds more like herself. She sits with Kathleen and Janna, and a nervous energy hovers around them. I'm sure Kathleen's told them of my questions last night.

Seeing that my eyes are open, they turn to me in a synchronized movement.

"Do you want to go outside today?" they ask me, careful with their tones and in the amount of enthusiasm they use.

I hear them go on talking, each of them listing descriptions and images, trying to tempt me into this outing. They don't need to, though; I've already decided that I will, and when I agree, I can see the surprise in their eyes. This will be my first time out of bed in months.

We call for assistance, and as we wait for the nurse to arrive, I listen to this group before me chatting happily as any other group of friends would do. A male nurse I've never seen before enters the room, and his annoyance is clear. He seems frustrated by the condition I'm in, annoyed that he has to help me, irked by the idea that he will have to move many machines and tubes and IV ports out of the way. I want to apologize to him for being such an inconvenience.

Knowing I'm too weak to sit up straight in a wheelchair yet, he rolls over a large, cushioned armchair for me to use instead. He takes two strides toward me, wraps his arms around me, and hoists me up in the air. Dropping me down in the chair, he has done his part. He turns to leave the room.

My bones scream in protest at all that just happened. My chest, in the middle of my ribs, where my sternum sits cracked in two, burns with a deep pain and my fingertips dig into the chair's armrests. But I keep my face from giving me away, refusing to show pain. I don't want to be impolite.

"Thank you," I say, forcing the words through my locked teeth.

As the door swings open and my chair moves forward, I catch my first glimpse of the hallways and its bustle of activity. We push past the nursing station of this floor, and those who sit there each wave an enthusiastic *hello*, smiles covering their faces, and I realize that somehow all of these people already know me. We move out of this small area and toward a hallway. Though all I've done is sit in this chair, the few feet we have traveled has already left me sore and exhausted. Someone presses the elevator button, and as we wait, I slowly turn my head, scanning the area. This is when I see the most beautiful sight I've ever seen.

When the group notices my awe-struck expression, they push me closer and stand beside me. We never move from this position, never leaving this hallway or entering that elevator. The bell dings, the elevator arrives, and the sound barely registers with me. I can't look away.

Three rectangular windows sit together, side by side, in the middle of this plain hospital hall. From these windows, I get my first glimpse of the outside world. I see the sky, so perfectly blue. I see the sun, so bright that I swear I can feel the warmth on my skin. I see the fluffy white clouds hanging so perfectly in place. The world is on pause, as I imagine that I am in this armchair, sitting outside, beneath the wide sky, the breeze blowing across my skin.

Mom wheels her chair up beside me and sits with her legs extended straight out and her feet, finally free from their casts, propped up on a bench. It's a tragic site, this mother-daughter pair both so viciously broken, staring up at the sky from the hospital hall in which they live. But for me, it's a perfect moment. It's a hopeful moment. It's a moment that tells me now, how lucky I am to be alive.

I'm not sure how much time has passed, but we head back toward my room. As my chair moves forward and I sit so perfectly still, I again take in all that is happening around me. Back inside my room, I remain in this oversized chair and turn to those around me.

"Tell me again," I say simply, but they know what I mean.

Kathleen pulls up my iPad and props it in front of me. I don't ask for help and slowly lift my arm and carefully type in each letter with one fingertip. Rather than reading the articles again, I move to the images and videos. I press "play" on the video at the top of my screen. I watch, as a boat burns before my eyes, and a monotone reporter's voice fills the air, but I ignore the words; I already know what's happening. I already know who was on that boat. Tears quietly stream down my face.

I feel my mom's hand land protectively on my shoulder.

"You don't have to watch this," she tells me gently.

But I want to. I need to. As the video continues, I watch as a bright red circle is being drawn around a seemingly lifeless body that's being lifted off the boat. My chest, spreading in a perfectly straight line down my ribs, seems to rip into two as I realize that this body wrapped in the bright-red circle is the body that belongs to me.

I turn to my mom who still stands behind me.

"I lost my legs. They're really gone," I say in a startlingly calm voice.

It's no longer a question. It is, this time, a realization. Her eyes are red and her cheeks wet as she answers me: "Yes…you did."

CHAPTER 7

There are only a few moments from that day that remain in my memory. Others might assume that it would be haunting, remembering the details. But to me, it is comforting. It's the missing moments, the gaps of time I can't recall, that sink my heart into a panic and lead my mind to the darkest of places. Because as I stare at my broken figure, my torn flesh, my scarred skin, my missing legs, I can't help but wonder, *What nightmares have I lived, but forgotten?*

But now, I've convinced my family to complete the story for me:

The explosion caused large pieces of metal, chunks of the boat itself, the awning that had been above us, to topple to the deck of the boat. But I had already been thrown from my seat, and so they landed on top of me, burying me beneath them and hiding me from view. The side of the boat's frame, either melted from the heat of the flames, broken from the force of the explosion, or maybe from a combination of both causes, had warped, causing it to bend and twist upwards, curling up and over my body. I was covered in metal from above and wrapped in it from below.

Once everyone in our group had each regained the slightest of understanding of what had just happened, they assumed, that like others, I had been tossed into the ocean. So, that's where they began to search.

This was when those two Bahamian men, strangers I will forever wish I could know, began making their way toward our boat, toward the flames, rather than escaping as many others would.

These men had looked for me alone. Hardly a moment after the explosion, our captain had thrown the boat into neutral, grabbed the young co-captain and leapt off the side of the boat. Not stopping there, he continued to make his way back to shore, back to safety. Leaving young children on his boat to fend for themselves. Leaving injured passengers behind. Leaving me there to die.

As my body was carefully floated toward the second boat that remained just behind us, this captain remained standing tall in anticipation. His decision to hold his position was heroic in its simplicity. If he had waivered in his courage and moved his vessel farther away, there would have been no way to rush me to shore. There would have been no way for me to ever have made it out of those waters.

This is when one of the few memories I can still recall comes suddenly to mind. The memory that makes my skin clammy and cold. I think to past pains of submerging a scrape or a thin, hardly noticeable cut in a pool of salty water and the burning sensations those had caused. Now, as I think of my torn-apart body and the choppy ocean water soaking into my skin, I multiply this sensation, over and over, with no end in sight. My mind has blocked out the pain.

Once shore was in sight, no one wasted any time. The same process was repeated one final time, floating me back toward land, though once we arrived, there was another obstacle to overcome: there was no ambulance. Onlookers yelled at us to wait, but everyone around me knew that I didn't have a moment to waste.

There was ongoing construction nearby. John and Paul found a large piece of leftover wood and placed me upon it as if it were the medical backboard I should have had. Sheila was off in the parking lot, where a parked pick-up truck sat in the perfect position. We didn't know who owned it, but she began emptying the contents of the pick-up's cargo bed on to the ground, and as the owner of the truck rushed to where we were, his eyes widened at the sight of my tormented figure. Sheila gave him simple directions, telling him to drive us to the hospital and to drive us there fast.

Thankfully, he knew those windy dirt roads like the back of his hand, but even so, it took nearly half an hour for us to arrive.

As we sped along the roads, Brooke sat beside me. She forced me down when I attempted to sit up. She fed me sips of water, commanded me to keep my eyes open, and helped me to hang on.

We arrived at the hospital, but the sight was both reassuring and confusing. The hospital's doors were locked. The group banged their fists against the doors until a nurse arrived and peeked outside.

"What are you doing here? The ambulance is on its way," she asked from behind the still-closed doors.

"We couldn't wait! She needs help now!" Sheila yelled.

Opening the doors to us, nurses went to carry me inside, but Sheila demanded a backboard first, knowing from my cries that something was wrong with my spine. Sheila has little to no medical training but her knowledge of the human body from her work as a personal trainer and survival training from her time in the United States Navy made all the difference.

We then ran into another problem: there were no doctors inside this hospital. Sheila watched, her eyes wide with horror, as the nurses gathered cardboard boxes, the type used to hold a six-pack of soda cans, from the floor, intending to use them to splint my unstable fractures. Next, as they worked to place an IV, Sheila shouted. My arms were both split open—there wasn't enough left of my arms to make finding a vein a simple task. Sheila pointed out a clear vein just below my shoulder, but the nurses continued searching along my arms. Eventually, the IV sank into my hand.

It was in solving the next problem that Sheila jumped into action. I'd been repeatedly saying, "I need to pee." It could have been a result of many things: the pressure in my cracked spine, the pooling of blood in my pelvis, or internal injuries. The nurses listened to me and set about inserting a catheter to empty my bladder. Sheila watched as they repeatedly tried and failed, while blood gushed from between my legs. This bleeding was likely a result of massive internal bleeding. It was too much to watch, and Sheila took over, successfully inserting the catheter herself—and wondering how she had just managed to do so.

Finally, a doctor arrived.

It was decided that I would be transferred to a hospital in Nassau. An ambulance would take me to a small plane that would be equipped with the necessary life-saving machinery and just enough skilled staff, it was hoped, that I would survive the flight. While we waited in the ambulance, eager to speed toward the waiting plane, Sheila sat beside me, asking me questions to keep me awake. But with each moment that passed, my answers came more slowly. My words began to slur. My eyes began to close. My face began to look distorted—less awake, less alive.

Sweat covered every inch of my body and continued to pour from my skin as we went on waiting in this stuffy ambulance. I asked for ice chips to quench my sudden thirst. This is when Tiran, Maleka's husband, lying across from me in the ambulance, asked Sheila, "How's she doing?" Though he was hurt himself, he was concerned for me.

As if I were answering him, my body suddenly shifted and my requests for ice ceased, creating the silence that all had been dreading.

My blood pressure crashed, and a long, intense moment passed. Then I broke the silence, and Sheila saw me in what looked to her to be the obvious process of dying. My silence was replaced with tortured groans and mumbled noises. My body began to convulse. My eyes seemed to be open but somehow remained hidden in the back of my skull. I was no longer awake, but I also wasn't asleep. I wasn't alive, but I also wasn't dead. I was somewhere in between.

Sheila reacted quickly, making demands, shouting instructions, taking command. She knew it was past time to get me to that plane. But they told her it was time for her to leave, that there wouldn't be enough room for her on the plane. A nurse grabbed her by the shoulders. She looked directly into Sheila's eyes, breaking through her unwillingness to leave, and she said, "I've got her."

Sheila measured her words, her tone, her demeanor, and she knew that she meant each word. A transition of care now began.

Though the distance to Nassau was short, I'm told I nearly died several times on the way. And as I arrived at this new hospital, my condition seemed to only worsen. The new hospital staff checked my vitals and saw a frightening reality. My vitals were deemed "unrecordable"—there was no detectable blood pressure.

They examined my legs. "MESS" stands for Mangled Extremity Severity Score. This scoring system was created to determine when limb salvage attempts are appropriate, and when an amputation is required instead. A MESS score of seven or higher signifies that amputation is needed. My legs presented in nearly identical condition: both received a score of eight.

I was rushed to the operating room. My legs were prepped, the surgery began, and two amputations were performed.

The wounds were packed and wrapped in dressings, and my blood pressure began to rise. It really had been a matter of my legs or my life.

I was admitted to the hospital's Intensive Care Unit, with full Advanced Cardiac Life Support protocol in place. Antibiotics, sedatives, pain medications, and countless other prescriptions, began to flood my veins.

Meanwhile, my mom, badly injured herself, had still received no medical care. After several hours had passed by, she was airlifted to join me in Nassau. But as she boarded the small plane, she was shocked to see the captain of *our* boat joining her. This is the man who had left us on our own in the midst of a nightmare. But now, he was being airlifted alongside her. Nonetheless, he walked on to the plane, his head hung low, unable to look at her.

The plane couldn't leave yet—they had to wait for the doctor. When he finally arrived, the doctor stepped closer to my mom. This is when she vividly recalls how a refreshing breeze of air swept across them, wafting the unmistakable scent of alcohol off of him and toward her.

Soon after, they arrived in Nassau. I see the pain, fresh in her eyes, as she relays this part of the story to me. Deep down she had known this moment might come, but her mind had given her a beautiful gift: until this moment, she'd been living within a place of denial. Her mind had blocked the images of my limbs and rationalized all that had happened. But then a surgeon walked into her room, and this is what she heard:

"Your daughter is still alive. But I'm so sorry, she's lost both of her legs."

She tells me how her head had instinctually whipped away until she faced the corner, unable to look at this man any longer. She shook her head, trying to push away his words.

"No … no … no," she repeated out loud, rocking back and forth.

The doctor eventually backed out of the room, knowing there was nothing he could say, nothing he could do, to help ease her pain.

Her heart had just broken, but with all of his medical training, this was not something he could heal.

She wishes she could go back to him now, to tell him she's sorry. To tell him she hadn't meant to place the blame on him alone. In that moment, it was all that she could do. But now, she's able to grasp on to and value that first piece of information he'd shared— that I was alive.

It was while we were in Nassau that my dad and my older brother, George, arrived. My dad had answered a phone call earlier, when my mom tried to explain what had happened. But shock and grief and pain had blurred her words, and she could not convey what she needed to say. Again, Sheila had taken control, grabbing the phone from my mom. "It's bad," she'd told him. "Get here now."

My dad is one of those people who, no matter the circumstances, is always sure of himself. He thinks rationally, makes decisions based on facts or numbers, and is always confident in his choices. I, on the other hand, could debate the most insignificant of options for days, changing my mind a thousand times. But he never waivers or changes his mind, no matter who might attempt to sway his decision, and he arrived just as those qualities were desperately needed.

With the amount of blood that I had lost, parts of my kidneys had died, causing them to shut down. I was in kidney failure and needed dialysis. The question was, Did we start dialysis, a timely treatment, here in this Nassau hospital, or did we wait until I could be flown to the United States and start there? The doctors in Nassau debated what to do. Some of them warned that I should stay, saying that I would not survive the flight home. Others disagreed, saying that if I was going to survive, I *needed* to get back to the States and that there I would have my best chance. There was no clear answer, but the choice was up to us.

My dad looked around. He weighed the pros and he weighed the cons, quickly, and efficiently.

"She's coming home," he said.

That was that. A decision was made. I was going home.

It was decided that Fort Lauderdale's Broward Medical Health Center was both the closest and the best prepared for my arrival. As we landed, not only did a quickly assembled group of skilled surgeons await my arrival, but unbeknownst to us, news of our boat's explosion had already reached the United States. And so a crowd of reporters were ready, eager to learn of these American tourists and their miraculous return home. They wanted our story, but as my comatose body was wheeled into surgery, none of us yet knew that in our fight, our story, and our battle to survive, we were still only in the beginning.

CHAPTER 8

*M*om stands in a shower with a floor stained from overuse. As the water seeps down her forehead and drips off her chin, her body shakes with the sobs. She needs the seclusion of this small patient shower to shed these tears because as I lie in my room, receiving one final session of dialysis before we leave, she must protect me from the burden of knowing how intensely she wants to go home.

Today, I am being transferred to a hospital closer to home, in Cambridge, Massachusetts, and she is going with me. She won't be going home to her kitchen with her favorite coffee mugs, or to her bed with her soft comforter and perfectly plump pillows. Her youngest daughter will go back to school and will re-join her soccer team. And Mom won't be home to help with homework, to greet her each morning with breakfast, to cheer for the goals she scores, or to console for the games that should have been won but had escaped them. She won't be going home, and she doesn't know when she will be again.

She knows why she is doing this. Why she is choosing to stay rather than sending me alone, when I haven't even asked her to do so. She needs me almost as much as I need her, and if we've learned anything from recent events—when just the other night, my lungs had filled with fluid, my breaths had come to a halt, and my oxygen saturation tanked, all while I was alone with only my mom beside me—it's just how desperately I need an advocate for my care.

But it still feels unnatural. Unnatural to give it all up, for a child she had already watched grow into an independent adult, who is now rocked back to a state where she cannot feed, bathe, or dress herself.

She had nearly lost a child. A loss that would have been too great to allow her mind to consider. And even though I am alive, she's stood too close to that ledge for far too long and her energy has been spent, as she fought for solid ground to hold on to. Her energy has been drained, as she looked over the edge, and the reality she tried not to consider stared back at her each moment. And even though I am beginning to heal, she often finds herself unsure of how to stand tall any longer.

She has no sufficient pain medication, yet she has been injured. She has no medications for anxiety or depression, yet she has survived a trauma, with its own memories and shadows that pursue her though each day. She is suffering. So today, she allows herself to cry, with her head hung low, staring at the stained shower floor.

Then she pulls herself together. She lifts her head and steps out of the shower. She dries her hair and changes clothes. And as she makes her way back into my room crammed full with dialysis machines and the nurses beside me, she spots me and can't help but smile. She can't help but relax at the sight of my open eyes and my naïve happiness clear through the grin on my face. I'm covered with countless blankets spread over every inch of me, even piled high atop my head like a makeshift top hat, as I'm freezing from the chill of dialysis. As I watch her return, I begin to speak with excitement.

"Ready?" I ask her, my grin growing wider.

She smiles and nods. But she doesn't look quite as excited as she should. Doesn't she know that today is the day we begin to get our lives back?

"Ready," she agrees.

Spaulding Cambridge Hospital for Continuing Medical Care is really a long name to help explain that the facility is partnered with the famous rehabilitation center Spaulding Charlestown. But this hospital is a sort of stepping-stone for patients who need that "continued medical care" before going on to the next adventure of focused and intense rehabilitation—patients like me, trapped in limbo between ICU rooms and rehab centers.

I am ready to begin steps toward rehabilitation, but this hospital offers the other, more important necessities. A dialysis clinic is located downstairs and the nurses and physicians are able to medicate, treat, and diagnose any remaining conditions—which in my case are quite a few.

This hospital is a building that comes with the charm and character of an older New England structure, with tall brick walls covered in vines that crawl toward the sky, and the surrounding area bustles with activity. To one side is a small café, filled at all times with students from Harvard University, who sip their coffees, teas, or freshly made juices hunched over textbooks and laptops. The city is so alive, so dramatic, so full of energy. Soon, I will learn that the inside of Spaulding Cambridge will feel quite the opposite. Within these walls, I will find myself feeling anything other than full of life, anything other than young, as my startling reality will grow clear; I am no longer the girl enjoying the cafés and exploring my favorite city, I am the girl within the hospital walls. The city outside will simply be a tease.

Our small medivac plane gets us there late in the evening. The seatbelt that stretches diagonally across me is undone, the locks of my stretcher click free, and we make our way out of the plane. The New England air sweeps across my cheeks with a comforting touch and a rush of familiar memories arrive in my mind. My eyes close, and I exhale in relief.

A parked ambulance sits waiting, ready to carry us the final distance from airport to hospital. My stretcher glides across the pavement, rocking slightly over each bump, until we arrive at the two doors opened wide at the back of this vehicle. Once I'm locked into place in the ambulance, we begin once more, traveling quickly now, and I silently stare up ahead, with a permanent grin on my face, while my mom happily chats with the emergency staff who sit beside her. This last stretch of distance passes in no time at all. We park, and the doors open wide once more at our final location. As the drivers work to unload the stretcher, my ears first hear what my eyes cannot yet see. I hear a familiar voice, and my grin expands even further, knowing who it is that I will soon see.

My Uncle Steve, only a few hours ago, had answered the phone to hear the heartbreaking voice of my mom, his little sister, expressing her worries and pain as we began our transfer. He hadn't asked many questions, but instead, with his typical calm and cool demeanor, he told her exactly what it was that she desperately needed to hear. He told her he'd hang up the phone, pack up his car, and meet us here.

I see them now, standing in a long embrace, both of them hanging on for a moment longer than usual. He's probably the person she needed to see today, more than anyone else in this world.

He's incredibly kind and easygoing, and his outward appearance seems to match this personality of his. His hair is slightly long, with newly grown strands of light grey. He wears his usual loose cloth pants and a unique graphic tee, but his most noticeable feature is the easy grin that can always be found on his face. He has the striking bright blue eyes that my mom tells me reminds her of her extended family, the same blue that can be found in my Grammy's eyes, as well. I know my mom would love to have eyes the same color, but hers are instead an always-changing-in-the-light shade of light brown that at times transitions to a light shade of green.

Her eyes don't match this shared family color because my mom was adopted. It's a simple fact, almost common even, but it's a fact about her that I've always loved. Countless times I've stopped to wonder how many decisions needed to be made *exactly* as they were for this family of mine to be created. It not only feels lucky, but it feels purposeful, as if we've all been perfectly made for one another, as if we've chosen one another. The first decision was made in that moment when my Grammy had set out to that New York City orphanage. She's told me the story so many times—how that very first moment that she saw my mom, the baby-version of my mom had looked up, made eye contact, and beamed with an enormous smile. My Grammy had known right then that this baby was meant to be her daughter.

So they went home. Later, they moved to a small town in Vermont, where my mom had grown up. And that's where she'd then meet my dad, in this one tiny town in all the world, and now, our family had been created.

I stare at my mom in awe as I think of these puzzle pieces being chosen and gathered together. I suppose I shouldn't be surprised at how my mom has held me up these past months because, even though she doubts it herself, I've always known the strength within her. Not only was my mom once that small child found in a New York City orphanage—leaving her with those perennial questions that I can't pretend to understand about how and why she was given up so early on—but, to compound those questions, when she was only seven years old, her adoptive father had one day without notice gathered his things and left her and that newly created family of hers. She's lived through the double impact of wondering *why* they left.

It was a time when both my mom and my Grammy represented in perfect clarity the type of strong women that they each came to be, or perhaps always were. My Grammy pulled herself together without hesitation, and my mom never complained about the changes in her life, even as they lost the house that she'd grown up in and moved to a smaller option. They are equally quiet and humble about the heroism with which they've lived, as if another option never crossed their minds. But their lives remind me to be thankful, both for them and for the life they've given me.

My stretcher rolls forward, toward the front door of this new building, as I lie here lost in my thoughts. My mom and uncle follow behind, and it's as if the air has changed, allowing my mom and I to both breathe once again. As we settle into this new room, a nurse by the name of Steph begins the routine that has been completed many times before. Each time a new patient is due to arrive at this hospital, nursing staff must first complete several steps. First, they read the patient's medical history, which informs them of all injuries and diagnoses, as well as all past treatments, surgeries, medications, and any information that might aid their care for the patient in the hope of avoiding repetitions or mistakes.

The second step is that once this history is read and understood, the intake nurse then calls for what's called "report" from the facility from which the patient is being transferred, to hear in their words the patient's history and diagnosis. In my case, this would be Broward Medical Health Center.

Steph always pays close attention to even the smallest of details so that she can be prepared for her incoming patient. Normally this is a somewhat quick and simple task, but today feels different. Her breath suddenly feels shallow, and as she continues to read, she feels her limbs beginning to tremble. Her mind races with all that she sees. There is nothing routine about this process today.

As she reads this history of mine, a list of questions she will need to ask Broward Medical continues to grow. She's never read such a complicated summary. She's never seen such a long list of these "current and remaining medical problems," and she's never needed to ask as many questions as she will need to in this report. Each injury she reads is carefully illustrated within her medical mind, but she is unable to put together all that she has read. Because, quite simply, her mind can't wrap its way around the idea that someone has survived all this. The dominant question in her mind now is a simple one: *How is this girl still alive?*

She gathers herself together, steadies her voice, and picks up the phone to call for report. It's a phone call that will last longer than any other she has done before.

⌒

As the morning sun rises and a new day begins, the warm rays sneak through the large window and land upon my bed. I hadn't had any windows in those Florida ICU rooms. It's a small change, but to me it feels nearly life-changing.

Steph walks toward my door, preparing for her first shift in this room. On any other day, she would stroll in with confidence and ease, her energetic and outgoing personality radiating around her until it fills the room. Today, she pauses.

As she stands before my door, those injuries she's just read about sprint through her mind once more. And she adds in some additional concerns as she wonders what else might not have been covered in that list. What else might she have to deal with that isn't revealed through a medical history? What's my personality, how am I dealing with the trauma, am I depressed, angry, miserable? Will I be terrible to be around?

With a deep breath, she puts the questions on hold. She shakes out her arms, rolls back her shoulders, and disguises herself with a mask of seriousness, obscuring her personality so as to avoid any possible triggers.

Realizing she's been paused before my door, not moving an inch, for how long she has no idea, she pushes herself into motion. The door swings open, and she takes her first steps into my room.

At first glance, she sees a childlike figure tucked within the bleached-white sheets. Sheets that fall flat too early. My body's slid down from the top of the bed, as my core muscles can't hold me in place. As Steph introduces herself, she gets a quiet, polite answer from me, as I have donned a mask of my own—one created from shame, embarrassment, and nerves. My mom is friendlier, and with a smile on her face, she limps around the bed and toward Steph to shake her hand.

Nurse Steph silently scolds herself. She's been so preoccupied with the patient and with her own fears that she hasn't given a moment's thought to the family that comes along with me.

She begins with a nervous joke, commenting on our matching names, but insisting she prefers the spelling of mine. Again, I'm nervous, so I reply only with a smile.

I have hopes for today, and in an unexpected moment of boldness, I speak up to this new nurse. I won't know this, but it will be in this moment that nurse Steph's opinion of me first begins to change. It will be this moment that she begins to see me with far more respect than even I see myself. The requests that to me seem so simple will take Steph's breath away, as she realizes all her expectations are proved wrong. She expected anger and withdrawal from the world around me, and yet she will instead claim to only hear strength and a quiet sort of dignity. I'm not asking for much.

"Can I take a shower?" I ask her.

That asking to take a shower suddenly feels so dramatic is a crystal-clear example of how strange my life has become. That it has been many months since I've taken a *real* shower, and not simply been sponge bathed or had my hair washed from my hospital bed, is a startling concept.

She smiles and says she'll have to check with her supervisors. That answer will have to do for now. I move on to my next request.

"Can I go outside today?"

This wasn't what she'd been expecting at all.

"Sure, we'll get you ready in just a little bit," she replies.

Now that I'm in Massachusetts, I'm only a three-hour drive from my dad and my sister. Since it's the weekend, they're here today, and will be every weekend from now on. As my sister walks toward me, my heart fills with joy, both at the sight of her and with knowing what it is she carries in her hand.

Behind her, she tows a small suitcase, packed full with my belongings from home. Not only has the fact that I haven't taken a shower for nearly two months rid me of all the familiar sensations of what it means to be a human, but another mundane task I have found myself craving is that of putting on clothing. Every day and night have blended together without that simple act of getting dressed for the day to create any distinction between the two.

In Florida, my mom had tried her very best. She'd gotten in her wheelchair and gone from store to store, purchasing the softest, easiest to get on, pieces of clothing she could find. And they were all far better than the hospital gowns that hung open even when they were tied, remaining uncomfortably revealing. But none of them were my own. Inside the bag in my sister's hands are *my* clothes.

The over-worn cotton fabrics piling before me look silky and beautiful and warm. I hold each piece, grasping on to the familiarity they each bring and the stories they share. Memories swirl through my mind: the T-shirts from soccer camps that somehow still fit me, the colorful tees with bold logos from each sorority event, the clothing I wore to the gym, the clothing I slept in, the clothing I wore as I lounged on my used furniture in those grungy college apartments, all of it bringing a piece of *me* back to me.

As nurse Steph walks back in to help me change, I already know that this is the moment that the shell of my modesty is cracked wide open. Gently, she lifts my arms into the air and begins to dress me like a life-size doll. She slips each sleeve over my arms and head. Slowly, and carefully, she slips my bottoms over the swollen ends of my limbs, pulling them up until they rest on my hips, as I lay still, entirely helpless.

I look down at myself and can't hold back the words that I've spoken far too many times in my life. The words that have made all of my friends and all of my family grow irritated with me countless times.

"I think I want to change."

Old habits die hard, I suppose. These clothes are familiar, and yet my own skin is not. A worn-in T-shirt can't disguise what is now so obviously different, and yet I continue to try. Believing that eventually I'll try on the right shirt and suddenly I'll look the same as I always have. But T-shirts are comfortable, they're not magic.

Each time I look at myself, the memories that just a moment ago seemed so sweet now taunt me relentlessly. The last time I wore this T-shirt there was no purplish scar tracing my throat. The last time I wore these bottoms my legs didn't end so abruptly. I wasn't so swollen, I wasn't so scarred, I wasn't so bruised. Nothing within this suitcase will ever feel just right.

It's strange for nurse Steph to watch this internal conflict. Here in this hospital, she rarely treats anyone under the age of fifty, let alone a young college-aged female, with every insecurity possible trampling through her mind. As she looks at me, she begins to take in these additional layers of conflict and injury that could never have been listed on those reports and could have easily been so invalidated.

She watches as I struggle to come to terms with the appearance of my clothes, hair, face, and body. And though she is not me, as she stands across the room, a witness to this, she *feels* it as well. She feels the weight and the gravity of all that I must accept, as I attempt to come to terms not only with disability and trauma but now with the added pressures so often placed on young women about how exactly to look. Like a sponge, she absorbs my pain.

When I am finally dressed and moderately content, Steph begins to help me out of bed. For someone who can't sit up on her own, a transfer from mattress to wheelchair is a time-consuming chore. A mechanical noise whirs in the air, and I wonder what it is. A claw-like piece moves toward me. Steph wraps my body in two black straps, and I'm still unsure what's happening. She picks up a small remote, and the mechanical noise starts up again, and suddenly, my body isn't against the mattress anymore. My little limbs go crisscrossed and a net holds underneath me. My eyes grow wide, and my face grows hot. I spin my head around, frantically looking around me as I float through the air, until I spot my mom looking up at me, a shocked expression of her own on her face. I'm above the bed, then I make my way across, and I'm being lowered down, landing now in a wheelchair. That machine was a Hoyer lift, used to transfer patients.

As I inspect the floor around me, my subconscious hunts for the missing items. Before we leave to head outside, I ask one last question.

"Wait, what am I going to wear for shoes?"

The room grows silent. My mom answers me hesitantly.

"Uhm … Stef, you don't need shoes," she says.

I pause for a moment, carefully considering her words. Realizing what I have forgotten, I burst out laughing, and the collective sigh of relief is audible.

"Oh my gosh, I totally forgot," I say. The concept of going outside with no shoes on feels too strange.

Following Steph's directions, my family and I make our way down the hallways until we reach a glass door leading out to the courtyard. The wide yard is filled with lush green grass separated only by brick pathways. The courtyard space is filled with a stone fountain and wooden tables, and surrounded by tall trees that seem to have withstood all time. This outside area presents a comforting New England air.

Hours pass as we bask in the sun, tucked away at a picnic table and chatting with ease, as if we've forgotten all about the past months.

Above us, looking out from a window on that fourth floor, Steph sees an ordinary scene that again sends a wave of shock through her. She sees a picturesque picnic table surrounded by a family. Each bench is filled, and on the edge sits a young girl in a wheelchair. She can't hear us, but she can feel the laughter from where she stands. She admires our smiles and our simple joy, and feels warmth within her chest as she catches a glimpse of a tender moment: Brooke leans over and rests her head against my shoulder, our hands intertwine, and I close my eyes, savoring the sun on my skin and the comfort of my little sister beside me. It's an act that came without thought, an act that though instinctive and unplanned wouldn't have happened had I been removed from the picture.

As we make our way back inside, my sister walks beside me while my dad pushes my wheelchair with a protective hand. My Uncle Steve radiates joy as he walks beside my mom, who finally has an expression of calm in her eyes. Together we make our way in through the doors, leaning on each other more than any of us yet knows. We're stronger together, happier together, and yet…entirely unprepared for what is soon to come.

CHAPTER 9

efore my dad and sister head back home for the work and school week to come, we first pause in the hallway. Looking at my dad, I reiterate my complete seriousness.

"If they come in here and tell me that I can't shower, then I'm leaving," I tell him.

"Okay, sure," he says with a grin. And I know he's just trying to placate me.

When I'd asked, what feels so long ago now, I was told that first a supervisor needed to be asked, and then his or her supervisor needed to be asked, and the idea of my taking a shower had turned into a highly debated subject.

Now Nurse Steph walks in with two others beside her, holding a pile of plastic in her hands.

"Good news, you can shower," she tells me. "We have to cover all your open wounds, any IV ports, and any recent incisions," she explains, pointing to the supplies in her hand. Each sheet of plastic will act as a waterproof barrier. They're large square sections, with double-sided tape on each edge, so that they will stick firmly to my skin.

She wraps each of my arms with two pieces, so that my forearms are now covered, with no skin remaining free. My stomach gets another piece, in order to cover my scar and my feeding tube. The ends of my legs first get extra layers of bandage, then a plastic bag is added over that, and then the plastic sheets are added as the final touch. A smaller piece is placed on my throat, and another on my bicep where my IV sits. And suddenly, I feel as though I've nearly turned into a plastic bag myself.

A large shower wheelchair, with enormous cushioned wheels and a waterproof seat, is wheeled into my room. The Hoyer lift repeats its work, moving toward me, lowering from the ceiling, scooping me up, and placing me in the chair. As I sit in this oversized chair, my fingertips grip the armrests as I secretly try to keep myself from slipping down and on to the floor. Slowly, my mom, Steph, two nursing aides, and I make our way out of this private room and down the hallway toward the spare shower. Keeping my eyes low, I pretend no one can see me as I travel through this busy lobby, wearing only these sheets of plastic and a thin cotton bathrobe.

When we arrive at a large empty room, it takes me a moment to realize that the enormous space before me is actually the shower itself. The overhead faucet is all that gives it away since this bath is as large as an entire bathroom would usually be, and the bathroom that the shower is within is the size of two rooms combined. My chair is pushed toward the faucet overhead, and I sit silently, looking at the people before me and patiently waiting for everyone to leave so that I can begin my shower. The silence continues until it feels entirely awkward.

Silently I begin asking myself questions, trying to figure out what is going on this moment. *Do I ask them to leave? What are they waiting for? Why are they all still standing in here?*

Then it hits me. They're not going to leave. This crowd of strangers around me are all going to help me as I shower. In a small way, I hate myself for believing it would go any differently. And I know that I should be thankful that I'm not lying in a bed and that I am in a real shower. I should be grateful that all of these people are here and willing to help me. But it's hard to feel thankful when all I feel is broken. It's hard to be grateful when I feel like I have been stripped of my right to privacy, like I'm no longer someone who has the right to protect her own body or to control how much people see of me.

I feel the rough cotton of my robe slipping off my shoulders as someone behind me carefully removes the last shred of fabric. I keep my eyes on the floor. The cool air and the many sets of eyes upon me both seem to bring a physically painful sensation that spreads across me. I want to cover myself. I want to pull the curtain round and slip into the shower alone. I want to wrap my arms around my chest and legs and hide myself from view. But all of this, I cannot do.

Staring down at the floor, imaging myself anywhere but here, I feel like a piece of myself has chipped away, flushed away by the water that's just turned on, and into the drain in the center of the floor.

I wait for the warmth of the water to bring some comfort, some relief. But the water sprays against the plastic, bouncing off of me, never even touching my skin. Only my hair is soaked, and my body begins to shake.

"I'm freezing," I mutter sadly. A splash of warm water hits the side of my abdomen. It does nothing to take away the chill.

A young girl moves to stand in front of me. She picks up the body wash and I look away, unable to watch, as this stranger begins to wash my skin. Someone behind me works their fingertips through my hair. They cleanse, rinse, and shave the hair that's grown along my skin. They wash my face, and a tear escapes my eye. I hope it blends with the water.

Finally, the water is turned off. My mom rushes for the towels, knowing how desperately I need them. They're stiff, bleached, thin hospital towels, and I miss the plush soft ones at home.

I miss my home.

With my bathrobe tied round me again, I feel my chair beginning to move. This time I'm painfully aware of the many eyes that can see me as I wheel past them, soaking wet, barely covered, and entirely embarrassed.

Back in my room, all the plastic now has to be removed. It was just put on moments ago, and the glue is still tight on my skin. Each strip sits so close to my injuries and incisions that as they pull each one away, I bite down on my cheek, pushing away the scream that sits on the tip of my tongue. One after the other, each square-shape of plastic is painfully peeled away, and it feels as though they've taken pieces of my skin with them.

Keeping my bathrobe on, I repeat the same mortifying process once more and patiently wait for the Hoyer lift. Up in the air my broken, wet, and shaking body goes, until I finally land back in bed; this time, with no desire to get up again.

⌇

Most of us probably know that feeling, often when you least expect it, when something hits you just right and knocks the wind out of you. It usually passes after a moment or two, but in that brief time, your head begins to spin, you rock back and forth in pain, and the moans escaping your lips are loud, ugly, and uncontrollable.

There's one memory, from years ago, that now plays within my mind. I'd been playing a game with my travel club soccer team. Our opponents had a defense consisting of girls who were each as tall as they were strong, and as we lined up before them, we had to crane our necks to look up at them. They were an intimidating force, making that goal and its crosshatched net seem an impenetrable fortress guarded by the strongest of soldiers. But though we were small, we were quicker than they were. We'd speed and twist and dance down the field, passing the half-line and breaking free. With the goal in sight, our hearts would race with the thrill of that prized moment that was sure to come. I'd made it there before, but this time, I knew I would go all the way. My right leg lifted in the air, my toes pointed toward the ground in the perfect and practiced angle, ready to lift the ball into the air. Out of nowhere, a harsh blow from my side instead sent me soaring while the ball was whisked away by my opponent.

The whistle blew, a foul was called, but I couldn't get up. My knees curled up toward my chest, and I rolled around in the shape of a ball. My mind raced, telling me to be quiet, telling me to get up. The heaves of my chest were guttural and low. I couldn't get a single breath in. I'd had the wind knocked out of me.

When I finally stood, the girl beside me apologized for the tough blow. I nodded in respect and gathered myself to get back into the game. It'd been a foul in the penalty box. I was granted a free penalty kick, and this time, the ball soared into the far corner of that goal. It'd all been worth it.

These first weeks here in Cambridge remind me of that moment. Except this time, the opponent and I don't shake hands or feel any respect or camaraderie. There is no ref to call a foul or grant me either enough time to get back up, and no retribution for the blow. Because now, as soon as I gather my breath, I'm hit just as hard once more.

It started as soon as I got here. Those medications I'd been on had created a blissful high that I'd been unaware even existed. Until now, my pain had been well-managed. Until now, I could push away the doctors' diagnoses and realizations as if they didn't matter. I'd been given the gift of ignorance, created by a steady stream of both morphine and fentanyl. In these two weeks, those doses have been safely decreased, and I'm now on no pain medication, and *everything* hurts. My bones feel as though they're continuously cracking in two. The phantom pain is no longer a foreign medical term but is the harshest of sensations, submerging the lower legs that no longer exist into a pot of scalding water from which I can't remove them. Even my insides hurt, with a pain I had never known was possible. But it is my back that is the very worst of all, creating a sensation that at times leaves me unable to speak, unable to breathe.

I can't blame this lack of pain medication on anyone other than myself. The nurses aren't cruelly withholding this relief; they're often pleading with me to take the meds. But once I'd refused them once, my stubborn nature set in. Not allowing me to give in and say yes the next time.

The only possible distractions from this pain are other horrors. The vomiting has only gotten worse, so not only am I in pain, but I am incredibly sick. Every five minutes, for all twenty-four hours of the day, my head is inside a bucket, vomiting up white foam and green bile since there is not a single drop of nutrition in my stomach.

My collarbone protrudes from my chest, my ribs are so clearly defined that they look like swords, and my cheekbones are gaunt and jutting out from my hollow and sunken cheeks.

My hair falls out each day, not a few strands at a time but in full handfuls, and the bald patch of bare skin atop my skull mirrors what is happening to the rest of me: my skin has begun abandoning this apparently decaying body, and it is a sickening process to watch. It began around my fingers and knuckles, and has now spread to my palms and forearms, and even to my thighs. First the skin turns a deep shade of brown, like the best tan I have ever had. Then the shade continues to darken, nearly reaching the color black, but before it does, my skin chips away like dried up paint, leaving behind raw patches of light pink skin. The shell of my past self is falling away before my eyes, leaving me vulnerable and brand new to this harsh world.

I watch as these people around me hold the buckets before my face, turn on my feeding tube in hopes that I'll keep something down this time, which I never do. They crush my medications and flush them through the hollow tube in my abdomen, and search frantically for answers. I want to yell to them, but I'm too tired. I want to thank them for trying, but to tell them it's clearly too late. We should all know it by now. We're watching, witnesses to the performance of this body of mine, making its overly dramatic exit, as I feel that I am dying in slow motion.

All this should be enough in itself for one person to have to survive. But now, while I lie on the ground, rolling in pain, feeling the wind knocked out of me, I'm hit once again.

On one of my first days here, this new medical team had unwrapped the layers of bandages round my limbs. We'd come here to Cambridge believing that this would be the place where I would get my prosthetic legs and I'd begin my newest journey. We'd assumed I'd had enough time, during those months in that Florida hospital, for these amputations to have healed. But instead, they saw a horrific sight.

The edges of my now circular legs have patches of thick, still-forming scabs in a horrendous shade of deep purple blended with the truest shade of black. The thin layer of skin-grafted skin, stolen from my right thigh and placed over these wounds, has created an almost polka dot pattern, and struggles to contain the swelling flesh beneath it. In many places, this tissue that is meant to be covered has broken free. Large, oval patches of an angry red remain uncovered, still oozing and shining and shouting their anger at what they have endured.

The specialist here told us that I was still at least two months of healing time away from being close to ready for prosthetic limbs. Then as they studied the remnants of my legs, they discovered a problem far greater than these unhealed wounds.

Even though my limbs are both classified as below-knee amputations, as my knees are both still intact, they're so short that they might not be capable of wearing a prosthetic leg.

How am I supposed to live as an amputee, without being able to have prosthetic legs?!

I gathered myself together. I looked to my mom, and we agreed; we'd figure this out when the time came—not knowing then that we were about to hear a realization that was just as disastrous.

I have a new nephrologist here who's monitoring my kidney function. Since being here, I've been going down to the depressing bottom floor of this hospital for dialysis every other day. But one day, as I lain in that room, this doctor called my mom and stepdad into his office.

He told them that it was still a matter not of *when* my kidney function will return, but of *if* it will return. He explained that my latest kidney biopsy, which had left us so hopeful, had taken a sample of tissue the size of a pinprick. Quite simply, that sample could have been taken from the only remaining viable tissue within my kidneys. He shared with them the harsh facts—that despite all the dialysis sessions I have had, which should have been jumpstarting my kidneys, my numbers showed there has been no improvement at all.

My mom's hands shook as she left his office, and her voice cracked as she called my dad to share the news. As she looked at me, and saw me then, so sick, so fragile, and hooked up to these machines, an uncertain future began to flash through her eyes. Right away, both my mom and my dad followed this doctor's next instruction and began looking into how to determine whether they were possible candidates to give me a kidney. Both of them were immediately willing to give me a piece of themselves. It created a beautiful moment in the midst of an agonizing reality.

Each night, my mom curls up in the small bed beside me and I lean my exhausted body into her shoulder. My sister sends me the brightest of messages, and though she is far away so much of the time, she still lights up this room. My dad sits on the phone with me each night, though so often neither of us speaks, and I simply cry into the speaker, with the comfort of knowing he is there. My brother calls and gives me the tough love that only a big brother can give, telling me I'm strong enough for all that is being thrown my way, and I try to believe him.

My nurses stand by, watching my shoulders shake with sobs each night, releasing the pain from the cruel hours of the day, and they watch as I get up each morning, always hoping that something better will happen.

My nutritionist, who has an infectious laugh that carries through the hallway, makes it impossible not to smile while she is around. She gives me doses of tough love and motivation when she sees me hiding beneath my pillows, and she talks to and comforts my mom, helping the both of us to cope.

The social worker here does what might not even be a requirement of his job, and he listens to me more intently than anyone ever has before in my life. He's so permanently joyful and selfless that I stare in wonder, contemplating how he manages to stay this way.

My new physical therapist, Danielle, with her nearly black hair and strong facial features that so perfectly match her bold personality and reassuring confidence, does more for me than simply help me to move my muscles. She's created a therapy gym that is my haven. She lets me be as angry as I need to be, using those pent-up emotions to fuel my workouts, and she takes my sarcastic humor and throws it back to me, making me grin in a familiar way.

My occupational therapist is a dose of familiarity I so desperately need, as her quiet demeanor feels akin to mine. Her comforting presence is more than necessary, as she works to loosen the scars that expand across my arms, scarring so tight that many movements have become impossible. She pulls and loosens; I clench my teeth and focus only on her soothing voice.

There's the young physician's assistant, and the easygoing attending physician on this floor. They both see me in the most difficult moments, the ones that most others aren't witness to. They guide me through the hard choices, the life-altering choices, that I never wanted to make.

Most of all, there is Nurse Steph, a brand new, main character in the story of my life. I'm not sure if it's because she sees me in the very first moments of each day, when I am sicker and in more pain than every hour from then on will bring, but whether she knows it or not, I cling to her presence for dear life. There's something magical about a good nurse that can truly change each day, and in turn, change each life. She's saving me in more ways than she'll ever know.

These people around me, they'd been no one to me just such a short time ago, and now they are everything. And this family of mine, they've seen me now in ways they'd never seen me before. While I lie on the ground, the wind knocked out of me, struggling to breathe, these people wrap their arms underneath my shoulders and help me back up again. Except this last harsh blow will be one that leaves me gasping for breath for far longer. This one feels impossible to get up from again.

The guardian of the front desk of this fourth floor, had gotten me an appointment with the impressive Dr. Smith at Massachusetts General Hospital. He's the chief of orthopedic trauma, and it was only supposed to be a routine appointment of him reviewing my case and checking the healing status of each broken bone.

He'd greeted us in his light blue button-up shirt, rectangular glasses, and a thick English accent that flowed so quickly I often couldn't understand what he'd said. His hair's a light grey and his eyes a soft blue, and though his looks and his demeanor left me intimidated, his expressions gave way to his underlying intense and genuine kindness.

He'd sat on a small stool that glided across the room on its four small wheels, and he peered at the computer before him, studying my X-rays and scans. He quickly turned to look at me.

The image of the metal plates in my spine was displayed on his screen, and he asked if I'd seen anyone in neurology here at Mass Gen yet.

"That's still in the process of being scheduled," I'd told him.

The staff at Spaulding Cambridge have been hard at work on this task and have one particular surgeon in mind they'd like me to see. But then, in our first glimpse of the efficiency and speed we will one day grow used to, Dr. Smith left the office and returned only a moment later with another man. He'd grabbed hold of a neurosurgeon who had been just a short distance away and brought him into this room for an impromptu evaluation.

They traded places. Dr. Smith stood by my stretcher now while this new doctor took his place on the stool. Neither my mom nor I took a breath as he peered at the screen, but I wasn't sure what had created such tension. Only a moment passed before he turned and spoke the words that stung like a slap across the face.

"There's a definite injury to your spinal cord."

I didn't know a lot about what this meant, but that word, that *injury*—it's one that everyone knows.

My future flashed before my eyes and a million questions paraded alongside it. I watched, though my vision was blurred by tears, as Dr. Smith rushed that surgeon out of the room and closed the door behind him. Then he walked toward me with a softer look in his eyes. His assistant, the tall woman with chestnut-colored hair, came to my side and handed me a tissue before grasping my hand. They told me I'd be okay. They told me I'd figure it all out. But they didn't know how tired I already was. They didn't know how drained I was of life and energy already. They didn't know I could hardly fight any longer.

When I first got here, I'd been filled with hope. I'd had a light within me. I spoke then with quick words of a promising future. I'd lost my legs, I was an amputee, but I would be fine, and I believed that. I believed I was here to learn how to walk back into my life with new legs and a sense of grace.

But now, I've lost my legs, and might not be able to be given prosthetic legs. My kidney function might never return, leaving me trapped on those dialysis beds, sicker than I know how to survive. And my back doesn't only throb with intense pain, it hasn't only shattered into pieces, but I have a spinal-cord injury. I'm paralyzed.

There's a look in the eyes of the patients here on this fourth floor of Cambridge. I'd once looked at them with pity, at their clothes that hung loose from their bony figures, at the dark circles under their eyes and their sunken cheeks, and worst of all, the blankness within their eyes. Now, I blend right in. I know exactly what it is that creates this look. It's the loss of all hope. It's feeling empty inside. It's having no energy to summon any emotion, so we stare blankly ahead, drowning, but somehow remaining alive. Passing through each day, and taking each breath, even though we feel only a ghost of a distant life that haunts us now.

CHAPTER 10

*I*t's far too early, and I hear myself groan in protest as the light beside my bed flashes on. It feels like only a moment has passed since I'd closed my eyes. I can't believe it's already another new day. There's no excitement or promise of the possibility of a good day. Instead, I fill with dread. I know what this day will be like, and how it will be just like all the others.

It's technically morning, but it's so early that it's still the night nurse's face that I see once I finally open my eyes. It's not even five a.m., and the early morning sun struggles to peek through the blinds. I close my eyes again, knowing that I can't do anything to help myself get ready, and decide to stay in a semi-asleep state of consciousness, as the nurse does everything for me. I've resigned myself to the fact that she will have to dress me, and that she will have to change the tubes inserted in my body, exposing me to the world. So I keep my eyes shut, pretending to be somewhere else, anywhere but here.

I feel the thick fabric of my sweatpants pulled over my legs, and I know she is now tying the bottom length of the pants together, pulling them into a knot that ties where my legs end. Instinctively I reach my arms out straight, and she pulls on each layer. Each day, I hope that with enough clothing, I will be able to stay warm, but

I never do. I've decided that there is no possibility of remaining a normal temperature when your blood is being systematically removed from your body and filtered. I know that dialysis is more complex than this, but to me, it is tortuously simple.

After another failed attempt at eating breakfast, the food is taken away, and the stretcher is pulled up next to my bed. The familiar face of the young assistant who'll help me now arrives at my side. Without having to ask, she goes to the end of my bed and reaches for the softest blanket I own and places it on the stretcher to take with us.

My mom stands up, her eyes still groggy from lack of sleep, and walks toward me. I wonder how many times I was violently ill last night, waking her each time. She squeezes my hand. "See you soon," she says kindly.

"Go back to sleep for a while," I encourage her, knowing that she won't.

My stretcher begins to roll out of the door and into the thickness of the silence of the hallway. The stillness, the emptiness, of the halls at this hour is almost peaceful. It's like a momentary escape from time, a momentary reprieve from all pain.

I used to feel uncomfortable, lying here on this moving surface, with a girl my age behind me pushing me along. But we've fallen into a routine. I'd thought I might resent her when I'd met her. I'd thought it would be too painful, that it might put an ache into my soul to see someone my age working so hard toward an obvious career goal while I lay on this hospital bed, each passing day filled only with therapies and dialysis sessions, pain, and sadness. But I quickly realized that there would be an ache in my heart for a long time to come, no matter who it was helping me.

The elevator dings, and we now have only a short stretch of hallway before we'll have arrived. The morgue, I call it. It's not actually a morgue, of course, but to me there are too many similarities. In what feels like the basement of the hospital is this room, all one bland color. Not quite white, and not beige, either. It's just dull.

No visitors or family are allowed in here, thanks to the strict privacy laws, and each bed holds a sickly-looking patient hooked up to the machines that are keeping each one of us alive. We spot the one empty bed that awaits my arrival. Carefully maneuvering the stretcher through the room, we arrive at my designated area, lock the wheels, and make the transition from stretcher to bed. Already closing my eyes, I feel my blanket spreading over me, and then footsteps quietly walk away.

Checking my phone, I see that I've slept through two hours of treatment. Four more hours to go. I never use my phone anymore. My fingertips are numb from nerve damage, and my shattered wrists have made fine movements a frustrating challenge. I read the texts that sometimes appear from family and friends, all of them checking in, but I put them away without answering, lacking both the ability and the desire to form any response. Dialysis is the only time I use this strangely familiar device. Tapping the Spotify app and grabbing my headphones, I begin to disappear from reality, while keeping my eyes wide open.

I remember the first time I'd done this. How for the very first time, there was no family around me, no visitors or even nurses around my bedside, and how I'd needed a moment to pause before pressing play. It was all too normal, this app, this phone, this casual act of listening to music. But now, all of it against a new background, the backdrop of a hospital bed and dialysis machines, and most tangible of all, a deep loneliness gripping my chest.

On that first day, the songs began to play, coming through the wires of the headphones yet reaching all the way throughout me. Every song carried a memory. Memories of nights out with friends, of sunny summer days when I drove with the windows down and the music far too loud, of the songs I listened to while going for runs or hikes, or getting dressed up in the rowdy and energetic apartments I'd called my own. Each song reminded me of the ease I took for granted, the life I took for granted, that in its simplicity had been pure happiness.

I had pushed those memories out of my mind as quickly as they'd popped in, as if in an instinctual survival response. I couldn't allow myself to remember those moments, not while I lay in this room, not while I lay attached to these machines, just not yet. Instead, I found new songs, ones I had never heard before, ones that held no memories, and this is what I now listen to each day. I listen to their words, their sounds, their melodies, and I let the tears stream down my face as they play.

There are so many parts of a dialysis day that are terrible, but they also grant me the gift of solitude, a gift I hadn't known I needed. Upstairs, the walls are covered with pictures of the past, the rooms are filled with smiling and helpful faces. But down here, down in the morgue, with my dialysis port plugged in and many hours to come without being poked, prodded, or even checked on, I can feel my grief in its deepest form. I can grieve in a way that I cannot while surrounded by motivational quotations and the faces of those I never want to hurt.

The time now begins to pass by, and eventually I check my phone again. I see that my treatment is almost done, but I pull my blanket a little tighter, since I can now hear the chattering of my teeth, despite my headphones in my ears. A nurse asks if I want another blanket, and I nod, even though I know the thin blanket they give me will only make a taller pile on my body and won't touch the deep chill I feel in my bones.

I close my eyes again, counting to sixty over and over, trying to keep track of the seconds and the minutes that pass. Finally, I open my eyes and see my nurse heading over to the phone, and I know she is calling for transport to bring my session to an end and return me to the familiar fourth-floor room. Relief floods through my body. One more day down.

The elevator rings again, and we are back on the fourth floor. I've dried my eyes, and glued a look of complacency on to my face. The halls that had been empty, as we'd made our way down this morning, are now full, and loud once again. Familiar faces give me a quick smile, not breaking from the task they are working on, and I can feel their sympathy as they take in the pile of blankets, my shivering hands, and the bucket on my lap. They all know what this treatment will make the rest of my day like, what it will make tomorrow like, and what every day here has been like because of this. They have been watching me wither away to nothing, sicker than anyone knows how to solve.

The cool sensation on my face increases, and my mouth begins to water intensely. I know that this means that once again I won't make it back to my room just yet. My stretcher is pulled off to the side of the hall.

Not even in the privacy of my own room, still in the middle of the fully staffed lobby, I begin to dry heave. I pull the bucket up to my chin as painful noises escape me, and I'm unable to quiet them or stop them. Lurching forward, my body tries to vomit, but with nothing in my stomach, I find no relief. The ugly sounds coming from within me seem to grate and echo against my chest, filling the space around me. My face is shining with sweat, my body shakes, and I reach up to wipe my forehead and upper lip.

We begin to move the final feet toward my room. I'm too drained to offer a look of apology to everyone around me. My head rests on its side as we move forward, staring blankly at those we pass, and my exhausted and limp body is carried forward into the day that's just begun.

CHAPTER 11

The visitors here today have forced their invitation, causing the hallways to buzz with an anticipatory energy. The hospital staff had planned every detail of today with a strict focus on my security and privacy. My health care providers, family, lawyers, and I, all believe this meeting is premature. In the midst of dialysis and extreme illness, in the midst of broken bones and physical pain that makes me weep each morning, it was obvious to us that it was not yet the time for me to be out of bed all day for this meeting. But the visitors' persistence was undeniable.

In addition, our lawyers had already stated to us and to them that they were scheduled for another engagement at this time and unable to fly from Florida to Massachusetts to be here. At any other time, they would have been sure to be here, sitting here with us. We saw this as reason enough for the officers to meet with us when I could have my lawyers present. And yet here we are, with no lawyers beside us, only our lawyer's attentive ears connected to us by phone.

We'd seen it in movies and dramatized scenes many times before—the questioning, the explanations conveyed with shaky voices, and the victims growing exhausted from sharing their very worst moments with the strangers before them as if being assaulted and harmed all over again. We'd simply wanted more time to gather ourselves, but it's time to pull on a layer of protection and face these fears. It's time to survive that day once more, because today, the Royal Bahamian Police Force has come to Cambridge, Massachusetts.

I feel like a young girl on the playground, facing her bullies for the first time, while holding the hands of my allies beside me. My lawyers have agreed to this meeting, but they've insisted that I not be forced to speak of the day just yet, arguing that to do so would not only be an act of cruelty, but would take unfair advantage of my vulnerability.

In brutal honesty, what I would have appreciated far more than this protection, would have been the Bahamian Police listening to our request for more time to heal. It was not a request we made lightly. It wasn't made with any intent to avoid this meeting, for it is a meeting we knew we would one day have.

Yes, this is a meeting we knew would eventually need to be held. It is not one to be avoided because all we wish for is that our suffering, and those horrific events, be taken seriously, and the re-telling of events to the police would feel like the first sign that it is being taken in this way. But one cannot feel that one is being taken seriously when pain is belittled or dismissed, as it appears to be now. I cannot feel respected when my reasonable wishes and requests are ignored, as they have been now.

Mom and Paul already sit in the reserved office room, so as Danielle and I wrap up our session in this gym, we make our way over to join them. My wheelchair moves slowly, as I push with minimal strength, and it's left me an easy target for interception. The foreign sound of stilettos clicking against the floor grows closer with unexpected speed, and now the tallest woman I've ever seen stands before me.

She's only inches away, on the thinnest of heels, which look strange on this hospital floor. Her dress is form fitting, her makeup perfectly done, and she begins talking quickly right away. As she speaks, she hands me one by one the items in her hands, with a speed that matches the unexplained urgency of this moment. My hands stick out awkwardly, fumbling to collect all that she hands me.

As quickly as she appeared, she takes off and disappears from view. The sound of her heels grows quieter with each step, as she nearly sprints away from me. I look up at Danielle, wondering what just happened. She helps me gather the items that are now slipping from my lap and sets them on the table next to us. We begin to investigate.

She'd handed me a card in an ivory-colored envelope, three beach bags, and an assortment of chocolate-dipped fruits. We start first with the card. The words within are few and simple, but they've managed to take my breath away in the worst way possible.

"Get Better Soon."

It's generic, brief, and should be read as a kind expression. I'm in the hospital, so it should only make sense that they wish for me to get better soon, right? Except that the reason this feels so strange is that there are many piles of cards already in my room, sent from strangers and acquaintances, family and friends, and not one of those cards has wished me to get well soon.

Instead, their words wish for me the strength to get through each day; they are expressions of hope and wisdom, and most of all, encouragement for the fight that I have been given. Not one other card says, *Get better soon.* Because it's an obvious fact that these are injuries that you learn to live with, and not injuries from which you can ever physically heal fom. I lost my legs on that island. They will not heal; they will only be replaced.

I suppose the thought was well intended, so I push away the anger and the shock before it can really grow, but I can actually feel the energy Danielle is expending as she holds back the words she wishes to say. We move on to the next items.

Three drawstring bags, made of a fabric that you tend to find only on a beach bag, are what we now hold. Each is a different color, but the decoration on each is the same. I begin to chuckle as I look at the sight before me. A small, stitched design of a tan patch of land with one single palm tree standing tall, surrounded by a patch of turquoise water, sits on the front of each bag. The single word *Bahamas* is stitched below. I feel Danielle's energy continue to simmer, until I hear her voice releasing a small fraction of her pent-up annoyance.

"Why would you *ever* want a reminder of that place?" I hear Danielle ask me, her voice dripping with anger, as if someone should have known better.

"I have no idea," I say to her, shaking my head.

We tuck the gifts into the corner of my room and head toward the office room with the firmly closed door. My palms feel cooler than usual and my stomach twists with nerves. The door swings open, Danielle protectively guides me inside, and a part of me wants her to stay. She gives me a look, silently ensuring that I'm okay before she leaves. I gulp but nod my head, and then the door swings closed with an intimidating sound. I take in my new surroundings as I settle in beside my mom.

Mom, Paul, and I sit on one side of the table, and three Bahamian police officers sit across from us. There are two men on each end, and a woman between them. Piles of paper, multi-colored forms, ballpoint pens, and recording devices sit before them, and a large office phone sits in the middle, connecting our lawyer into the conversation.

The room has remained silent as I've entered, and not one of them has stood, extended a hand, or offered any introduction or greeting. I move about in my wheelchair, awkwardly attempting to get close enough to the table, and they still sit sternly and silently. Mom and Paul look to me, checking I'm settled and okay, but still, these strangers don't speak.

I'm terrible in tense situations, and always have been. So, in my typical fashion, I look up at them and give a huge, face-covering grin. My eyes bulge slightly with the intensity of this unnecessary expression, and I fight back nervous laughter. I want to shout, "Okay, so this is awkward!" but I simply place my hands on the table and remain silent.

Paul carries on answering a question he's been asked. He's recounting every detail he remembers from that day. As I hear his words and each visual description, I focus on my breathing. I look over to see my mom's delicate hands wringing her fingers together just beneath the table, hidden from everyone else's view. She's covered in layers of blankets, and I wonder why, as it's not cold in here; in fact, it's rather warm. It won't be until later that she'll explain that she was bordering on an anxiety attack as the memories tormented her, and the nervousness had left her freezing cold.

The officers interject at odd times, seeming to have heard one sentence or another that holds some unknown meaning for them. It's when the part of the story involving the car rental company is involved that they force the words of Paul's answer to be repeated an agonizing number of times, seeming to me as if they're hoping he'll eventually change his response or twist the words around. But how can the repeated words change when you are only telling the truth?

The car rental company had told us, directly and clearly, to use and to trust Four C's Adventures more than any other company on the island. Of course, we hadn't only taken their word for this, as it had been one of many recommendations we'd seen and been given along the way. Both my mom and Paul explain it to them once more.

"They said to use Four C's," they say clearly, as they have many times before.

The police officers take a long look at one another, finally write down these words on the pages before them and move on with their questioning. Later on, when we explain this moment to the same volunteer on the island that had helped my family that day, it will be explained to us that most likely the police officers knew that someone at that rental company either worked with the owner of Four C's, in some off-the-books way, or was related to him in some way or another. And if this were the case, it would make the recommendation not unbiased but possibly self-benefitting.

As they move on to their next question, they again seem unwilling to accept the first given answer. This time, it's my mom who speaks, and we are now to the details of that first Bahamian hospital. They've asked my mom which doctor it was who treated her, and what care she received. She answered quickly and with ease, but it seems they do not believe her. Their unforgiving voices command her to answer this question with a nearly degrading amount of repetition. She again speaks her words calmly.

"I received no medical care. No one treated me," she repeats one last time.

There's nothing else that she can say, and no other way to form these words, because she simply hadn't been treated. She hadn't even been given an Advil, even as she began to faint from pain.

I'm silently wondering why this moment even matters. If all they are really here for are our statements to help determine what happened that day, statements they've claimed they need to pursue criminal cases against the company's owner and the boat captain, then why do these moments in the hospital have any importance? How could our medical treatment, or the lack thereof, have any relation to the cause of that explosion—the topic they claim to be here investigating? My thoughts continue to wander, wondering if they are even here for this reason at all. Perhaps they wanted to speak with us early on hoping we'd slip in our words and give them some information to protect themselves against us, the victims of their damaging actions and choices. But that can't be true, can it? The Royal Bahamian Police Force can't really try to work against us, can they?

It's in this moment that a quiet knock is heard at the door, and Nurse Steph makes her entrance. She walks in hesitantly, but still with confidence, as she is not about to apologize for entering this off-limits space. It's time for my afternoon medications. Living with kidney failure seems to be a game of balance, and my latest blood work has revealed many out-of-balance numbers, tipping the scales either too high or too low. So now the medications within that Dixie cup have increased not only in number but also in importance. Right now, the most startling result revealed by these tests is a dangerously high potassium level. This morning, a nurse had arrived early with two large white pills, speaking of the risks to my heart, and with wide eyes I'd watched as they'd administered that first dose. The second dose is in that Dixie cup.

The conversation fades while Steph works. I wheel my chair out a few inches, creating space between myself and the table, and Steph reaches for the feeding tube that hangs from underneath my shirt, the tube that is now a new addition to my life. As we begin this everyday routine, in which medications are crushed up and injected directly into my stomach, since I'm still unable to swallow any mediations without my body immediately rejecting them, I laugh silently at the idea of interrupting this tense gathering with a sudden and violent heaving of my body. I can feel the eyes of the officers drifting toward me, and the energy they expend trying to force themselves to look away is obvious.

A quiet crunching sound interrupts the voices as Steph crushes each pill into a fine powder. This is followed by a slight clinking sound as the substance is combined with water, and then sucked into a syringe and plunged through my feeding tube. Their questions have stopped now, and they can no longer hide it as they look on at our performance, with new expressions of what seems to be horror on their faces finally breaking through the business-like looks they'd held consistently before this.

Steph moves with a practiced speed, knowing if the fluid goes through the tube either too quickly or too slowly, then it will immediately wind up in the grey container that sits beside her. One after the other, each pill is flushed into my stomach. My face grows pale and my eyes are intently focused as I will myself to keep each one down. As this process comes to an end, I pull down my shirt, covering the tube as much as I can, and wheel myself back toward the table, keeping a blank expression on my face, as if nothing strange at all has just happened.

As the conversation picks up once more, I take notice of what's gone unsaid—they've dropped the questions of medical care and have moved on to the next topic.

The interview is relentless and the hours continue to pass. I'm exhausted, and my back screams to me in pain, telling me I can no longer sit so straight in this chair. I'd tried to tell them that I couldn't yet endure a meeting like this, but it'd felt like they'd taken my words to mean I might perhaps feel some slight discomfort from today's conference-room meeting. In fact, my frayed spinal nerves and nearly severed spinal cord are quite furious at being put through this. The meeting continues, but I am done. Mom walks me back to my room.

We're greeted by a group of nurses, each of them curious and craving details of the going-ons behind that closed door. It feels like a slumber party conversation, the sharing of secrets, as I lie back in bed now and everyone stands around me asking questions. As I repeat each word and share each painful moment and its details, I feel a heat within my chest and my voice only grows louder. As I start to think of those Bahamian men and women visiting today, the woman in her stiletto high heels, the officers with their blank expressions, and how all of them will now fly back home, having felt no impact at all from that day that's ruined and forever altered my life, my hands begin to shake and the fire of anger roars.

They'll go home to their sunny island and those white-sand beaches, and I will stay here. I'll fight for my life in this battle they gave me.

Not once did I hear an apology today. Not once did I hear recognition of my survival or my fight today. Not once did anyone look at me as though they even care about what's happened to me. Not once did they even speak my name. I want them to remember my name! I want them to *care*! The anger seems to physically crush my chest, pushing me against this mattress, pinning me in position, and leaving me gasping and tingling and aching with anger.

Those Bahamian beach bags sit on the floor, staring back at me, and the card sits on the counter beside the fruit basket. I don't want them here. I don't want to look at them. My next words are meant to sound hatefully angry, but as I speak them, I break out in laughter at the sheer stupidity of my request.

"Can I smash the damn fruit basket?" I ask them.

"Absolutely," they each reply.

But as I look at it before me, I'm momentarily distracted from my anger, because those chocolate-covered strawberries really do look good.

"Okay, but can I just eat one strawberry first?" I ask, still laughing.

The nurses have left my room, we've given them the fruit basket, and the silence is so clear after hours of nonstop questions and answers. As Paul walks in, he holds in his hands a packet of papers that have been given to him. My stomach drops because I know what these are. They're going to explain what happened aboard that boat that day.

I skim the pages that are crammed full with information, conveyed by stern and official wording that holds no emotion. I read sentences about improper fuel lines, and improper welding, with images of the work that's so poorly done that even I can tell it was left messy and incomplete. Reading the description of a valve that, though it was safe used only with water, was used instead on the fuel tank. Page after page, and one paragraph after the other, outlines an incredible number of faults in that boat, and how each one is a possible cause of the explosion.

A diagram of the boat includes the rows of seats, and a small letter is beside each one. I don't remember a lot about that day, but I can still see the image of the seat that I had chosen and where exactly I had sat. That moment, and that image, are permanently engraved in my mind. My eyes go directly to this spot, to my seat, and I find a circle drawn round the location, and an arrow pointing to where I would have been. I follow the arrow toward the side of the page and read the text beside it, seeing now, that this marks my seat as the exact location of the explosion. I read it once, twice, ensuring I've understood each word correctly. My eyes grow wide, and I look to my right to where Mom and Paul sit reading these same pages.

"I sat right on top of the explosion," I say to them, feeling unsure of how to phrase these words any differently.

They look up from their pages with a look of confusion, which quickly changes to horror. I sit in shock for a moment, trying to understand what this would have meant. I can't help it, or stop it from happening, as my mind begins to visualize what must have happened to my body as I received the blast's first and strongest impact. I no longer imagine only my body within a terrifying, massive, destructive blast of an explosion. I see it now, hitting my body first.

I can hardly breathe with this thought in my mind. I shake my head, trying to clear the image, but instead it only changes. Now I see myself sitting there, having no idea what was about to happen, and how just underneath me, those diagrams show me now, there was some sort of ticking bomb, waiting for its moment to strike.

The day has passed, the lights are off, but I can't sleep tonight. That image haunts me, and the silent countdown I had never heard now beats its drum within my mind.

Everyone has left, or is asleep, and it's only me lying here, alone with these thoughts, staring wide-eyed at the darkness. I'm frozen in fear, feeling as though I'll never sleep again. I feel my eyelids beginning to droop, and I'm so tired, but I fight the fatigue, protecting my mind for a while longer. But eventually, I can't fight it anymore. My eyes close, and those images find me right away.

Each nightmare starts so simply. I sit with a smile on my face, chatting easily with everyone beside me. Their lips move as they shout their warnings, because they can hear the countdown that I cannot. I don't hear them, their lips make no sound, so I stay where I am. I'm blissful and ignorant and happy and naïve, and then, it's too late.

I never see the blast, but I know it has happened. The dream comes to an end, but instead of changing to something new, it begins to play all over again. That same countdown plays once more.

Over and over, it plays. Some aspects change, different scenes and backgrounds, but each time the result is always the same—my body taking the brunt of all the mutilation and destruction.

These nightmares are the first of many more to come, each one seeming to remind me that just maybe it wasn't only that boat that wasn't safe. Just maybe the whole world is no longer safe. Just maybe, that unheard countdown is possible to begin anywhere that I go.

Just maybe, I'll never breathe easy again.

CHAPTER 12

I'm lying so still. My arms are extended perfectly straight out to my side, floating beside me. As I stare up into the sunshine, I keep my eyes wide open. With one deep exhalation, I slip a little lower. My fingers slip underneath the water's surface, and then my chin follows underneath. Inch-by-inch, I fall deeper, until my body is beneath the waves. The sun's rays are blurry now, but my eyes stay open, never losing sight of the dazzling light above. I'm drowning, I realize.

The silence is mesmerizing here, and the water is so cool against my skin.

Lower, and lower, I go. My eyes stay open, but the sun is getting smaller.

The silence is so peaceful.

The water's growing darker—less bright blue and more a deep black.

I'm really drowning now. I think those words with a feeling of peace; acceptance.

My arms still stay straight out to each side of me; I'm like an angel, falling through the air. I fall in slow motion, the water protecting me, slowing me down, but still I fall. There I go, disappearing, into the silence of nothingness.

A sudden noise pulls me away, out of the imaginary water. Annoyed, I open my eyes, seeing now my crushing reality, seeing the hospital walls, seeing the nurse who's come into my room, medications held in her hand. I see the same ceiling that I stare at every day. That daydream was far more peaceful. I close my eyes, trying to return to the ocean, but the feeling of my feeding tube being pulled straight, yanking at my sore flesh is too distracting. A rush of cool hits my stomach. I stare upwards, my eyes open and my mind now focused on reality. I know what will happen next. A bucket appears under my chin, and I lurch forward, as agonizing sounds escape my mouth. The force of my efforts hurts my stomach. Several minutes pass, and I continue creating an awful symphony of sound.

I collapse back against the pillow and close my eyes once more, wishing to return to my imagined escape. But the day is determined to continue. I submit myself to its torture, knowing today will be the same as each day before. I'll be in pain, and I'll be sick, and I'll go through the motions—pretending to be alive like everyone tells me that I am.

A woman enters my room, someone I haven't met yet before, and I wonder if she's a new doctor of mine. I'm so sick of doctors and tired of our awkward introductions.

"Hi," she says. "It's nice to meet you, I'll be your psychiatrist." She settles into my room.

I scan the room, looking for an escape, but see none, and I know I couldn't reach it even if there was one. Apparently talking with this woman won't be an option, seeming to be instead a necessity.

Taking in her perfectly matching clothes and her hair pulled into a simple and elegant ballerina bun, I can't help but assume there's no way she'll be able to understand what I'm going through. The difference between us is painfully obvious. Staring down at the remnants of my figure, I take in all of my physical reminders of why I now hate myself.

A discreet noise grabs my attention, and I watch as my mom quietly makes her way out of the room to give us privacy. I'd forgotten she was in here. As she turns to shut the door behind her, I catch an unfamiliar look in her eyes—one I am sure she has tried to keep hidden. My guilt screams within me. I saw the pain in her eyes, and I know that it comes not from her suffering, but from mine. My daydreams, of disappearing into the darkness of the water's depths, have been a retreat from my pain. But it seems that, without even knowing it, I've been reaching out beside me, and pulling her down with me.

I know the dimness of her eyes, the fatigue within her, comes from the times she's seen me sob with such intensity that we both hold our breath, waiting for the wails to fill the air. But instead, I've found that when you cry, *really* cry, you make no sound at all. Your lips shudder, your shoulders shake, and your ribs feel as if they're pulling apart, but you make no sound. I know her pain comes from watching me refuse to bathe or even speak. It's from my inability to find the desire to join in on anything at all.

But I know her, and I know she's hoping this person will begin to heal me. So, I suppose I have two choices: I can keep my jaw clenched tight and not speak a word, or I can give this a try.

The door closes, and the woman begins.

"You've obviously been through a lot. I'm just here to listen and to help you navigate your feelings. Eventually, you and I will decide if you need any type of medication to help you through this. There would be no shame in needing anti-anxiety or depression medication to help you some." She sits back, holding a pen and clipboard on her lap.

I wait for her to begin the session, unsure how therapy actually works. A long silence passes, and I realize she's waiting for me to say something. I'm not sure where or how to start. Then, as if the connection between my brain and my mouth has been cut off, I hear myself speaking, and the words begin to flow without any mapped-out plan.

My darkest thoughts, which have been carefully tucked away, begin spilling out.

"I feel like they picked up the pieces of me, stitched me together, and left me to live the rest of my life like this." I'm getting louder with each word.

"They should have known I was too far gone…." My voice grows quiet.

She pauses before speaking, giving me a moment to catch my breath.

"When you think about it, do you feel angry that they saved your life?"

Startled, I think about her question. Everything in me aches to deny it, to push her words away and exclaim that of course that isn't true. But that would be a lie. My hands stop shaking, and I slowly look back up at her.

"Yes," I answer simply.

"I don't want to live like this." My voice is steady for the first time.

My shoulders drop lower with relief. As if some tightly wound doll had finally been released back to its natural state. It's out there now, my very worst thoughts. There's no taking it back, and oddly, it feels the slightest bit peaceful.

"That's understandable," she tells me.

I nearly break out in laughter, which tends to be my default reaction when it comes to dealing with stressors. Maybe my darkest secret wasn't as terrible as I believed it to be.

"The question now is, Do you think you're suicidal? Do you have any intention of harming yourself?" she asks intently, but kindly, in the only way a question like this could be asked.

The pause between us lengthens as I give the question honest consideration. Contemplating the question and what it means, knowing the daydreams I have had and the depression that consumes me. Carefully, with my voice steady once more, I give my response.

"No. Definitely not."

More weight seems to have lifted off my chest. Her questions were the ones that without even realizing it, I've been asking myself. I've wondered if I am suicidal, and if I really wished to no longer exist. But as I heard those words within her straightforward question, I came to a realization that suddenly feels so obvious that I wonder how I hadn't known it this whole time: that daydream that plays on repeat in my mind has never once been about my life ending.

In those imaginings, I only dream of myself finding that absolute calm and silence that cannot be found in my life. Beneath those waves that I see in my mind, there are no new harsh realities being thrown my way; there is no illness or pain. There is nothing, and no one, at all. It's blissful, serene, calm.

Every day, I feel as though I've been struck by the force of a strong wave, dragged across the gritty sand, and slammed into the sharp coral. It never ends: the needles piercing my skin, the sickness, the nerve pain, the new discoveries of more to overcome. The limb loss, the paralysis, the brain injury, the organ failure; the injuries to all that is needed to survive. I need it to stop. I need a moment of peace, and that is what those daydreams give me. That is what I've found beneath those waters.

Talking with this psychiatrist for one hour had been like turning down the heat on a boiling pot. I'd been spilling over with anger, and with this last hour, suddenly there is now a sliver of room within me for an emotion other than that one alone. Suddenly, I can think more clearly, this room around me seems brighter, and I am no longer blinded by hatred.

I look toward my window. There's one lone tree that I can see from my bed. It's all that I see each day. But somewhere along the way, some time ago, its leaves have changed color. And I wonder, *When did this happen?* How had I not noticed? I used to go outside, when I'd first gotten here. I used to breathe in the crisp New England air and relax, finding a peaceful pause outside of these walls. I don't do that anymore. When did I stop? How long has it been? It's been too long.

Mom walks back into my room, and I take a deep breath. For the first time in a long time, as I speak, my voice is less strained, and recognizable once again. Almost as if the daughter she's always known has finally returned.

"Want to go outside? I think I need some air," I ask her.

She does a double take. Then her face cracks in relief.

"Of course," she says. "That's a great idea."

With one last look over my shoulder, back at that tree, as my mom pushes my wheelchair toward the door, I decide now that it is my turn to change. It's my turn, my time, to create of myself something new—perhaps a brighter version of myself too.

CHAPTER 13

*M*y body has endured a lot; it's demanded all our attention and all of our time in order to survive, but when the care transitioned to check in on my mind, thoughts, and emotions, that is when the real healing began. These last weeks have been a whirlwind of always-changing activity.

My bones are healing, my pain decreasing, and my strength returning. I can transition myself across a slide board to get myself into and out of bed on my own. My wheelchair glides across each room, as I have now gained some of the strengths necessary to propel my own chair, and I now sit up on my own with ease, with the threat of toppling over no longer crossing my mind.

Everything began to get better when those five-minute intervals between having my head in a gray plastic container extended from every five minutes to every several hours. It was the simplest of explanations; I can quite literally see the good around me again, now that I'm able to see beyond the bottom of that bucket. It was my psychiatrist who prescribed me the medication that brought this relief. The name of the prescription had taken me by surprise—I questioned whether they really were willing to give me this in a hospital setting. It was a prescription drug by the name of Marinol.

Marinol is an FDA-approved medication containing the active ingredient Dronabinol. Dronabinol is a synthetic version of THC, one of many cannabinoids found in marijuana. It's used to control nausea and improve appetite, and it is most commonly given to cancer patients who are enduring the dreaded side effect of treatment known as chemo-induced nausea. It's used when other treatments have failed, which is exactly where I had been. Without hesitation, I'd taken the Dixie cup from Nurse Steph's palm and swallowed my first dose.

For months now, I haven't had a single moment when the waves of sickness within me didn't crash against my insides with such strength that even the thought of food made my stomach twist and turn. But it hadn't taken long, after that first pill, before I looked up at those around me with an unfamiliar feeling. I was *hungry*.

Overjoyed with my announcement, Mom propped her injured foot atop her scooter and nearly disappeared into thin air as she flew out of my room. She returned, not much later, with the basket of her scooter filled with a large cardboard container. She then presented to me the most beautiful sight I'd ever seen—a family-sized box of extra cheesy Goldfish crackers.

The first problem was now checked off that too-long list, as day-by-day I tasted each food for what felt like the first time, and in turn, I began to regain strength. My psychiatrist hasn't saved me with this prescription alone—it's in the moments that she spends in my room that I begin to heal. It might be easy to assume that the reason for my grief has been the loss of my legs, since this is the most obvious of all losses. But this is not what I grieve. Of course, there are many moments when I find myself attempting to explain how intensely I miss them, and how it's a sensation that isn't the result of vanity.

This is the body that I was born in and had lived in each day of my life. Those feet were the ones I crammed into too-tight shoes, sprinted across playing fields on, and hiked my way up mountains with. Those legs were the ones that carried me through each step of my life, and I ache knowing that I've lost them, that they've been taken from me, and that a part of me no longer exists. It's not vanity, and yet I feel unable, or simply not allowed, to miss them as deeply as I do. Because somehow it *feels* vain. But still, this is not what I grieve.

I'm grieving for the loss of myself. This is a subject that feels impossible to explain, so like some dirty little secret, I share these thoughts only with this doctor who is bound by the permanency of confidentiality. The life I was creating, day-by-day and choice-by-choice, has now been utterly changed. In fact, it feels like that life has ended, like who I was died on that boat and a stranger took her place. And when I think of all life's goals, responsibilities, and slightest of tasks, my heart races and the nerves and grief set in. I think of finishing school, beginning a career, driving a car, traveling, dating, marriage, starting a family, and every little thing in between—each task comes with a giant question mark and a feeling of helpless impossibility. These thoughts are ones that terrify me and pull me under that line of depression I try so desperately to stay above. Because I don't know how to survive, live, or be a *person* at all.

But as I speak each sentence aloud, in this quiet room with only the two of us, and as I feel and weigh and contemplate the uncertainty of my future, I now also see that future in a growing light of possibility. As if the tasks ahead are all challenging me to get out there and figure out how to check them all off my list. I'm now at least trying to look at things in a new way.

The most important thing of all about these sessions and these conversations is that I can actually feel it as it happens—the weight of the suffocating pain slowly leaving my body. This therapy is like the greatest detox of all time. We all know the type, the ones that are supposed to leave your body refreshed and re-energized, and that's exactly what's happening. I believe it, with every fiber of my being, when I explain to everyone around me that just maybe those thoughts of self-pity and anger had been toxic to my physical self, because the more that I speak my thoughts aloud, releasing them from existing within me alone, the more I may be allowing my body to mend. And with only days to spare, my body seemingly thanked me in the greatest way possible.

Maybe it's only ironic timing, and I know that my doctors believe that it is, but I would like to believe otherwise. Because each day after these conversations, my blood work reveals improved numbers. This, to me, is proof enough that my mindset can impact my healing and recovery. Because for months before this, before these conversations, when the treatment had remained the same, there had been no changes and no improvements at all.

I'd been sitting down, not paying attention, when the commotion first reached my ears. I looked toward the sound, and watched as someone ran closer to me, seeming to be unable to contain the news they held. That was when I'd heard it. Only days before being put on the transplant list, I was out of kidney failure.

My heart had raced. My eyes shed no tears but instead began to sting with intense emotion. I couldn't speak, knowing I would choke on any words I tried to form. Taking a deep breath, before addressing the bearer of this news, I looked down toward my abdomen. I know this isn't their exact location, but it's where I've settled upon, and I spoke to my kidneys one last time, giving them my deepest thank-you.

My surgery was scheduled shortly after, and I was brought to Mass Gen to have both my dialysis port and my feeding tube removed. The disappearance of all the tubes from my body was almost startling, because now, I had to survive all on my own.

Without needing dialysis, without needing the feeding tube, and having learned how to do the simplest of tasks on my own, I no longer need to be here anymore. I'm not ready for home. I'm not ready for the amputee program at Charlestown, and I also can't stay here. The question now is simple: Where do I go? Today, we have a meeting to find an answer.

As the meeting begins, I sit at the head of the table and the physician assistant immediately begins the usual discharge process, during which the patient's medical history from the day of injury on is read aloud.

I know all of my injuries, and I know all that I have been through, so it takes me by surprise when it suddenly feels harder to catch my breath and my hands feel cool and clammy. It's something about the way that they're being read today. It's not in its typical list-form, and it's far more than simply bullet-point facts and terms. It's read today, more like a story than ever before. Not only is each surgery, injury, and treatment listed, but they're read as if the moment is happening right then and there. Each moment leading up to each procedure is replayed and described, explaining for the very first time *why* they were necessary.

Right now, she's at the early part, explaining why the two slices within each side of my chest were necessary, how my lungs had filled with blood. Sharing how I was acting, presenting, and suffering.

There is no break, and as she continues reading, I realize now just how intense those moments had each been. One injury flows into another with a speed that is hard to fathom and a transition that feels too easy. I'd been so broken, and each choice had been so careful, so precise, and so necessary. These scars on my skin are no longer a patchwork of randomly collected pieces, but are instead connecting with one another, creating a patchwork quilt of a story of the battle for survival.

My fingers lie flat on the table, as if I'm holding tight so not to collapse. She looks up at me, as if she can feel the air being sucked out of the room, just as I can.

"This is a lot. Are you okay? I can stop if you need me to…," she says to me.

I feel all the eyes in the room staring at me. They don't seem as fazed by her reading as I do. This break in her words has given me a moment to catch my breath, so I tell her to continue, and the rest of the meeting now passes in a blur. Opinions are given, listened to, and considered, and a plan is created.

Spaulding Charlestown's floors are separated and categorized by injuries. For example, I had thought I would arrive on the fifth floor, where all amputees stay, known as the comprehensive rehabilitation floor. After much talk and debate, the answer became perfectly clear. Instead of scrambling to find a time when both injuries, spinal cord and amputations, can be addressed at the same time, why can't we simply separate them into two separate stays?

I'll be admitted to Spaulding on the sixth floor, the spinal-cord injury floor, where I'll focus on regaining strength and mobility while also focusing only on the complexities and treatments for a spinal-cord injury. That in itself is certainly enough to focus on for now. If the last remaining areas on my legs heal while I am there, we can then address fitting for prosthetic legs and rehabilitation for this additional concern. But for now, we'll focus on only one concern at a time. Just the conversation alone, the decision to take these steps one by one, has dropped my shoulders many inches lower in relief.

With a look to my mom, and a nearly synchronized nod of our heads, the plan is finalized and approved. One week from today, I will begin the next, and final step.

I said most of my goodbyes throughout the day and night yesterday. My door had been on a steady rotation, as one after the other, each nurse came to find me in this room for one last time. I've always been noticeably awkward with emotions, and goodbyes always feel the most emotional of all. I can pick the perfect gift for someone to show them how much I care and I'll act as though it took no thought or time at all. I can write the words I wish to say in black-ink pen and look away while they are read, and I have mastered the silent and anonymous acts of kindness which are always an attempt to avoid any real emotional intimacy in all forms. But finding the spoken words to give an adequate goodbye—that I can't do.

I've known these people only a short while, but somehow, the words for each farewell were not nearly as challenging to find as I'd thought they might be. There was no reason to keep any walls between us when they'd all been broken down so long ago. And I know that even though these moments may be the last time we'll see each other in this same setting, each and every one of them has carved a place in my memories, and they've all done so in different ways. There are the stories they've shared with me of their families and children. I've looked through photos of wedding dresses with the newly engaged nurse and cheered from a distance for the soccer teams of the kids that they coach. But what I will always owe them for is their kindness, their care, and their genuine friendships.

Nurse Steph had left her morning shift first, but before she did, she'd handed a small white box and a black-and-white card to my mom and to me. Just as I would have done, she'd told us not to open them until she'd left the room. Mom and I opened the matching gifts at the same time and found two delicate silver bracelets with inscriptions of hope engraved upon them. The cards made tears stream down our faces, and I was thankful in that moment that she was not beside us to see. The words within my card left me with a confirmation that I hadn't known to expect: that not only had she touched my life, but that I had touched hers as well.

I just want to thank you for being such an amazing patient. Your strength puts me to shame. I am so impressed with your progress and how much effort you put into your healing process. You have made me a better nurse and taught me compassion and empathy. I was hesitant when I heard you were coming, because I have a hard time with tragedy. But with you, my fear subsided, and I am no longer afraid to ask hard questions or cry with a patient. I have cried many rides home after my shifts, good tears and bad, thinking about you. You are a miracle, don't let anyone tell you otherwise. You are such a beautiful, strong woman, and despite this setback, you'll be on your "feet" in no time. You've got a long way to go. Be patient. You WILL be an amazing woman with a lot to teach people. You're going to be an amazing girlfriend/wife/mom/daughter/co-worker/athlete... etc. whatever you want to be! And through it all, you will always be in my heart.

Love,

Steph

The card is now packed carefully in my bag with the rest of my belongings, as I wait for the ambulance to arrive. Steph and Danielle stand beside me and pretend to tease me as I show my excitement, saying things like, "You better not forget about us now," as if I could ever forget either of them. The heavy wooden door to this room swings open, and a shout from outside announces that the ambulance is here.

As the stretcher carries me outside, I can't keep myself from fidgeting with excitement. My eyes scan frantically around me, not wanting to miss my final sight of any of them. I see the front desk, the receptionists and doctors, and they all cheer as I make my final lap round this hospital floor.

My stretcher is loaded into the empty space within the back of the ambulance, and Mom sits beside me. I shout one last goodbye and then I catch my last glimpse of Spaulding Cambridge.

The ride to Charlestown is quick, and I'm immediately, to say the least, impressed with my new surroundings. The building is tall and elegant, extravagant yet also simplistic. The colors of each side are of cool grays and long stretches of glass windows that reflect varying shades of blue. It looks more like some science-fiction apartment complex or business building that shouldn't yet exist than it does a hospital. The reputation of this place has been high, so high I thought it impossible to meet, but somehow, they already seem to have earned it.

As we enter, I first see banners in a beautiful bright blue, showing the center has been ranked number two of all rehabilitation-focused hospitals in the country.

We head up to the sixth floor, the spinal-cord injury floor. My heart drops as the elevator rises. The fact that I am now a person living with a spinal-cord injury is still sinking in. Of course, no one ever expects to live with this injury, but you'd think that if it were to happen to you, there would be a moment when you would simply know it to be true. You'd think you'd feel so remarkably different that you wouldn't even need someone to share with you your diagnosis, because you would already know. But I keep waiting for that moment. I keep waiting for it to sink into my cognition, and it never does. In fact, for too long now I have tried to deny that this is real, that those who have handed me this cruel diagnosis were simply mistaken. But its effects are far too real to deny it any longer. It's time to learn to live with it. I won't, however, ever allow this term and its relation to me, to take away anything that I still want out of life.

We've wound our way through the hallways and have arrived at my new room. When you hear the word *hospital* or the phrase "rehabilitation center," they sound so sterile and boring, serious and bland, but that's not what I see before me. Yes, the bed still has the controls and bedrails beside it, and the cabinets and counters are still basic and plainly colored, but everything else makes it seem to appear more like a modern apartment than it does a hospital room. The wall across from me, and beside the bed, consists mainly of windows and overlooks the city of Boston. It's a million-dollar view, of both the city itself and the harbor and boardwalk just behind us. The view of planes landing at the airport so close by makes it seem as though everyone here has chosen these rooms for the ideal location, and not for necessary rehabilitation from life-changing conditions and injuries.

As excited as I am to have made it to this center, there is one upcoming introduction that is foremost in my mind. There's a doctor here who oversees all patients with limb loss, and now I anxiously await my turn for an introduction of my own. Becoming an amputee has felt like being picked up and thrown into an unfamiliar world, with no one to guide me on how to get around. I need advice and answers, but most importantly, I need hope. I know of so many others who have gotten all of this from this very same doctor. He's seen many others go on to live full and successful lives, and now, I need him to tell me how to get there.

As this doctor walks through the door, the room seems to fill with his presence, just as it always does when someone impressive stands before me. He has the aura most successful people seem to have, and it's one of confidence and composure. He doesn't wear the typical white coat I've grown so used to seeing among doctors, and instead wears a simple button-up shirt and tie, and khaki pants—seeming both medical doctor and college professor at once. My nerves are now at an all-time high, as I wonder what he's going to say, what he'll ask me, and how I could manage to impress him.

He begins with a brief introduction and the usual greetings. He fills me in on the center here and what types of rehabilitation they have to offer, telling me of the equipment, the aquatic therapy, and the recreational therapy, all of which is downstairs. I nod my head in excitement, eager to get started. Then he asks me a question I've never been asked before, and though it's clear and makes perfect sense, I feel lost for an answer.

"So, what do you know about prosthetic legs?" he asks me.

"Uhm, well I know I'm going to get them," I say simply.

I want to lift my hand up and smack myself in the forehead. *What a dumb reply,* I scold myself silently. I scramble for something a bit more impressive to say, and then I continue.

"I know it will be hard work, but I know it's how I have to walk from now on, and that's okay," I continue nervously.

He sits beside me and seems to be contemplating my words. Then he continues. His next words confuse me even more. He begins with a quick explanation about how I am not a *typical* amputee, due to the additional injury to my spinal cord. Then he begins to lay out options for me. They're options I have never considered, and they each feel like a punch to my gut. The clearest of them all, went something like this:

"Well, society has come a long way, but it's still not very accepting of people being different. So, what you could do is you could get a pair of cosmetic prosthetic legs, and they'll look nearly exactly like your natural legs did, and then you can remain wheelchair bound."

Those two words are each so simple, and yet when they're strung together, they seem to have a brand-new meaning: *Wheelchair bound.* I repeat it to myself.

My head feels like it's spinning, and I can see that he's still speaking, but I no longer hear his words. I look just slightly above him, attempting to look focused and intent, while all I'm really doing is forcing the tears to stay behind my eyes. I cannot cry in front of him. I won't allow it. I'd wanted to come off as strong and mature and give my very best first impression. I refuse to be the girl who cries at hard news on her very first day. But I feel like I'm back at the beginning, back to being the girl who wanted to give up more than she wanted to fight. I feel the familiar urge to pull the covers over my head and hide from the world that continues to prove just how harsh it can be.

The moment he leaves the room, as soon as I hear the door close firmly behind him, the tears begin to stream down my face. I stare down at my short, little legs, and only one thought repeats in my mind: *Amputees are still supposed to be able to walk. This isn't supposed to be taken from me.*

It's now as if someone's just looked at my life, leaned forward and pressed replay, and an all too familiar scene begins once more. Mom walks toward me, crawls into bed next to me, and attempts to console me. But I only shake my head, because she can't understand.

Mom was in the room when those words were spoken, and Paul's just arrived. They both spend all night trying to cheer me up, but how could anything they had to say help me to feel better? They have never been told words such as these ones. They have never been told they won't walk again. They have never felt their future taken from them. They have grown and lived full and successful lives with careers and families, without ever being told those two limiting words that I've just heard. They can't understand, and I can't be consoled.

Suddenly, this room feels massive, and I feel so alone here in this place away from home. As I face this new reality, I'm taken over by an intense need to share what I have heard, unable to be alone with this for another moment longer. I text my two closest friends, sending only a short and simple text.

"I don't think I'll ever walk again.

Their replies arrive on my screen almost immediately, the perfect combination of condolences and motivation. But my eyes have once again become blurred with tears, and I cannot steady my shaking hands enough to reply. I put the phone away.

For the rest of the night, I remain silent. I can't find the strength or the will to speak a single word. I can't feel anything any longer, and I seem to have gone completely numb. I can't make myself care that I know my family wants me to be okay. I can't care that I've gotten myself well enough to have arrived at this hospital, a transition that had once seemed impossible. I can't care about anything at all. I'm empty inside.

I let the new team of nurses come into this room and check off each of their tasks. I swallow my medications, chew my dinner without tasting it, and go through all of the motions, but I'm only a broken, damaged, and incomplete shell of a person.

The tears have left me exhausted in the deepest of ways, and though it's still early, I lie down to go to sleep. I feel the tears traveling down my face until I drift off, finally escaping the pain.

Each night so far, my dreams have been filled with detailed images of my healthiest self. In these images, I am standing, sprinting, or jumping upon the very legs that I was born with. So, each morning as I wake up, the lingering pictures are still so clear within my mind that I am given a half-second of a nearly euphoric state, one in which I believe that my legs and my health have returned. Then I look down, and see the sheets flat against the mattress. Reality replaces those optimistic thoughts. It's like relearning about the loss of my legs every morning, and it's a routine I cannot escape.

Tonight, this is not the dream that plays behind my closed eyes. Instead, I have one that is new but clearer than all of the rest:

I see myself with such clarity. My hair has grown back to its full thickness and has remained its new and natural shade of light brown with strands of shimmering blonde. I'm thinner than I used to be, but no longer look unhealthy. There are no dark circles beneath my eyes, and I look well-rested. I stand on a road, one that is made of gravel but is somehow still smooth. Dark green grass has grown thickly on each side. I see no end to the road. It has slight curves, creating a snake-like pattern as it expands into the distance.

I watch myself, as I walk as tall as I can, with my back perfectly straight, and a not-quite smile on my face, but a simple expression of pure content. My eyes stare ahead, and step-by-step, I walk forward.

There's no one else in this dream and nothing exciting happens; all that I do is continue to walk. Except this time, in this dream, I am standing, and I am walking, on two prosthetic legs.

I wake up to the sun beginning to pour through the tall windows beside me. I sit up, but today it's only a way to start my day, and not part of some desperate search for the legs that are not there. Because for the first time, I don't have that crash of a letdown. I feel at peace.

Mom sits before me, and I can see it in her eyes—the nearly crazed thoughts running through her mind of how to approach me and how to console me today.

"Morning," I say to her with a smile.

She replies, but then continues to stare at me with worry in her eyes. I decide to put her mind at ease and share with her the complete calm with which I have awakened.

"Maybe he hasn't had a patient with my injuries before. Maybe he's never seen someone with both amputations and a spinal-cord injury who has walked before. I guess I will just have to be the first," I say to her now.

I watch as her entire body relaxes with relief, and she instantly agrees.

The morning continues for only a short while longer, and then we hear a slight knock at the door. It's the weekend, so even I know it's a surprise when I hear the doctor's voice from behind the door. He peeks his head in, and then begins to speak.

"Are you guys hungry? There's fresh bagels and cream cheese downstairs. I can get you some," he says before he disappears once more.

When he returns, over bagels and coffee, we begin the conversation from last night one more time.

"Was that news hard to hear last night?" he asks.

"A little," I say hesitantly.

"A little?" he asks, clearly knowing this had been a lie.

"Okay, maybe a lot," I say now, surprised at the grin that's formed on my face.

He takes his time before speaking again.

"I am going to do everything I can to get you walking."

I nod quickly, thanking him, and that slight grin now widens.

CHAPTER 14

The gym of this Charlestown center is its most well-known feature. It's an impressive, wide open, and expansive space on the third floor of the hospital. The windows in every wall fill the gym's floor with bright natural outside light. The outskirts are lined with a hemisphere shaped row of low sitting and cushioned exercise tables, while the middle is filled with every form of exercise equipment imaginable. From the ceiling, and stretching across the front of the gym, extends a harness system into which patients can be safely strapped before they begin walking along its course, with the security of knowing that with any trip or beginning of a fall, the system is designed to catch each patient. This harness system can be adjusted to hold differing amounts of body weight, allowing patients to walk more freely, and with specifically chosen amounts of assistance. Just behind the gym is a fully equipped kitchen with height-adjustable countertops, used for patients to practice preparing and serving their own food. There's a basic model construction of a car, used for patients to begin practicing transferring into and out of each seat, and next to this stands a tall shelf that holds countless board games and puzzles and many other creative pieces, all of which are used to aid in fine motor movements, sitting or standing balance, and memory.

The gym is impressive with its advanced technology and the sheer number of equipment and tools, but there is more to it than that. I'm not sure if it comes from the brightly lit space, its modern appearance, or what exactly it is, but there's something that makes the air simply feel *different* here. It's a place filled with hope and possibility, two feelings that are often lost, and always needed, in the patients who pass through these doors. Without hope, they could have all the machines in the world, and still they would need that one missing aspect.

I work in this space, each day, side-by-side with my two new physical therapists. The reason I now have two therapists rather than just one is that one is still a student within the doctoral physical therapy program and is in a clinical rotation here at Spaulding.

It's a good team, the three of us. The newer therapist of the two explains each exercise clearly, as though he's been working in this field for many years. As I fearfully attempt each one for the first time, his presence assures me that I am both safe and capable. He's always serious, while the other is consistently joyful, in a way that's clearly honest and not put on. Besides her radiating happiness, it's also her extreme intelligence that's obvious. She fills the air with a stream of knock-knock jokes that only she can make funny, and when she interjects, it's always with a note that makes me really stop to think about what she's just shared. I've quickly become comfortable with the two of them and look forward to our sessions each day.

My body is unfamiliar and awkward, so as I move into position for each exercise, I either flop over with far too much force or get trapped in an awkward in-between state, having not used quite enough. We often begin each hour of work together with an exercise that is simple yet wholly frustrating. I lie on my side with a floor-length mirror rolled in front of me, used in hopes to form a greater mind-body connection. One of my legs is propped up on to a small table or stool, just slightly higher than the exercise table I lie upon, and all I need to do then is move that propped-up leg backward and push it behind me. I can swing it forward with ease, so this should happen just as quickly, right?

Except each time I stare into that mirror, giving the exercise every drop of strength, energy, and focus that I have, my reflection remains unchanged. That leg stays firmly in place, as if glued into position. This easy-enough movement is one that requires the activation of glute muscles in order to move backward—quite clearly one of the many muscle groups that have begun to display its firmly held state of paralysis.

It's a strange phenomenon, the realization that your mind gives your body an instruction, but it now goes ignored. To feel that you are using all your strength but see no result. It is like being trapped within a body that is no longer yours. As if your soul and spirit and mind are the same, yet there you are, captive in the wrong container. I want to yell at my limbs to listen to me, to do as they are told, as they always have before. Yet their silence and ignorance and stillness continue.

After a disheartening number of failed attempts and a frustrating number of repetitions, something finally changed. The reflection before me finally began to move in that desired direction. That very first time I got my leg to swing, maybe even less than an inch or so behind me, I felt an excitement so great and so obvious that an onlooker might have thought I'd just won the lottery. With beads of sweat on my forehead, the three of us cheered, and I tried once again. My leg swung backward one inch all over again, and it felt as though I'd just won the greatest fight of all time. My limbs were beginning to listen.

There's another exercise that is my favorite. I lie on my stomach on this same table, and a chair is placed in front of me. After grabbing on to the legs of the chair, I climb my way up, inching my hands upwards until I'm standing on the ends of my legs. The position that

I end up in is more akin to kneeling than it is to standing, but when I look up at the gym before me, seeing all the activity in the room no longer from a seated position, it's in that brief moment that I get to feel that familiar and so taken-for-granted sensation of what it's like to simply stand once again.

This exercise is a stepping stone in preparation for the day I am given the gift of prosthetic legs. Because when that happens, I will essentially be doing the same work that I have done in this exercise, except my legs will no longer end at those knees that I stand upon, and that kneeling position will be replaced with manmade legs and creatively constructed limbs.

But this exercise is excruciatingly tough and perhaps this is part of the reason why it is my favorite, as I feel the pride of the work put in. Not only is it clear that I lack strength, as I feel as if I'm summiting some mountain as I desperately inch my way up the legs of that chair, but I lack endurance, as well. From a month in a coma, combined with weeks of bed rest, and just recently being given a wheelchair to minimally use on my own, I breathe in loud puffs of air. My athletic self has been replaced with wheezing and coughing, a racing heart, and a bright-red face.

Other times, in hopes of regaining both some sensation and some strength in my muscles, I work alone with the female therapist of the two. As she puts it, we then "stim my bum" as the rectangular pads of a neuromuscular stimulation device are placed on my skin. She increases the intensity until I can feel the tingling sensation within my muscles.

A neuromuscular device sends electrical impulses to your nerves and forces the muscles to contract. This is used to prevent muscle atrophy, or the wasting away of muscle, of my glute and hamstring muscles, which are vitally important for me ever to attain the goal of walking again. This device contracts the muscles in a way that I cannot on my own.

I lie on my stomach and hold my breath, anxiously waiting for that first detection of any tingling, or any sensation at all, to alert me that I have noticed the device's presence. As the sensation grows and spreads throughout my muscle, I release one giant sigh of relief and allow the machine to continue. The reason waiting for that first sensation is so tense for me is that this is not the first place that I have used this same machine. Back in Cambridge, Danielle had placed these same sticky pads on the same areas of my skin. She'd intensified the device as high as it would go, and I'd felt nothing. She'd quietly tucked the device away; we'd changed our plans and moved on to doing something else, and never once was that moment ever mentioned. For me, knowing that something that should have burned and stung and worked its way through my muscles had gone completely unnoticed, was a concept I could hardly understand. So now, I lie here, savoring every moment that my muscles sting beneath those pads.

After physical therapy ends, I then have occupational therapy. My therapist walks into my room, seeming never to be bothered by a bit of stress. I always hate the beginning stages of working with someone new in these medical settings—the awkward introductions and the phases of time when you don't yet know each other but have no choice but to work so hands-on, in such a personal way, answering all of their seemingly invasive questions. In a hospital, I've found that I have no privacy at all. But I hadn't even had time to worry about what it might be like to work with this newest therapist, because on her very first day of working with me, she began with the lessons that banished all modesty and privacy.

As I learned to bathe on my own, a task I was desperately eager to learn, I'd transferred over to a small shower chair, and she stood directly before me. I cautiously stripped each piece of clothing off and she'd reached her hands out, still chatting easily as if nothing out of the ordinary was happening. Then, she took each piece of clothing from me and placed them in a waiting pile on the counter. It had only been day one, and I'd already stripped naked in front of her, all while she remained completely unfazed. Then I closed the curtain around me, and took my very first shower on my own. I was ecstatic, and strangely proud, staying underneath the water longer than I should have as she stood outside, patiently waiting.

When I was done—my hair washed and conditioned, my body cleansed, my face exfoliated—I realized I had no idea what to do next. Looking around, I saw the door that was so far away, the clothes that were out of reach, and the towels that were too far, too.

"Uhm... I'm all done. What do I do?" I'd nervously yelled.

My curtain swung open and there she stood. She began chatting again to fill the air with a needed distraction. She brought my wheelchair closer to the shower chair, helped my still-naked-self transfer over, and then I dried myself off. Our session was finished. I was clean and I was happy, and I smiled as she left my room, setting out to find her next patient.

Physical therapy is an up-close and personal relationship in many ways, but it's occupational therapy that takes it to a whole new level. It's in these sessions that each aspect of recovery that no one wants to talk about is addressed—showering, going to the bathroom, dressing, personal hygiene—and each day she moves us through these tasks with complete normalcy. Not only am I thankful for her in each minute of these days, but it's at this same time that I've begun to notice the changes within myself.

I'm able to ask the questions I would have once kept to myself. I'm able to yell for help when I'm trapped naked in the shower with my wheelchair too far away without my skin burning red with shame. I'm more comfortable in this new, broken, scarred, still-healing skin, than I ever was in the undamaged body I'd had for so many years.

That is an eye-opening moment, as I wonder how and why I'd always managed to detest the body that had been so healthy and able to do everything I asked of it.

Why was it then, when I had the legs I'd been born with, all I could focus on was the thighs that I felt were too big? Why is it that it took literally losing pieces of those legs to begin to love them a little more? Why is it that when I was capable of doing everything on my own, without help or needing an emergency call bell beside me, that I often found myself too anxious or even depressed to breathe or move or do the activity I so wanted to do?

The biggest question of all: *Why is it easier to notice what you don't have, than it is to see all that you do?*

In all those moments in each of the hospitals before this one, when I'd claimed that I could feel "pieces of myself chipping away," had I really only simply been forced to grow? I might not be physically healed yet, and have so far to go, but just maybe, I'm healing a little bit more in ways I never knew I needed.

After both of these sessions are done, I then have speech therapy. Before this, I'd always thought of speech therapy as something entirely different from what it really seems to be. I'd thought it was only for speech-related concerns, such as stutters or mispronunciations, but they include so much more than that. My therapist was given the neuropsychology evaluation I'd taken recently, and we work to improve and manage each of the concerns that were revealed within this report.

As she hands me a Monday–Friday pill container with a.m. and p.m. boxes for each day, I read each of my prescription bottles and confidently drop each dose in the correct space. Some pills are taken each morning, some every other morning, some every night, and some every other night, but still, it should be an easy enough task to read each direction and place them in the correct space. I slide the container toward her, she inspects my work, removes each one that is wrong, and then slides it back toward me. Each time, I sit there thinking, *How did I get any of those wrong?* This is the task that's convinced me that speech therapy isn't some unnecessary inconvenience but is something that I actually need.

I take tests and fill out mazes and puzzles and games, and after each session when my mom asks me, "How was speech today?" I am entirely frustrated each time that I hear myself answering those questions with sentences like, "I got stuck by the llamas in the zoo and never made it to the zebras." She'll stare at me with no idea what I am talking about. I'll explain it then, telling her of the maze I was supposed to complete with one single line, and how I couldn't yet find my way through its design.

Mazes, puzzles, and games should be easy fun. Yet my head throbs with the headache that's formed. Throbbing from the focus that now takes physical work, from feeling fried from the pushing for progress, and from the frustration of it all.

My mom has remained by my side here in Charlestown. She listens to each of my doctors, stays updated on my care, creates never-ending to-do lists, and keeps track of all that I forget. Both of our days are filled and always busy. While I am downstairs in that gym, Mom does physical therapy of her own, in Spaulding's outpatient clinic. On the rare days when the weather is not freezing cold, she'll spend her time walking round the boardwalk of the harbor as far as her slowly healing feet will carry her.

Many times, though, when I arrive back upstairs, I find her sitting cross-legged on the small couch that she will sleep on later that night, with countless pages of paper before her, as she focuses on the mind-numbing tasks of insurance coverage, applying for grants for home adaptations, planning and learning how to install hand controls in my car, researching outpatient therapy clinics for the two of us at home, and all of the tasks that continue to arise.

When trauma occurs and your life changes in an instant, it feels as though the world should simply pause, and that it should give you a moment to just breathe. But the world doesn't know what's happened to you, and so it continues to go on, expecting you to keep up. Bills arise, payments are due, and everything that needs taking care of still needs taking care of. It's an incredible responsibility— keeping up, while trying to take care of yourself, too.

At the end of each day, when the sky has grown dark, lit only by the bright Boston skyline, mom settles on her stiff and uncomfortable couch, and I settle into my stiff and uncomfortable hospital bed. We pull our matching sleep masks—from the gift shop downstairs— over our eyes, attempting to hide from the still-lit machines around us, and we close our eyes to rest for another day.

Not every night, but many of them, as we lie in this room across from one another, one of us repeats the same sentence that's been said many times before. "Can you imagine if we didn't get along?" one of us will ask the other, quietly laughing each time.

In between the words of that question, and hidden in the gaps, is the real meaning. How neither of us has any idea in the world how we would have survived this without the other.

＿＿

Just over a month has passed. This same routine being performed each day. The same therapies at the same time, the same menu of meals served at generally the same time, the same timing of closing our eyes, and waking to begin once more. But now, today, the routine has changed.

A quick knock taps against my door.

"Come in," I yell.

The door swings open, and my doctor takes a step inside.

"You ready?" he asks me, looking serious but with a slight smile on his face.

I try to act casual, refusing to release the emotions I feel pent up within me.

"Yes!" I say simply.

I hadn't slept last night. Kept up with excitement, like a child the night before Christmas. But today is better than Christmas. Today, I'm getting legs.

Everything *looks* different today and everything *feels* different today. The same surroundings look brand new, and I'm charged with energy. Typically, I'm running late for my eight a.m. start time. Always keeping my eyes shut until the last possible minute, skipping breakfast, and often caught pulling a T-shirt over my head as the door opens and the day begins. Today is different. I sit ready, dressed in a navy-blue zip-up athletic top and gray shorts, and my hair pulled into a high ponytail with a scrunchy. My white sneakers sit by the doorway, finally unpacked from my suitcase, and ready to be worn.

It's not only my room that feels electric with energy: this entire hallway feels different, as if I can sense the energy and silent cheers spreading from my fellow patients on this spinal-cord injury floor. Nearly bouncing up and down, I wait until my physical therapist arrives. Finally, he appears in the doorway—and pauses. Quite the crowd has gathered.

The news of my injuries had crashed through my family's and my small hometown. So today isn't a holiday celebrated by me alone, it's one that everyone wants to gather for. My mom and stepdad are here. My dad has picked up my sister from school, and my brother from his apartment, and they arrive next. The neighbor I grew up with on that mountainside road of my childhood home has made the drive to visit; she's picked up my grandma, and the two of them sit in this small room. Sheila and Haiden are here. Elliott, a patient who was discharged from this floor just as I arrived, but who I like to think is one of my very first friends in this new community, sits outside my room and is ready to cheer me on. Jake, the patient in the room next to mine, has demanded that today they do his physical therapy *only* from machines that allow him a view of my session. Many Spaulding physicians are here, and the woman delivering my legs is here. It's a combination of my past life, current life, and a collection of professionals from these halls. As my physical therapist stands paused, he seems to be taking a moment, assessing the massive amount of pressure within this room. Then we make our way downstairs.

The far-right corner of the gym has been sectioned off, leaving us space with an exercise table, parallel bars, and a harness. A tall mirror stands at the end of the bars. We make our way to the table; two legs rest against its edge. My heart drums against my chest.

"First of all, how are you feeling today?" I hear my PT ask.

It's a valid question. He's not asking only because today is a big day; he's asking because I had surgery yesterday. It was truly horrific timing. I could've put off my "leg delivery day" until a different day, but there was no way I was waiting. Besides, it was a minor surgery, I tell everyone.

In the early days after my injuries, I'd been marked as high risk for blood clots due to the extensive list of fractures within my body. Because of this, an IVC filter, or Inferior Vena Cava filter, had been placed, ensuring that if any clots formed, they wouldn't travel to my heart or lungs, something that could have been deadly.

Yesterday morning, this filter was removed. Though the procedure itself was minor, the pre-op visit had left me unnerved. The surgeon was new to me, a vascular surgeon whom I only got to meet in his office once before he wheeled my sedated body into surgery. As he'd explained the procedure to me, he lifted his palm in the air. In between his index finger and thumb he held a ballpoint pen. "So I'll place something that's only about this wide," he said, indicating the width of the pen, "and this will travel through your vein [he pointed now to the vein in my neck] and down to where the filter rests." The filter, he explains now, has been placed in my inferior vena cava, which sounds to me like a large vein in my heart. So, this large, pen-shaped tool will be traveling through precious veins that I imagined to be not-so-sturdy and not something you wish to be bumped or cut into with any pen-shaped devices and entering my heart. I swallowed, and then quite simply replied.

"Uhm…that's a big pen."

"And if the filter seems to have gotten stuck, we won't pull on it; we'll just leave it," he said. Ending the appointment with that last sentence that put this procedure in my mind with far too much imagery. Suffice it to say, the pre-op appointment had not calmed my nerves.

"I'm good," I tell my PT now. "I'm used to surgery by now," I say, trying to laugh it off, even though the hangover of anesthesia still fogs my brain.

The crowd meets us at the table, forming a semicircle around me. Normally, I'd be embarrassed by the attention, especially now, as other patients come down to begin their sessions in this gym, but today nothing can bother me. First, this strange process is explained to me. The woman from my new prosthetic clinic hands me two tan-colored gel liners. These go on first. I lie on my back on the table and feel the cool gel slide against my skin.

My prosthetic legs are different from any I've seen before. They're a combination of prosthetics and orthotics. Trying to make up for the weakness from my spinal-cord injury, two tall black-plastic components have been added. These will extend all the way up to about where my hips begin. On each leg is a circular piece of metal on the back of each knee and jutting outwards; these are the components that will lock and unlock the leg into and out of a straight position. Since my knees are incapable of bending, these hinges will unlock instead. Rows of silver metal extend vertically on both the inner and outer sides of each leg, from the very bottom to the very top. She hands me a pink, almost flesh-colored, spherical piece.

"This looks like a thumb," I stupidly say.

Clearly, I'm nervous if I'm already making bad jokes. To my relief, those around me laugh and agree.

I put the thumb-looking piece over the end of my right limb. This is the shorter limb, with only skin-grafted tissue that constantly breaks down and cracks open with the slightest touch covering the end. In fact, today was nearly canceled, as two stubborn open circles sit on the edge of my leg. To my relief, nurses had applied a healing cream and two padded bandages and said that this would do. These are now both tucked carefully into these skintight liners. This right side is the limb I will always have to be the most careful with, hence the need for the thumb piece.

Now I slide the black plastic around my thighs, line the end of my limbs up with the "socket" part below me, and begin to push them on, making sure to stay straight so that the pin-lock system matches up. All the terms become muddled in my mind—sockets, pin-locks, liners, thumb piece, I try to memorize them, repeating them in my mind. We struggle to get the lock on tight. No one seems to be able to get it lined up just right. My doctor's stood quietly watching, and hands me a small silver coin.

"It's good luck. Just hold it," he says.

I look to see if he's serious. He seems to be, so I reach over and grab the coin from his hand. The lock finally clicks.

"Now you use a coin or something to tighten this," my prosthetist explains, pointing to a straight line within the lock that must be turned.

"Go ahead and use that," he says.

After using this lucky coin to tighten my legs, I'm finally all set to go. My physical therapist looks at me seriously now. He can tell I'm nervous.

"Focus on me and you, don't let anyone distract you," he says.

Taking a deep breath, I nod my head. "I'm ready."

I transfer into my wheelchair. These prosthetic legs can be locked completely straight, or unlocked so they hang toward the ground. Right now, they stick out straight, leaving me stiff and unsure of how to move. A once easy transfer, across about one inch of space between table and chair, now feels dangerous and extreme. I'm off my game already.

Finally in my chair, I push myself toward the parallel bars. I make my way up one last, small ramp, and then I'm in the parallel bars. My reflection stares back at me. *Huh.* It's an odd sight.

Somewhere along the way, I'd gotten used to the reflection of a sort of half-person. It had grown familiar, seeing myself with no legs. Replacing that now, with these two heavy-duty prosthetic legs that stick straight out from my chair, is quite a difference. Nervously, I play with the tape on my neck that covers yesterday's incision. *Stop doing that,* I silently remind myself.

A thick vest wraps around my waist and chest. My face flushes red as they decide it's too loose, and I hear someone say, "Can you see if we have a children's size somewhere?" I hadn't expected to hear that.

This weight loss has been such a contrast from the curvy body I'd always known that it's only added to the disguise I feel as though I'm wearing. It's hard to feel like myself when nothing looks the same any longer. I look at my reflection once more and feel the wind slightly knocked out of me. The crowd around me is busy chatting with one another and we're in a moment of pause until the new vest is found, so no one notices my momentary hesitation. *Who is this girl looking back at me?* I wonder, still stuck staring at the image of the girl in the mirror. Her hair has slipped down from a high ponytail. It's too thin to be held tight by the scrunchie she's used. Deep dark circles, nearly black in color, surround her eyes, looking like she either hasn't slept in months or she's healing from two black eyes. She looks sick. A thin piece of tape, with edges darkened with dirt, dust, or some unknown substance, curls at the edges and lifts slightly off the skin. The small-sized blue top fits loosely, and her gray shorts look far too baggy, as she has neither muscle nor fat within her hips. Her legs bizarrely stick out too straight, making her look like a mechanical doll.

What has happened to me?

I snap back into focus. They've found a smaller vest, and I change into it. A small rectangular remote lowers the harness toward me. We lock the vest into the harness, and they ask me if I'm ready. Each step is completed with ease.

"Ready," I tell them.

A goofy smile sits on my face, but I can't wipe it away. I always smile when I'm nervous. The harness rises back into the air, pulling against my chest as it moves, and I feel myself sliding toward the edge of my wheelchair. Quickly I grab onto the bars beside me. My physical therapist sits on a stool in front of me in a prepared position. He grabs on to my hips to guide me upwards, and suddenly, I'm out of my chair.

"You're standing!" I hear someone say.

"I am?" I ask, confused.

"I can't feel the ground!" I say, laughing now.

So, this is what it's going to feel like now? My hips stick out behind me. My palms grip tight on the bars. I can't feel the ground. I'm uncertain about what's going on. Again, I feel my face turn pink.

"Beautiful!" I hear my PT exclaim.

I give a sarcastic "Ta-daaaa!" but secretly, I'm thrilled.

"Time to start running, right?" I ask him.

The gym has filled with patients and I can feel the eyes of those interested by the activity here in our corner. We begin by working on shifting balance from right to left, and front to back, a simple enough task that is now hugely challenging. I ask if I can try to take a step.

"Not yet," he tells me.

I continue the strange tasks, hanging on to every word of advice I hear from the two doctors beside me. I'm unbelievably surprised and grateful that they have stood by and taken the time to watch. My palms are sweaty and a hue of bright red has clung to my cheeks.

"You're shaking," someone points out to me.

I know they want me to take a break. Without hesitation I reply, slightly sarcastically and with a determined smile on my face: "I don't know what you're talking about."

They laugh, and they let me continue. Finally, I hear the question I've been waiting for. It's a good thing I heard it now, because in reality, I am shaking like a leaf. I'll need to stop soon.

"Do you want to try a few steps?"

My face lights up. Of course, I do. They explain what to do, and I can't help but think how weird it is that I now need instructions on walking. I do what they tell me. Holding on tight, I shift my weight to my right side, but really, I'm still holding nearly all of my weight with my arms. My left leg feels glued to the floor. I push forward with all my might, until it seems to pop loose. Not simply stepping forward, but instead kicking forward, higher into the air than I would've liked. I land with my feet crisscrossed.

"Does that count as a step?" I ask, only half-joking.

He nods his head. He's always so serious.

"We need to work on it, but yes," he finally agrees.

I doubt he meant it, but I'll take what I can get right now.

"Let's keep going," I encourage them.

A new, female physician steps up now, giving me advice that I imagine to be simply priceless. She's the head of the entire physical therapy department, and here she is, giving *me* advice on what to do. I hang on to every word. She adjusts my posture. She tells me to look into the mirror. I'm set, back into position, and ready to go.

"Come toward me," she says.

I feel my frame shift toward my right. The mirror gives feedback and clear instruction, her voice is my guide, and this time my leg swings forward more easily, staying low to the ground, and landing exactly where I needed it to. Instinct now takes over. She's giving instruction on what to do next, but my body has already seamlessly transitioned to the next step.

"Yep!" she says, nodding her head.

"Beautiful," someone else agrees.

My heart soars with their approval. All I'd done was place my weight on to the foot that just landed forward. It was instinctual. But now I'm in position for the next step. It looked easy and felt almost natural, but my eyes are glued to the reflection before me. I've never been this focused in my life. The crowd around me has disappeared. I can't hear any voices other than these two beside me. I'm locked in.

I repeat the process again. I'm in a groove. Voices break through my focus, and I hear my mom's emotional cheer. Then I look down, seeing that my feet have landed crisscrossed again. Time to adjust. Gathering myself, I get ready to start once more. I straighten my back and lean into their voices; shift my weight, swing my foot, and repeat. Four steps come right in a row.

Three black lines of tape mark the end of the parallel bars. That tape had once looked so far away. I look down and my feet stand on top of them.

"This is exciting," I say, and the crowd laughs.

I want to scream how proud I am to have made it. Instead, I settle for the short proclamation of emotion, always hiding my real thoughts and not wanting to boast over something that is so simple.

We finish up, and I sit back in the familiar wheelchair. We head toward the elevators. Everyone else follows behind. A sign-out sheet, allowing my family and I to go out for a celebratory dinner tonight, has already been signed. The combined effects of yesterday's surgery and today's activity have left me starving, so we keep it simple; we're going out for burgers. I can't remember the last time I've eaten a burger, I think, laughing. As if walking only a few feet has earned me this divulgence.

My therapist helps me get settled into my room, congratulates me on today, and walks away. Elliott gives me a hug that's made complicated by our two wheelchairs being in the way, and then he wheels toward the door, heading back to his apartment. Jake shouts his cheers and then stays in my room until his nurse calls him away. My brother and sister say goodbye, and I thank them for coming. My dad tells me how proud he is. I'm riding a high as my mom and Paul walk the rest of the group to the elevator. In my room alone now, I enthusiastically spin my wheelchair around. There they are, my brand-new legs!

I hadn't had a chance to really look at them until now. The door's shut, so I push my way forward, and pick one of them up. *God these are heavy.* I push the metal circle back and forth, watching as it locks and unlocks the bottom portion. *How strange.* I hadn't noticed the feet before, but now I look at them closely. They're an off-white color. Similar to the color someone's skin might turn if they were both intensely pale and sick with the flu. Thin lines, looking as if they were drawn with pencil or pen, outline the five toes. There's no indent or shape to them. The toes are less creative than a stick-figure drawing. The soles of each foot are completely flat. Suddenly I feel sick.

In that entire hour-long session, I only took about six steps. That was with the help of a harness holding nearly all my weight, and two parallel bars that nearly burned off my skin with the intensity of my grasp. How am I ever going to do this? How am I ever going to use these? How am I ever going to walk without my legs?

Suddenly it all makes sense. I won't ever walk with these.

My world is crashing down around me. I was so high, and now, I'm so low. The entire floor and the hallways outside seem empty, which is a blessing, as I break into sobs.

Earlier, as my session had been coming to an end and my mom had hung back in the hallway, my doctor had briskly walked away, in search of a printer. He printed off a sheet of paper, returned to the gym, and handed it to my mom. It was a prayer of hope.

He told my mom that it is the moment after using prosthetic legs for the first time that is often the hardest for amputees. Before you put them on, it's just an idea in your head. Your imagination can create any reality you desire. Then you put them on, and often they're stiff and uncomfortable, or there are spots that are painful, and your reality comes crashing back. It's no longer a figment of your imagination; it's a brutal reality. A reality you will never be able to escape.

He'd told her to stay hopeful. He passed along a new form of his wisdom, this time not in medical terms or diagnoses, but in the printed words of a prayer and a kind gesture.

She walks back into my room with that piece of paper sitting carefully folded in her pocket. Instantly, she's thankful for his warning, as she sees me now. My cheeks are wet and she hears my cries. She pauses for only a moment at the door, and then she rushes into action. She kneels before my chair and listens to my explanations. Then, she extends her hand and passes this piece of paper to me.

As I read the words, my breaths return to a normal rate, the tears cease to fall, and I feel calm once again.

It's exactly what I needed, to know that this sudden fear and crashing reality is often a harsh part of the process and not something that only I have felt. Knowing I am not the only person to have felt this way after such a long-awaited moment, for some reason, is the news I needed to hear. I push the negatives out of my mind. I focus on the fact that I have stood, instead of how hard it had felt. I remember those steps I just took, instead of counting how many I had taken. I think of how hard it was, only to congratulate myself for the work done and not chastising myself for how challenging it had seemed, not telling myself it should have been easier. I tell myself that I am not weak, but that I am simply working my way through the fight that I have been given, and that is the strongest choice of all.

The fatigue I now feel reminds me that time and time again, I've wanted to give up but have instead gone forward. Today didn't need to be perfect. I was strong enough to try, strong enough to have made it here today, and that is victory enough to celebrate.

Mom pins that printed paper on the wall across from me, and with that rush of emotions now released, we return to our plans. I swipe one brush of mascara along my lashes, and head out the door in pursuit of my grease-filled, oversized, and highly craved reward of a cheeseburger, and for tonight, that will be enough.

CHAPTER 15

As I lie on this thin mattress, turned slightly on to my side with my arms wrapped round my stomach, a text appears on the screen of my phone. It's from my friend Tati.

"Are you being discharged today?" she asks.

"Supposed to be on Wednesday, but might have to push it back," I reply.

"You're pushing it back? Why?"

"Yeah, we might have to. I just can't seem to get better."

On the very same week that I was meant to be discharged from the hospital and set to return home, this is what happened instead.

Alone in my room, I roll on to my side and begin scrolling through social media posts, only half paying attention. Then, out of nowhere, I gasp in pain. Something has just jabbed through my stomach, grabbed hold of my organs, and is twisting with excruciating strength. It's so painful I can hardly breathe. I look down at my stomach, seeing only my oversized T-shirt. There's nothing protruding from my abdomen.

There should be something there, I can feel it! It's too painful to not be real.

As my mom walks back into the room, she pauses at the entrance, gawks at me, and suddenly exclaims.

"Oh my gosh! Are you okay?"

"Something's wrong," is all that I can say.

My body rocks back and forth. Each of my limbs begins to shake and spasm. Every inch of my skin has begun to sweat. And now, to make things worse, I begin vomiting.

"Something's wrong," I say once more, though the words are now slurred.

It's the weekend. Anyone who's been in a hospital before would likely agree that you don't want to get sick or have any complications on the weekend. Your everyday doctor will have been replaced with a weekend physician. Of course, they are equally talented, but the relationship that has been established is no longer there. They can't know your pain tolerance, they can't know what your usual and healthy physical appearance is, and the slight signs or symptoms that might be noticed by the other can often go unnoticed through no fault of their own.

The next days pass by in a blur of pain and confusion. I won't eat for days on end, and my feeding tube has been removed, so it feels like I'm losing all of the muscle I had so recently restored. I'm nearly delusional with thirst and hunger and pain. I can't sip on a glass of water without it immediately coming back up, and the dehydration has reached the point of being dangerous. My veins sit collapsed against my skin, and an IV is painfully inserted in the back of my hand. My skin has turned an odd shade of gray. I can't lift my head or my arms, or move at all. I simply alternate between moaning in pain and falling into a deep silence.

One moment remains clear in my mind. With much help from the nurses beside me, I'm picked up and transferred to a stretcher. I hadn't known there was an X-ray machine here, but I travel down to the lowest floor, moving through an odd series of hallways, finally arriving in the cold and quiet room. A friendly woman greets me, and my nurse, using all her might, helps slide me on to the exam table. The friendly voice asks questions, and I try to reply, but words are nearly impossible to speak.

The X-ray of my abdomen is quick, and I'm soon making my way back to my room once more.

The hallways are brightly lit, though I suppose no brighter than usual, and my eyes hurt as I look above me. I feel my stretcher come to a stop, even though my room is still far off, and my nurse quietly, and without giving a reason, disappears. Patients and their therapists mill about, all heading toward their sessions, and I wish I could disappear. I know how I must look, and can't tell why I've been left here in the middle of the crowded hallway. My stretcher rests tucked to the side of the hall, and I feel painfully exposed. Everything is fuzzy and moves so slowly, as if I'm stuck within a dream. Then my eyes close.

"Stef?" I hear the voice of my occupational therapist calling, the sound breaking through my disconnect.

My eyes open, but I can't lift my head. I'm too tired. *Why am I still out here? How long have I been out here?*

"What are you doing out here?" she asks me.

"I have no idea. I got an X-ray and my nurse left me out here," I explain groggily.

I'm not on any medication, but my surroundings blur and my consciousness seem to have left my body. She brings me back to my room. Before she leaves, she takes one last look at me, and her eyes betray a deep worry.

"I'm going to check on you later, okay?"

I nod. I don't know this yet, but she now goes to find my physical therapists, sharing with them the scene she's just witnessed. They know that something is terribly wrong. What I'm also unaware of is that my favorite nurse here has been convinced of the same idea. This group have all concluded that I need to go to the Emergency Room.

The X-ray image reveals nothing wrong, but my regular doctor has returned now and agrees that something is dreadfully wrong. He begins my transfer to Mass Gen.

The familiar faces of the ambulance drivers that I've come to know so well arrive in my room. Mom chats with them as I lie with my eyes closed, trying to ignore the stabbing pain.

The Emergency Room at Mass General Hospital is something out of a movie. There are no patient rooms left, so my stretcher is placed in the crowded hallway. To my right, a woman stands screaming at the police officers who surround her. We hear the words "detoxing" and "withdrawals" coming from their direction. A man sits groaning in pain in the wheelchair beside me, and I turn my head just as he vomits into a paper bag held in his hands. The commotion around me is loud and constant, and I want to shrink in size. I'm only here for a CT scan, and finally it's time.

I'm taken into a small room that is all too familiar in its appearance, with its plain white walls, fluorescent lights, and a cold flat table for me to lie on. I hate the rooms that look this way. A man in scrubs helps get me on to the table.

I'm so desperate for an answer, for something to end this pain, that at this point it doesn't matter to me how terrible it is. After the scan finishes, the ambulance takes me back to Spaulding, saying the image now needs to be read. Groaning, I wonder how impossibly long this will take.

We make the drive back to Spaulding, but I don't even make it back into my room. My doctor stands before my door, anxiously waiting.

"You need to go back to the ER…now," he says plainly.

The results of my scan have been read. My stretcher is turned around, and we make our way back. When we arrive again, this time I'm rushed into a room and not seen only in the hallway. A young male doctor greets us and explains what he will be doing. Essentially, they're going to pump my stomach. A long tube is inserted into my nose, and he instructs me to make swallowing motions as the tube travels toward my stomach. At first, nothing happens, other than the massive discomfort throughout my throat. Then the tube travels just slightly farther, and without any warning, my body remaining in its exact same position, sitting in a nearly perfect ninety-degree angle, I begin projectile vomiting a bright green substance.

This doctor, clearly unsure of how to handle this, reacts instinctively. His hands reach forward, with a plain piece of paper within his palms, attempting to catch the fluid, as his eyes look frantically around him. I can't even apologize because this plastic still sits in my throat. Apparently, the tube had been inserted too far. As they pulled it out a touch, the vomiting relented, and my stomach began to empty into the plastic container beside me, as it was supposed to.

Only a few moments later, everything changes. I'm not sure what's prompted the need to change, but our plans now switch in an instant. The reason my stomach was being pumped was in the hope of avoiding surgery, but clearly, that is no longer an option. Most of the surgeries I have had before this were done while I was either comatose or highly medicated. Or they were at least planned well in advance. So, I'm unprepared for what is now happening. Everyone's movements around me occur with a frightening speed. My stretcher

is unlocked, each wheel making a sharp noise of release. Palms grasp
on to the stretcher's railings, and without a look back, I'm whisked
away, heading toward the operating room.

As I lie on a new, and even colder table, a man stands before me
listing all the possible complications of some surgery that I seem to
be having, though I'm still not entirely sure what for. It's a long list
of risks. I swallow deeply, and exhale slowly, trying to breathe away
the terror. That tube still pushes against my throat, distracting me as I
try to listen to this man before me. The tape attaching the tube to my
skin has begun to burn against my nose. I can't listen to these worst-
case images; I want to beg him to just start already!

My mom stands with wide, terrified eyes. I see her being rushed
out of the room. She walks quickly, but she walks backwards,
seemingly unable to look away from me. I lay down. I stare up into
the brightly lit room. Looking up at the ceiling that looks the same
as all the others, contemplating all that could happen, all that could
go wrong.

Then, the familiar darkness of anesthesia washes over me.

There hadn't been time for the standard introductions between the
patient and the surgeon before this procedure. He'd rushed into the
operating room while I was already deeply asleep on his operating
table. Just over a day has passed since, and today is the first time that
I'll meet him.

He walks into my room around five a.m., but I'd only been
half-asleep. I can only lie on my back, can't roll over to adjust or
get comfortable. The pain is intense. My abdominal muscles have
been cleanly sliced through. Any slight movement is excruciating,

and it's only the morphine that forces my eyes shut for a few hours each night.

I first notice that he's tall as he stands above my bed. His hair has a slightly red hue, a typical match for his green eyes. He sits on the edge of my bed, and though the room is still dark and it's far too early, he launches into conversation, explaining what he'd had to do within that operating room.

All the way back in Florida, when I was suffering from internal bleeding, I had a life-saving surgery to stop it. This is the surgery that's left a long scar throughout the center of my body. Now I'd known about the scar that is visible, but what I hadn't known is that these scars can actually create more scar tissue, inside your body. Like a sly predator, this tissue has been silently forming, likely since the day of this earlier operation. I wonder now, if the moment of pain that I can recall so clearly, had been the exact moment that the scar tissue had wrapped round my intestines and cut off all blood flow.

"I had to make an incision that was a few inches long," he continues. He holds up his fingers, gesturing to the approximate size. I nod my head, not wanting to admit how unfair this news already seems to feel. He'd done his job; I really shouldn't be concerned about the addition of another scar. But it feels cruel, imagining yet another straight-lined permanent marking sitting beside the other.

"But I went over your previous incision, so it's actually slightly smaller now," he finishes saying.

My eyes open wide at these words. He asks if I want to see it and I enthusiastically nod my head yes. I can't yet sit up, so I crane my neck, until my head is lying sideways, and my eyes can finally see. He lifts my hospital gown up, somehow in a way that remains holding a shred of privacy, and I see a bandage in front of me until he lifts this away, too.

The top of my scar looks the same. The bottom of it hasn't changed, either. But right in the middle, about three inches of this scar is now only about a quarter of the width of the rest of it. That area in the middle is now more of a pencil-thin line, more of a tracing or outline, than it is the thick, overly-stretched, rope-like wound that is the rest of it.

My emotions are high. I'm medicated, tired, and still slightly out of my mind. But I swear, in this moment, I would kiss him if I could. Instead, I choke out a simple "Thank you," my voice cracking.

Before this surgery, I'd been trying to bargain and plead with the staff at Spaulding to convince them to allow me to stay awhile longer. Just days after getting my first pair of legs, and as I remained unable to even stand on my own, they suddenly began throwing around discharge dates as if I was anywhere close to ready to leave. As they'd begun talking of going home and finding a new outpatient clinic, everything within me knew that I wasn't yet ready for this step. But now, after this brutal procedure, I've quite simply had enough. I want to go home. I *need* to go home.

The staff here at Mass Gen has been working with my insurance to send me directly home rather than back to Spaulding.

My mom and sister have been here in this room with me. But today, the two of them are going home. We'd thought that I would be going home with them. Brooke had curled my hair into perfectly loose waves, just tight enough to stay in place. I'd changed from my hospital gown into comfortable clothes, and she'd applied my makeup with the gentlest touch. It was something I hadn't worn all this time, but I felt joyous at the thought of this miraculous and long-awaited homecoming. All my belongings sit in zipped-up suitcases, packed and ready to leave.

I'm ready, and everything I need is ready. I need only to sign those final discharge papers. But as the door swings open, I see there are no papers and their faces now tell an entirely different story than on their previous visits.

Before I hear any words, I know what I will be told. But I listen anyway. There's been a change in plans, they tell me. I'm not going home.

I'd gotten ahead of myself with the daydreams about this plan. I'd been ecstatic at the thought of this nightmare coming to an end. My hopes were up. I'm only able to repeat one single sentence: "It's been *five* months. I want to go home," my voice cracking each time.

As another one of my surgeons comes up to my room, I am at this point crying ugly tears. My mom and sister have already left for the airport. I'm alone in this unfamiliar room, so recently split open to the world once again, and I can't get the tears to stop, even as he calmly stands before me.

I'm not sure why this doctor has come up to see me. It's not something he'd had to do, or should have felt any need or pressure to find the time for. I've come to know my surgeons as the people who are so busy and always-needed that they quickly disappear after they've finished each procedure, and only see you in their follow-up appointments. Him being here, I know, is an extremely kind act. Perhaps he just feels bad for me.

He's probably not much older than I am. He hadn't been my main surgeon but had been a resident in the OR with me just a few days ago. And because of that, he's read my medical records. He stands before me; again he looks so tall, but different from the other surgeon. He has nearly black hair and dark brown eyes. But, like the other, he's also speaking in a kind and gentle way. I try to keep the tears from continuing to fall. I wish that I could silence the ugly sounds that escape me, but my shoulders heave up and down, and my face has grown red and puffy.

Some of the words he says break through the noises I'm making, and I try to smile, and say thank you, or at least simply nod my head.

He's sharing how difficult it was for him to read the story in my medical records, and how unfair this all has been.

"You weren't expecting any of this…." Those words break through my sobs, and his voice seems to crack, too.

He says he wishes he could send me home, but it just isn't possible. I nod my head, and thank him for trying, and try to put on a brave face.

As the ambulance drivers arrive to take me back to Spaulding, I have tissues tightly grasped in my hands and headphones in my ears, and I've wiped my face and pulled it together. I ask them if they would mind picking up my things for me, and watch as they kindly collect the packed bags, my prosthetic legs, and everything that we'd brought here in the hopes of heading home with them. Instead, they will be stowed in the ambulance.

I pass through the brightly lit hallways and enter into the dimly lit surroundings of the back of the ambulance. I keep my music playing and hardly speak. They leave me be, seeming to be aware of my need for silence. I feel so alone. I'm not sure if you can feel as deeply alone anywhere else as you can lying in the darkness of the back of an ambulance.

As I arrive back at Spaulding, it feels different, though I've been gone only a few days. The hallways are silent and dark; everyone is already in their rooms. No nurse is there to greet me, and it is only the ambulance drivers and me, until they leave, as well. I feel empty. A nurse finally comes in to my room. She has to re-do all my intake information, as if I'm a brand-new patient and not someone who has basically lived here apart from my brief disappearance. I've missed dinner, so she hands me a bowl of cold soup and half a sandwich, and walks back out the door. I return to staring up at the ceiling.

I hear a slight knock and a familiar voice. Looking like a child who's just snuck out of the house, the patient whose room is next to mine wheels his way into my room with a look of worry on his face. He pushes toward me and hands me a small container and a card with cursive writing. He stays for a while, his booming and cheerful voice helping me to find my smile again. He leaves now, as his nurse can be heard frantically searching for him. Once the door closes, I open the recently wrapped gift he's handed me.

In my palm, I hold a small wooden angel, her hands folded in prayer and her head bent forward. A light pink heart sits delicately on the front of her gown.

"My family and I were so worried about you," he'd told me, and the card was signed by each of them.

I hold the carved figure in my palm and lay back against the pillow. I don't stare up at the ceiling any longer, and instead simply close my eyes. This room might be empty, but I can rest, as I finally seem to know that I am anything but alone.

CHAPTER 16

*L*eaning forward, I rest my arm against the back-seat car door. We pull out of the parking garage and the late-afternoon sun pours through the windows. I take in my surroundings with wide-eyed amazement. It's all so simple, yet looks so beautiful. The November air is cool, but I open the window anyway, desperately craving the wind against my skin. The sky's the perfect shade of blue, the type of shade that's so ordinary yet feels so rare.

Our car speeds along the highway, while others surround us on each side, weaving in and out of traffic with skill and speed. What feels like a lifetime ago, this all would have passed by my eyes without notice. Today, I watch with wonder, at the goings-on of the world; so complex, so combined, and I'm a part of it all once again.

Today marks exactly five months of this twisted extended vacation. Five months, two countries, and five hospitals later, I'm finally on my way home.

Home. The word calls my name with the sweetest voice I've ever heard.

I continue watching these outdoors scenes passing by until slowly I feel my eyes getting heavy. I'm so tired. This latest surgery has ravaged my body. The incision in my stomach is raw and tender, making it painful to sit straight in this seat. I slip lower, easing the pain. My eyes close, and I fade away.

The sharp turn of the car jerks me awake. We've pulled into our driveway. There it is—our house. The tan-colored home with its cream-colored trim, sharp-angled roof, and porches extending from each end. There's the expansive yard and that charming stone wall, and it's all the same. Nothing's changed. Paul swings my door open.

"Ready?" he asks.

I nod. Carefully, he picks me up, avoiding my stomach and holding only my legs and underneath my shoulders. I hate how easy it is to pick me up now, like a baby being cradled. But I'm home earlier than we'd thought, so there isn't any ramp or accessible way into the house just yet. We walk up the deck and toward the back entrance, the door slides open, and we step inside. He sits me down in the kitchen, and I stare around the room, scanning every inch of the space. Everyone around me talks with enthusiasm. Their words escape my ears. The world is muffled. I feel like some alien, finding her way to a new world and needing a minute to adjust.

"I want to see my room," I announce.

He scoops me back up and carries me up the stairs. When it was clear I wasn't ever returning to that second-floor duplex with the narrow stairway and that small room tucked in the far corner, my roommates had packed up all I'd left in that apartment and returned them here. My plush white comforter lies perfectly flat, without a single crease. Everything is organized and clean. It feels so empty, more a museum than a bedroom. The floors should be cluttered with clothes. My sheets should be crumpled and tossed aside from a night of deep sleep. Shoes should be scattered across my floor, and my closet door should be hanging slightly open. It's familiar, yet unrecognizable.

I lie on my bed, and my eyes continue to scan the room. Everything is intensified. My bed is softer and my comforter thicker. My pillowcase feels silky against my skin, and the sheets wrap around me in the kindest embrace. From my bed, I have a perfect view out my window and into the dark sky. I toss the sheets to the side. Sitting back up, I inch my way closer, until I'm sitting at the edge of my mattress, staring out the window into the evening sky. The world remains silent, and time seems to remain on pause, as I continue to sit so perfectly still.

I have no idea how long I've been in this position. It isn't until I feel a single tear rolling down my cheek that the spell is broken, and my eyes break away from the sight. I'm hit with a whirlwind of emotions, unsure of which to land upon. I'm heartbroken, but I'm thankful. I'm content, but disoriented. I'm thrilled to have made it, but I'm grieving the battle I've been given. The familiar is comforting, but also painful. I'm here, I've survived, and yet I feel as though some stranger has taken my place.

Every inch of my room carries a memory of a past life that I would give anything to travel to once again. The stairs remind me of the mornings I sprinted down them, running late, keys in hand, and dressed for the day to come. The kitchen is where I brewed my coffee and spent hours creating dishes for the family to taste. The lawn is where I chatted with my mom, glass of wine in hand, savoring a moment of sunshine in this often-gloomy climate. I want it all back. My heart rips into pieces.

You're home, I remind myself.

Mom comes in to say goodnight. Neither of us says it, but I know we're both pretending this is normal, pretending we both can't feel the enormous and obvious changes that have taken place within us. I'm not sure about her, but I know that for me, a part of my mind wants to run from this house and all that is familiar because I feel only a trespasser. Instead, we say goodnight, as if nothing's changed, as if we're not terrified, as if we're not anxious at the thought of the nightmares that might find us or for the time our alarms will ring and we'll have to begin to live this normal life again. We don't say any of this. The fan switches on, and my lights turn off. I lean into the breeze, and watch the door close behind her.

It feels strange to be here in this room, even stranger to know that no nurse will wake me up in the night to check my vitals, flashing on the lights and talking so loudly. It feels startling to know that no one will sink any needles into my veins or ask for samples of blood, urine, or flesh. I'm home. It's over. So why does it all still feel so incomplete, so unfinished? Why do I still feel so unprepared for this sudden cessation of all the things I'd wished would disappear?

My mind remains determined to keep me awake with past memories and pointless questions about the future that have no answers, but I feel myself melting into the soft surface beneath me, a far cry from the thin hospital beds. I can think about the future tomorrow. Tonight, I am going to sleep. The world around me disappears, and for the first time in a long time, I fall deeply asleep.

This first week of being home has seemed a vividly detailed nightmare. Everyone seems to have some purpose, and my life seems to be on pause. My family wakes up and sets out each day, heading toward their routines and their obligations. And my mom and I, we wake up terrified for the hours to come, suddenly feeling alone in our struggles. She's hardly able to walk, and limps her way throughout the home. I can again barely sit myself upright or roll myself over.

After this last surgical intrusion, my body seems to have quit on me. Some mornings, I wake up with urine-soaked sheets or blood-covered bandages, as well as dealing with a rotating ailment of fatigue or nausea or weakness. There's no handbook on how to transition into this new life. We're castaways, thrown into the waters with hardly any idea how to swim. And yet, we must. We splash about, our arms flailing in the air, crying for help with no one to hear. We don't drown, but we make no progress. We're simply treading water.

As each new day begins, I stare up at my ceiling fan, wondering how long I can lie here, watching the blades turn round and round, before I must get up. I suppose I could stay here all day; it wouldn't really seem to matter.

In a small burst of courage, I set out on my own, attempting to brave the treacherous surroundings. With a push of my palms against the mattress, I lift slightly in the air, moving across this bed. It takes far longer than I'd ever known it could. I sit at the edge, looking down at the floor, wishing I could simply get up and walk across. My wheelchair sits waiting to be put into motion. With one last push, my wrists now beginning to ache, I land on the cushioned seat. I'm going to take a shower.

The only bathroom that can fit this wheelchair is my parent's master bath. So now, within their ivory bathtub sits a brand-new addition of a gray-plastic, sturdy-looking shower chair. As I sit before it, I angle my body. Placing my hands in position, one on the shower chair and one on the wheelchair, I lift into the air with a practiced confidence. Expecting to cross this insignificant stretch of open space, I feel my stomach drop with the realization that I'm now hanging in open space, somehow in between both surfaces. My palms grip tightly above me, but I can feel them slipping.

My mom's hands suddenly appear, gripping under my arms, keeping me from landing on the tiled floor. For a second, I exhale in relief, but as she pulls against my arms, I see that we're still in the same position. She can't get me up either. After what seems like hours, though it's been hardly any time at all, both our efforts fail and I crash to the ground. My wrist, so delicately held together with metal pins and plates, slams against the cool white floor. It throbs with a steady rhythm. But as the pain beats its drum in the background, my mind focuses on the cruelest injury of all—the realization that I can't even take a shower on my own.

I try to get myself up—using every skill, movement, exercise that I've learned—and still I fail. I push on to the surfaces above, and I lift myself higher, but each time I only slip and fall to the ground once more. If I had any sensation in my hips or tailbone, I'm sure I'd feel the bruises that are forming.

Without uttering a word, I move with noticeable silence. Picking up my phone, I call my dad. I don't bother with any conversation and simply tell him what's happened. He hangs up the phone and picks up a blank piece of paper. Using a thick black marker, he creates a makeshift sign. The sign reads: *"Will return in fifteen minutes,"* and he hangs the notice of a momentary closure on the front door of his shop and rushes down the road to his stranded, pathetic daughter.

With ease, he lifts me into the air, and places me on the shower bench. Then he leaves, and I start the shower. As the hot water streams down my hair, my arms hang limply by my side. My eyes stare blankly at the plain-white shower before me, but without seeing anything at all.

The next day brought an emotional change, going from one extreme to another. Today, I've landed upon pure anger.

This time I haven't fallen but have purposely planted myself on the carpeted bedroom floor. I inch my way across until I arrive at my closet. Staring back at me is a collection of items that belong to a person who no longer exists.

I'd begun aiming to create a pile, with the thinking that this was simply a practical task to complete. But with each throw, I'd only grown less practical. The strength of my throws increased, as a newfound anger fueled each pitch, and now the floor of my room is covered with mismatched shoes. My chunky-heeled shoes, too high for my perfectly flat feet, land with a startling noise. The tall boots that would no longer fit over my massive prosthetic legs follow. The sandals that would surely slip off these feet are added to the pile. In my closet now remains only one pair of sneakers.

The words I've been told so many times ring through my ears. Words that might have consoled another, but only fuel my rage: "Prosthetics are amazing; now you'll be able to do so much."

These are the words that I had once believed, until I reached another crushing realization. A truth that no one around me seems willing to understand. That I am not an amputee; I am a paraplegic who also happens to be an amputee.

The technology of prosthetics will only be a tease, because for years to come, I will struggle simply to walk once again. I won't use running blades, and I won't have adjustable ankles to again wear high heels. I will use basic, sturdy materials as I push forward for a goal that will remain close, and yet so far out of reach. My heart aches, my mind silently screams, and I'm left feeling utterly alone with these combined punishments, wondering what I have done to deserve them.

I can feel every inch of me shredding to pieces, as I feel so lost, with no idea how to figure this all out, no idea how I'm supposed to survive this. Both of these injuries alone are too painful for words, yet combined, I feel myself drown under the weight. As if their palms rest atop my skull pushing me further and further beneath them. *You've won!* I want to yell to them, *Just leave me alone,* I want to plead with them.

Why does this paralysis have to be so sly, such a disguised villain of my story? While I feel his presence every moment of the day, he slips past the eyes of everyone else. They see me only as an amputee. I feel him smile, pleased with his success at evading another's detection. My mind fills with my own torments, wondering what everyone must think of me.

Do they think that I am lazy, and that's why I'm not yet walking on these prosthetic legs? Do they think I'm too scared, or that I'm not dedicated? What story fills their minds to explain why I am unable to walk on these brand-new feet? "Amputees can do amazing things!" I hear their voices within my mind. "Prosthetic technology is incredible," they silently continue.

I wish there were a sign around my neck, a sign that reads, "I'm paralyzed, too."

I move on to my next task—emptying the socks from my drawer. It only makes sense to make room for something more relevant. Strangely enough, this task feels harder. A quiet laugh escapes my lips as I can't help but find a sort of twisted comedy in this image— me holding these used socks so close to my skin. Tears begin to fall, and I realize that this isn't funny at all.

A pain pierces my chest, as if someone's stuck a large pin through me. I'm not tearful over this goodbye to each pair of socks, I'm grief-stricken at the realization that I will never again feel the soft fabric beneath my toes. I'll never have a cold Vermont winter morning when the chilled hardwood floors brush against my feet until these soft plush socks bring a luxurious relief.

I'll never have feet again.

Because I am an amputee... who also happens to be a paraplegic. And the unfairness of these double-punches knocks the wind out of me until I can no longer breathe.

CHAPTER 17

I've left nearly no time between my return home and the beginning of this newest chapter of outpatient physical therapy.

I'm trying to find the outpatient clinic that feels like the perfect fit, so as each new therapist evaluates me, I am in a way evaluating them. If my inpatient time has taught me anything, it's that my future is uncertain and the milestones I might one day reach are unclear, with nothing certain. So I quietly evaluate, hoping to make what I deem to be the correct decision.

I sit in my wheelchair, staring into my dresser as I prepare for another new trial, and feeling envy, I remember when the process of getting dressed was enjoyable. When it was a process spent in crowded bathrooms with friends, yelling from room to room over the music that blared throughout the house. Here I sit, in the silence of my room, alone, staring into my drawer.

Today, I'm making my way to my first appointment at a new outpatient center, to work with a new physician, though I cannot recall her name. Perhaps this is due to some effort of my brain, once again hiding the less-pleasant memories into some hard-to-reach place.

Mom and her friend Kathleen sit in the front seat of the car, driving me to today's appointment. When we arrive, Kathleen drives toward the parking garage while Mom and I rush through the cold air and inside the front doors. We've arrived late, and we frantically look around for a clue as to where to go. I check my emails, re-reading the steps that I have been given while searching for something to match the words that I read aloud. It's a confusing series, filled with elevators and hallways with no signs, before finally we arrive in a brightly lit and completely empty waiting room. I feel as though I'm intruding as I wheel toward the desk and wait to introduce myself.

Only a moment passes by, with us sitting in silence, before the physical therapist arrives, and we make our way toward the gym down the hall. Mom sits behind me as the therapist and I get to work. Since today is our first appointment together, I'd known that it would consist mainly of getting caught up with my case. Medical records can share only so much, so each appointment is always first a series of tests and exercises, highlighting each muscle and pointing to which require priority in treatment, which will be concerns to consider, and where there is remaining strength. As I move about, focused on each request, we chat easily and already comfortably.

After finishing up, I get back into my wheelchair and follow the therapist into a smaller, private office room. She beckons my mom to follow along. This step was expected, too. This is where we'll discuss what the evaluation revealed. I'll pass along any further information required to answer any questions that have been formed. Then we will create a schedule.

Mom and I sit side-by-side, and the therapist sits across from us, hands folded on the table. The conversation begins just as I'd known that it might. We discuss my amputations and the spinal-cord injury. We discuss all past surgeries so she has a complete overview of past care. I fill in gaps about what was focused on while I was an inpatient. The conversation is smooth and easy, and the exercises I've just finished have left me fatigued. It was a great session. I can't wait to work here.

Before we begin scheduling, this therapist ends with one last sentence. It's one that changes the mood in the room. My hands grasp each other more tightly. I sit straighter, and lean a touch farther away from the table. This physical response is a way to keep my distance, to protect myself from the words coming my way. I recall the physical therapist saying: "You *might* one day walk, with a walking aide, across a flat surface—for a few steps. But you won't get up a curb. You won't get up a stair. You won't go up a hill or down a decline."

I lean farther away. I wonder if it's noticeable. I can feel my mom's eyes glancing toward me as she tries to keep her observations unobtrusive.

My mind goes blank. She continues to speak, but I hear no more words. The small office is now claustrophobic and seems to only grow smaller. My eyes burn. I bite down on my cheek as a distraction, refusing to allow anyone to see my tears.

When she begins pointing to a calendar and asking when I'd like to come back, I finally speak.

"We're going to go home and look at things, and I'll call if I'd like to schedule," I say without a drop of emotion in my voice.

I leave the office, making my way toward my escape, entering once more into that silent, empty waiting room. The complete quiet now feels haunting, as if I should've known it was a warning of what was to come. I don't hesitate. I don't pause. My wheelchair glides across the carpeted floor, and without a look back, I leave that office behind.

Kathleen, who's sat waiting in the hallway, takes a look at our faces until her own eyes fill with concern. She speeds up her steps to keep up with us. The sky is dark, and the air now painfully cold, harshly stinging my skin as I glide through those hospital doors and burst into the night air. My hands fall from the wheels of my chair, and one tear slides down my face as the wheels continue to carry me forward. I lift a palm up to my face, wipe that one tear away, and refuse to allow another to fall.

I transfer into the back seat of the car, my chair is stored in the trunk, and Kathleen begins driving us home. Mom, sitting in the passenger seat, turns to look at me. Her arms are spread across the front seats, and her body's twisted until she can look directly into my eyes. She doesn't have to say a word. I don't pause before I voice my decision.

"I'm not going back there," I say with a finality that she doesn't dare to question.

She nods, and quietly turns to face front again. I don't speak the entire ride home, but my mind is anything but silent. I wonder if this therapist was right. I wonder if I should listen to those words and change my expectations. Maybe I never will step up a curb, and maybe I'll never make it up another step in my life, but right now that wasn't the problem. The problem, and the reason that I cannot return, is that there was not an ounce of hope within that room. We'd spent less than a full hour together, and the finality of her outlook for me was startling. Maybe there will come a day I will let go of this dream of walking again, but until every sign points to the need for that, I will hold on. I will hold on, with every fiber of my body filled with hope, and I refuse to let go of this yet.

I can't work with someone who has no hope for me, who sees so little possibility in the future. I need creativity and encouragement and someone who dreams alongside me, pushing forward for all that is uncertain. Sure, it might be easier to work toward a goal that you are one hundred percent sure will happen, that you are sure you will not fail to attain, but where is the excitement and the pride and the worth to all of that?

If I give up now, if I settle only for what I am sure I can do, won't I always wonder about those dreams I gave up? Isn't that what life's about—pushing for the uncertain, moving the lines and the boundaries just a little bit farther away?

I will draw the finish line one day, but only when I am too tired to go another inch further.

In the months that follow, I'll think back to this day often. Each time this thought crosses my mind, it will be a confirmation that the choice I made in the back seat of that car—to ignore those words predicting a limited future—had been the best choice I ever made.

I'll think of this day the very first time that I step up a curb. I'll think of this day the very first time I walk up a set of stairs, and I'll remember it as I make my way down them, too. I'll think of this day when I carefully walk down an icy hill and when I climb my way up our driveway, which feels *so* steep, and each time these moments occur, I will be surrounded by people, and every person around me will be filled with one feeling, and that will be the feeling of hope.

But of course, none of this could I ever have known. In between these moments will be the times that I tried to get up a stair, a curb, or a step, and instead fell to the ground. There will be the months of work filled with blood, sweat, and far too many doubts as I wonder whether I am simply torturing myself with these hopes.

It will remain my greatest and most constant battle—when do I draw the finish line?

CHAPTER 18

*M*y stairlift beeps three times, announcing my arrival at the bottom of the stairs. I feel a slight sting of embarrassment as I wheel into the living room where my mom and two women sit waiting. I glide forwards, reaching out to shake their hands.

The women in the living room, Kate and Lindsey, co-own a physical therapy clinic located just down the road. It's a small clinic with a close-knit staff, and I'd assumed they wouldn't take me as a patient. I've had several larger clinics tell me that the combination of my injuries was too complex for them to take on. So, the thought of choosing this clinic for my care had never crossed my mind until now.

Kate and Lindsey are longtime friends with similar personalities. In my opinion, the two even look alike, with their dark hair, and their tall, strong figures. They're both confident and enthusiastic. Their type-A personalities seem to keep them in constant movement, their minds racing, their words quick, and their bodies keeping up with the speed of their thoughts. It's more than slightly intimidating, and as I look on at them now, I can see how focused they are on containing this energy, most likely trying not to overwhelm us.

I'm already certain I want to transfer into their care. It's the nearest option and will create the least amount of stress on my family in me getting there, since I haven't yet gotten into the course to relearn how to drive myself with hand controls. But they're here today so that we can gain impressions of each other.

I listen as they catch up with my mom. They're smiling and relaxed, but as they turn to me, their faces grow focused, and we dive into business.

As I fill them in on my rehab so far and the tiring list of injuries, they seem to notice certain sentences that have significance to them and nod, glancing at each other and silently communicating. I sit waiting for something I say to scare them off, waiting for them to decide that I'm a waste of time, too broken to attempt to help.

They want to see me in action, not wanting only to listen to my descriptions but to evaluate for themselves. Mom grabs the gray-blue cushioned table that stands folded in the corner. It's really a massage table, a tool to manage my chronic pain, but it also works for my physical therapy exercises.

I start on the table. Responding to their requests, my body flips and adjusts, as I move from one side to the other, trying one exercise, and then moving on to the next. They watch, and observe, and point out certain muscles and movements to one another. When we're finished, I sit up straight and listen as they begin to speak.

"Honestly, we didn't expect this," Kate begins.

My mind races. *Where did I mess up? I knew they wouldn't want to work with me. I'm too broken. I'm not worth it.*

"I mean, really, you're so much stronger than I expected," Kate finishes.

I hear Lindsey agree enthusiastically. The look that passes between them sends a thrill through me. There's a look in their eyes that matches my own.

"We don't want to push you, but we would really love to work with you," Kate says now. "I would work with you, Stef, and Lindsey would work with your mom," she continues.

I feel myself nodding in agreement.

"I want to work with you," I say with finality.

"Okay, then, how about you come in tomorrow?" Kate asks.

I slept deeply that night. There were no worries parading through my mind. I had created a plan. A plan that I felt in my heart would work.

Nervous excitement quickly sets in as I begin dressing for this morning's appointment. But for once, my morning routine seems to go smoothly. My prosthetic legs each slide on with ease. I pull my hair back, not into my usual ponytail, but instead into a carefully brushed and meticulously done, half-up and half-down situation. My hair's been freshly chopped, gently brushing against my shoulders and ending an inch or so below. I get dressed, my clothes seeming to fit just right today. Looking in the mirror, I see the reflection of someone who appears healthy and strong; ready for the day to come.

The drive down the road is short, and as we pull into the parking lot, we realize that this must be their day off. There are no other cars here.

As our car rolls to a stop, their office door swings open, and Kate and Lindsey head toward us. Mom pops the trunk, beginning her usual routine, and walks toward the rear to retrieve my wheelchair. She stops short; they've beaten her to it. I watch from my passenger seat, as my mom stands still for the first time in a long time, and Kate instead pushes my chair toward me. The change is sudden, nearly strange to see, as Mom's always-moving self suddenly remains completely still.

We make our way inside, and pair off, both of us getting to work right away.

I've been on the far table, going through a routine that Kate has clearly been considering deeply since I last saw her. From the corner of my eye, I can see my mom, as they work to strengthen her foot, and hopefully, in turn, reduce some of the massive pain that's on full display throughout her in each moment. Kate walks away as I finish up one last set of this final exercise.

Hearing a loud noise now, I look up. Moving in dramatically slow motion, my eyes drift to my left. Finally, it comes into view. Kate stands with a silver walker in hand.

"Ready to walk?"

This walker, something I might once have seen as a hideous reminder of pain, now glistens in the light as though it's the pearly gates of Heaven before me. Far too slowly, my wheelchair carries me toward the frame. I come to a stop, put the brakes on my chair, and reach forward. Placing my hands on either side of the walker, I await Kate's instruction, eager and impatient to begin.

With my prosthetic legs locked in their straight position, to keep the hinges from swinging loose, only the heels of my feet rest against the floor. I lean forward, keeping my eyes glued to the black floor beneath me, and my arms will work alone to push myself upward to stand. Focusing only on my palms pressed against the cool metal, I use all my strength, until I feel myself standing upright. As my body begins to wobble and sway, my eyes grow wide, and I realize I've pushed much too hard, and my feet now hang in the air, rather than being planted firmly on the floor.

I lower myself slightly, until the toes and heels of my feet are both on the ground, but my hips sway back and forth, unsure of what to do without a cushion to sit on. My palms begin to burn, but my grip grows tighter, and I struggle to remain on my feet, determined not to fall over. Every second that passes feels like a battle, when really, it's just about to begin. Kate's instructions fill the air, and she tells me to begin stepping forward.

The walker rubs against the floor rather than gliding smoothly as I'd hoped, and I push it forward while also seeming to dig it into the floor. With the walker now ahead of me, my feet step forward, one by one, until they're both back within the center of the frame. I've just taken my first two steps.

My shoulders drop many inches lower. Letting out a long exhale, I regroup. One more push forward, and now, two more steps. One more push, and two more steps.

Kate's hands are protectively against my hips, but she surprises me now.

"I'm not doing anything! This is all you!" she nearly shouts.

Tears steadily glide down my mom's cheeks.

The room has, in my mind, turned into a racecourse. As I push the walker's frame toward the right, rounding my first corner, I pause for a moment. Without daring to look up, I speak to everyone beside me.

"I'm never going to stop walking," I say to all of them. The tone of my voice is one I've never heard before.

They simply laugh at my words, but I mean them more than I've ever meant anything in my life.

CHAPTER 19

We should be leaving now. In fact, I think I've officially just made us late. We should have already begun making our way along the winding roads that lead the way to Plattsburgh International Airport, a remote little airport so close to the Canadian border and the province of Quebec that the signs read in both English and French. There aren't many airlines that fly in and out of here, but luckily for us there's a direct flight to Ft. Lauderdale, Florida. But I've made us late, as I always seem to do. Except today it's for a frustrating new reason that I have yet to learn to manage.

We aren't running late for my usual reasons, such as insisting that I couldn't find an outfit that looked just right, a claim usually disproven by the pile of clothes tossed on the floor beside me. It wasn't from my typical procrastination about packing, or even from a last-minute realization that I'd forgotten a toothbrush or phone charger. My tardiness today is due to a new reason. I can't get my leg on.

I've just barely managed to force one prosthetic leg on, but the other lies uselessly on the floor beside me. I pick up the prosthesis to try again, but my flesh only bulges over the socket no matter how hard I push. My face is red and beads of sweat lie on my forehead and lips, threatening to ruin the fresh layers of foundation and concealer. I bend over at an awkward angle, trying to use all my body strength to try once more. Again, my now-red flesh groans in protest, refusing to conform to this tight space.

"Just let me ice a few more minutes," I plead with my family.

I'm hoping the cool ice packs will bring the swelling down, not wanting to leave until the prostheses are both on. Not wanting to travel through crowded spaces with nothing to disguise what has happened to me. Not wanting to have to ignore the stares, or worst of all, the looks of pity. This is the first time I will be traveling since losing my legs, and the idea of leaving the house with nothing covering my short limbs crushes me, bringing the feeling of hopelessness I had hoped to avoid this vacation. Yet here it is, before we've even left.

I look over and catch a look pass between my mom and sister, so brief and secretive that I'm surprised I caught it. It's a look that says that this is a moment they knew was sure to come, though I doubt even they had thought it would happen this soon. These moments are not the result of one single feeling but of a combination of many. I'm frustrated. I'm heartbroken that having to manage to don a set of prosthetic legs is something I have had to experience. I'm infuriated by the unfairness that one single moment and the poor decisions of another human being have changed my life so completely, and I am lonely. Lonely in feeling all of these feelings by myself. These are the emotions that flood together, as any ordinary task turns into a struggle.

But I had hoped to avoid this type of emotional collapse more for my family's sake than I had for my own, so I push the emotions away and agree to leave.

"Fine. Someone just carry my leg to the car for me then," I say, not bothering with any politeness.

I wheel toward the door quicker than usual, throw open the sliding door and burst outside into the cool air. I rush down the ramp at a speed that threatens to tip me out of my chair, and I reach the car that sits waiting at the end of the ramp. But this is as much as I can do, and as far as I can go, on my own. Now, I silently wait for my family to meet me at the locked doors to help me into the car.

They give me a boost, holding underneath my arms, as I make the still not well-practiced transition from wheelchair to car. After putting my headphones in, I sit silently in the back seat, now dreading this vacation.

The two-hour drive has passed, and I've iced my limb the entire ride. But when we park the car, open the doors, and try the prosthesis once more. It still won't go on. I simply sigh in resignation, and we make our way inside.

This process is new to me now. I've always traveled, I know the routine, but I've never traveled in a wheelchair. I can't carry any of my bags other than the one backpack that hangs on my push handles. I can't reach over the desks, and I struggle to weave my way around the crowded space.

Then there's security. I think of the many pieces of metal inside my body that hold my bones in place. I think of the metal on my wheelchair, and the materials that make up my legs. I'm taken aside to wait for a female agent to pat me down, rather than heading through the metal detector that would surely sound its alarm. It's awkward, and we struggle to make the experience less uncomfortable through forced conversation. I watch as onlookers purposely avert their eyes—while others stare with a focused gaze of interest.

Our seats are in the front row of the plane, a fact that fills me with at least some form of comfort as I realize that with only one leg on, I can't stand up, and with the plane aisles too narrow for my wheelchair, my stepdad will have to pick me up and carry me to my seat. Swallowing my pride, as I've gotten so good at doing, I wrap my arms around Paul's shoulders as he lifts me into the air and carries me through the plane.

The rest of the trip went by with ease. The flight attendants were gracious and kind as they brought my belongings and assisted me with getting safely off the plane. I'm still getting used to accepting offered help. I'm getting used to telling myself not to feel ashamed, telling myself that they are being kind, and not judging or looking down on me. I'm still learning to ignore those harsh words I hear in my own mind, trying to replace them with kinder thoughts.

My mind whispers to me: "You're pathetic. Look how much help you need. You're worthless. You're such a burden. Everyone must be so sick of you."

I silently remind myself to replace these thoughts and now repeat: "You are strong. You are still worthy to be here."

These inner thoughts are not a well-kept secret, as they change everything about my appearance, from my posture to my voice. Those harsh thoughts bring tears and frustration. My shoulders rise higher, and lock in a tense position, and my voice either fills with anger or cracks with grief. The kinder thoughts, repeated back to me, lower those shoulders; they smile through the struggle, and my voice turns kinder, gentler, to everyone including myself.

We're here now, in Ft. Lauderdale, Florida. The place where my life had once been in the hands of others, as I lay peacefully unaware of what I would soon have to face. This is the place that saved my life.

After a few minutes of driving from the airport, we pass a tall gray building that seems to be reaching up toward the blue sky. "The hospital," I hear someone explain.

I scan the building, my eyes locked on the sight as it continues to grow smaller in the distance, surprised that it looks so unfamiliar.

I'd expected to feel at least a flicker of recognition. But there is none, which feels odd, when so much happened to me here. But I left this place through the ambulance exit, and had never been well enough to gain much of an outside view. I remember the few moments I'd spent outdoors in that intense Florida heat. My shame so intense I refused to remove the thick blankets I'd used to cover the remnants of my legs. I'd sit in the shade and I'd sweat and I'd be so uncomfortable, but I thought it was necessary. Believing that if I removed the blankets, the others who sat outside would grow sick at the sight of me. Thinking that I wasn't only doing them a favor—it was necessary for me to stay hidden. Not only did I not want others to see me, but I couldn't stand the sight, either. Tears threaten as I remember how disgusted I'd been in my own skin.

I'll be back there in a few days. This is the main reason for our visit. We've come to see those surgeons and nurses. We're here so that I can say thank you. But we plan to have some fun, too. Life for all of us has been challenging, to say the very least. So we've planned a few extra days to soak up some sunshine and get some much-needed relaxation.

As we arrive at the hotel, we all agree to head right to the pool after throwing our suitcases in the room. I throw my bag onto the bed and get ready to change. None of my bathing suits fit anymore. My frame is more skeleton-like now, a stark difference from the once curvy and muscular body I had once had. Years of sports had made my thighs and calves strong, and the years of college and too many calorie-filled beers had added to the curves.

The person I see in the mirror is unfamiliar, an image that still takes me by surprise every time. The scars are everywhere. My ribs peek through, showing their shape and their sharp definition. My legs and arms have healed but are still mangled and slightly distorted. But I expected this.

I look at my sister, her hands rummaging through her suitcase behind me, and I know she must have lost so much innocence and trust in this world, as she spent her days and each weekend visiting me in hospitals. She told me once how she can no longer hear any sudden or high-pitched noises; they remind her of the machines that swarmed around me in that ICU room in which she could hardly force herself to stand. I think back to the day when she'd been going through her school-day routine, pretending to feel normal, as though her world as she'd known it hadn't quite literally burst into flames. Along with her class, she'd gone on a field trip, and only hours into the day, they visited a famous battlefield. And the topic, along with descriptions, of amputations were casually mentioned. Her classmates were curious, intrigued by the subject. But she knew more details than even her teacher could ever share. Her head had spun. Her knees grew weak. She'd nearly fainted, and her class getaway that should have been memorable was effectively ruined.

She's had a tough time since the day that changed our lives, tougher than she'll ever let any of us know. She tries to be so much stronger than she needs to be. She deserves a normal vacation, one that doesn't end in horror. She deserves a few easy days that don't revolve around me or my thoughts. So I don't let this mirror image get stuck in my mind.

Instead, I now have to make it worse, I joke to myself, as I take out the large container of zinc. The thick white substance is much different from the tanning oil I'd always used. I cover all of my scars. I cover the skin graft on my right thigh. I cover the long thick lines on the fronts and backs of both of my arms, and then I draw one long line down the middle of my stomach. My scars are now protected from the sun, keeping them from turning the permanent purplish color that I'd been warned could result from exposure, I now put a thinner layer of lighter sunscreen on the rest of me. I put a quick swipe of concealer over the red line on my throat, as if hiding this one scar makes some type of difference, and now I'm ready to go.

I push myself out to the pool. I'm surprised by the noticeable absence of the anxiety I usually feel. I'm surprised by this rare confidence and lightness to my spirit, despite the wheelchair and the exposed residual limbs sitting atop the cushion being bared to the world. It's as if there's something in this air that's turned back time, bringing back the familiar easygoing young woman I had once been.

I sit on a pool chair and take off my tank top and shorts, revealing the strapless red and white striped bikini I've borrowed from my little sister. It still hangs too loose, but it fit the best. My shoulder-length hair is braided into two tight French braids, and my small oval-shaped black sunglasses seem to complete the look.

Brooke and I put our headphones in and lie down, basking in the sun. With my eyes closed, it's almost as if nothing has changed. I'm just a young girl, lying in the sun, as I have a million times before. And somehow this time doesn't feel any different.

The sun is strong, and I've quickly grown uncomfortably hot. I open my eyes, waiting for a sharp pang of reality to hit me as I see myself once again, but it doesn't come. Instead, I see my sister next to me, lying on her stomach, giving her back a chance to match the fresh tan she'll surely see on her chest. I look up to the clear blue sky, and the warmth on my skin spreads throughout me, as my heart seems to fill with thankfulness for this ordinary moment.

I decide to cool off in the water—which feels like a daring choice for someone who has not yet relearned how to swim. Transferring back into my wheelchair, I head to the edge of the pool. I lift myself up into the air, and awkwardly manage to lower myself to the concrete. Looking into the pool, the water is so close, but I wonder how I'm going to get into it. I'm not really sure if I can swim without any feet, so throwing myself in seems like a bad idea. After a few moments of serious contemplation, I decide I need some help.

Paul jumps into the pool first and stands in front of me. Placing his hands under my armpits he lifts me up and into the water. I quickly grab on to the edge. Already laughing at how strange this sensation is; the cool water feels so different against my paralyzed muscles. I wonder what in the world I do next. Do I have to cling to the edge this whole time? I push myself off the edge to give it a try. Hoping I don't sink. My hands move quickly under the water in a circular motion, and my short legs try to keep up. With no feet or toes to move the water, and lacking the muscles to push backwards, they struggle to make much of a difference. My arms complain about how much work they now have to do.

Then I realize something and I shout to my family: "Guys, I'm kind of swimming! Or, I don't really know what this is, but at least I'm not drowning!" I shout through my laughter.

I dog paddle my way back to the edge, holding on for a moment's break. Looking around, I see the others at the pool. Some of these strangers look away, while others throw me a quick smile. Maybe it's a smile of sympathy, but I don't give it much thought.

We spent hours going from tanning by the pool to cooling off in the water. I had a few spiked seltzers to drink, and then we went back inside, exhausted from the heat, and each of us many shades darker than we'd been just a few hours before.

The next days were full of countless beautiful moments. We had nice dinners on sandy beaches as we watched the sunset over the clear water. We'd driven out to Key West, where we ate fresh seafood and made our way along the rowdy boardwalk. We drank margaritas, and got our nails painted—they had let me sit in the spare massage chair, my prosthetic feet up on the foot stand, as the rest of my family got pedicures. We had the best key lime pie of our lives. Every moment of these last few days was filled with laughter as we made new memories.

It was a vacation that felt both eerily familiar, and entirely different. This is exactly how that last one was supposed to go.

Now it's time for what I have been looking forward to. The reason that of all places we could have chosen to vacation, we've chosen Ft. Lauderdale. Tomorrow we go back to the hospital.

We pull up in front of the entrance, and my heart beats quickly. My phone chimes, and I exhale in relief, as I see Alison's name on my screen.

"Alison just got here!" I tell my family, thankful that her familiar face will be with me.

News channels and cameras surround the car, giving the appearance that we're celebrities. I suppose in a strange way, at this hospital, we might be just that. My walker is placed in front of my open door. I take a deep breath and double check to make sure my sundress is situated just right. My prosthetic toes are painted with a nice shade of light blue polish, and I put them on the ground. It's time to walk in.

I repeat everything my physical therapists have taught me. Put my weight on my left foot, swing the right foot forward. Squeeze all the necessary muscles, tighten my core, then repeat. One step at a time. The camera flashes are bright, but I remain focused on making it through the doors in front of me. I haven't looked up, too focused on the view of my moving feet, so it's not until the refreshing feel of ice cold, air-conditioned air envelopes my skin that I realize I've made it inside.

"Do you want your wheelchair now?" a voice behind me asks.

I feel the adrenaline in my veins. The idea of showing off what these healthcare workers here in this very building have allowed me to do is stuck in my mind.

"No, I'm good." I say, feeling determined.

"It's a long walk," someone warns.

I nod my head, look back down to the floor, and begin my way forward. One step at a time, I remind myself. We slowly make our way to the elevator, go up a few floors, and then head down a long hallway to the conference room they have reserved for us. Each hallway feels too long, so as I stand at the beginning, I wonder how I will manage to cross the way. But I look down toward the floor, forgetting about the distance ahead, and focus only on moving one foot in front of the other. And somehow, each time, the walk comes to an end. A door opens, a chair arrives, something marks that I have done it.

My palms are sweaty and my cheeks are hot as I step into this final destination of the reserved office room. I stand in front of a chair at the long table; my hands beginning to shake, and I nearly crumple into the cushioned seat behind me. Finally, I can relax.

Feeling like a mess, as if I've just run a marathon or done a long workout at the gym, I try to gather myself together again. I push back my hair, I take a deep breath to lower my racing heartbeat, and then I turn to give Alison a long hug.

"You look so good," she says, her voice full of emotion.

There's a reporter in here waiting, and while the woman who's greeted us sets out to alert my past surgeons that I have arrived, I turn to her to begin the interview. The answers flow naturally, with an unfamiliar confidence in my voice. Then, the woman who'd just left returns, the interview comes to an end, and I hear her announce with emotion that Dr. Roberts is on his way to this room.

I don't remember who Dr. Roberts is, but I don't have time to ask. We all get up and make our way to the hallway. By the time I make it out there, I see a man standing at the end of the hall, clearly waiting for me. He wears a light blue cap tied around his forehead, evidence that he's just left surgery. His dark blue scrubs reveal his importance, and his relaxed stance and thin gold chain necklace hanging on his chest, peeking through the scrubs, give off an air of ease.

I feel no familiarity yet, as I'd hoped I would, but I continue walking toward him. Dr. Roberts stays in place, one hand on his hip, and the other rubbing his forehead, giving way to the emotion he seems to be trying to hide. I finally reach him. Seeming to move without thought, as if I'm reacting to some subconscious guidance, I lift one arm off of my walker to give him a hug. He holds me with a grip so tight it takes me by surprise. We hold on to one another for a long time.

Even though my mind tells me that I can't remember who he is, there's something deep down within me that knows him anyway. There's part of me that somehow knows he has touched my life in some huge way. My eyes may not have recognized him, but it feels I've known him my whole life. In this moment, he doesn't seem a stranger; it's as if he's a long-lost friend, or someone I've been waiting my entire life to meet. An assortment of intensely strong emotions washes over me.

He pulls back, slowly shaking his head. He shakes Paul's hand, and my mom's, and they greet each other in the way you only do if you've either spent much time, or been through an important moment, together. For them, I suppose it's both of these things. I see his eyes now. They're red, and his cheeks seem wet.

"Do you remember me?" he asks.

Embarrassed, I shake my head.

"That's all right; most of my patients don't," he kindly offers.

"He was your neurosurgeon. He did your surgery on your spine," I hear someone explain.

I remember being told I'd had a nine-hour-long surgery on my spine. I remember hearing of the doctor who had walked out of the operating room, just as my mom's nerves were about to snap as she wondered what must have gone wrong if this was taking so long. He'd greeted her with confidence, a thumbs-up, and a coffee in his other hand. Looking at him now, I grin at the story, at his ease, at his comforting presence, and the knowledge that he'd done that surgery with flawless precision.

We walk back into the conference room. Alison sits next to me, and Dr. Roberts sits next to her. My heart feels full as I hear them interviewing him. I don't know what they've asked him, but I do hear his reply: "To actually see someone that you touched like this, and walking like *that*...nobody warned me about that. It was a hell of a surprise."

I'm bursting with emotion, thrilled to have walked to him today. To have been able to prove to him how hard I have been working. To be able to show him that I haven't let him down. He is the person I credit for ever having this chance. If that surgery had gone wrong, those steps he'd just seen would not have been a challenge; they would have been an impossibility.

Because he came into my life, because he was my surgeon, every step I take and every moment I stand, will all be a gift from him. I'll never be able to thank him as deeply as I wish that I could.

Dr. Roberts checks the time and announces that he has to get back to work. After a quick hug and a promise that, one day, the two of us will ski together, he sets out and we follow just behind. Slightly exhausted now from the activity of the day, I sit in my wheelchair and push toward our destination. We're going to the ICU. We're going to see the place where I'd spent my days.

~

The elevator doors open, and we cross a stretch of hallway and arrive at the tightly sealed entrance. With a swipe of a badge, we're granted access. The door opens and the first glimpse inside, and the first feel of the frigid air, takes me right back. The sterile rooms, the silent halls, they give the sensation of being frozen in time.

As we make our way along, each nurse we pass by takes a second glance, shocked to see that it is the patient they all remember. Shocked to see the familiar features of my face from when they saw me last. My face is no longer bruised, the swelling has gone down, and the tubes have been removed. I am the same girl they saw every day, yet in so many ways, I am a person they have never seen before. I am the girl who has finally healed after they so carefully cared for me. The word "miracle" can be heard in every other sentence. The same word that I've now had tattooed upon my skin.

"Your room, I mean it was full of machines. There was no room for anyone to even stand in there," one of them says to me. "You had every single machine you could possibly have," he continues. He has a daughter my age, so these words come through his tears.

"That's what I've heard," I tell him.

We make our way toward the room that was once mine. It sits tucked into the corner of the hallway. I stare into it, trying to imagine myself lying there. Trying to imagine my family sitting there beside the bed, as they talked to me, unable to know if I could hear them. I think of how they begged and they prayed that I would wake up again. It's hard to visualize yourself so fragile, so broken.

Quickly, I beckon for my walker to be brought closer, and I stand up from my wheelchair, feeling an overwhelming need to stand defiant in the presence of these memories. As if I need to prove something to this organized and empty room before me.

I turn my back, and I walk away from it, leaving it behind me.

At the end of any vacation or weekend getaway, no matter the destination, I almost always feel a temptation to remain in each newly found place. The pull of each town, state, or country is magnetic, as the appeal feels greater than any desire to return home, back to routine and reality. I find myself imagining what type of life I might discover if I stayed a while longer. I daydream of exploring the local coffee shops and of finding a perfect booth or corner table at the local café, of shopping at the area's boutiques and farmers' markets, and of all the interesting people I might come to meet. This time, though, I only feel excitement as I board this plane to head back home. It's not because this trip has been any less appealing than the others—in fact, it exceeded even my highest expectations—but because there is so much waiting for me once we arrive.

This vacation had been my very first after the last had gone so terribly wrong. So, when I lay out in the sun, my damp hair pulled back from my face, it not only felt familiar, but it also felt brand new. When I'd kayaked in those Florida waters, the sun and the wind against my skin had left me feeling more alive than ever before, and each sunset had been the most beautiful sight I'd seen, leaving me awestruck and asking those unanswerable questions about life. I'd felt so humbly insignificant, and the world felt intensified in its magic.

I've learned the value of a life, the magic of being alive, and as the breeze caressed my skin and the sun warmed my soul, I was keenly aware of each breath and each single moment. So, I don't dread going back to routine and reality as I once might have. Instead, I see it as a gift.

But before anything routine about life sets in, we have one new item to cross off the list first. It's something that will add some highly craved love and excitement to each day. As soon as this plane lands and we make the drive back home, I get to pick up the newest addition to this family. Someone who will be completely mine—a 16-week-old, English Cream Golden Retriever puppy.

We have one photo of him, which sits in its frame in the living room next to the photos of the rest of the family. He's coming from North Carolina, and my stepbrother and his wife are driving him up to us today. I'd found him online during one of those early days that had felt so impossibly hard that I wondered how I would ever survive. Returning home to the house filled with memories and reminders of the family who had left for a vacation one day, expecting to return home just one week later, had been so intense that it had begun to feel physically painful. But when I saw him, that pain was felt just a little bit less.

As we board the plane, I can tell already that the trip home is seeming quicker and easier than that first attempt. The flight sped by as I chatted with Brooke about each day we'd just spent, savoring the feeling of completeness after meeting my surgeons. It had felt as though I couldn't truly move on without knowing them, and now I have given them my thanks, and my mind is at ease.

The plane landed, and my wheelchair was brought to the front of the plane. I waited for each passenger to exit, and then I stood on the two legs that had both slid on without struggle. I held on to the rows of seats on either side and made my way forward, smiling as I heard the cheers of the flight attendants beside me, strangers who found joy in my steps. And now, though I am exhausted from the trip, we have made it home.

My mom and stepdad bought this house about five years ago. It's an old farmhouse, built in 1885, so as you might expect, there was much to do to fix it up. There were some outdated furnishings such as the coral-colored kitchen counter, teal-colored living room carpet, and floral wallpapers. But these were all fixable. The house itself was what we had all fallen in love with.

The downstairs level is nearly entirely open, without a single wall darkening any area. The kitchen has hardwood flooring and a long butcher-block island. This connects to the living room, where your eyes are drawn to a large bay window with crosshatched window panes, looking out toward the green lawn. From there, if you walk down the somewhat-narrow hallway, you'll find a door that leads out to the rectangular, screened-in porch, where we've added a delicate antique set of white table and chairs, as well as a comfortable sofa, perfect for a cup of coffee or a glass of wine.

The backyard has another, uncovered deck, where the grill and fire pit are. There's much space in the backyard that expands until you reach the stone wall, with berry bushes and grape vines crawling along the stones, that separates our house from the neighbors' a distance away. Maple trees and oak trees fill the yard. I love everything about it here.

When I'd finally returned home, after those unexpected hospitalized months away, I was recovering from that unplanned emergency surgery, so everything had been intensified in its challenge. But even as I grew stronger and life returned to being the slightest bit easier, the pain I felt never seemed to be even close to erased.

One day I had done what it sometimes felt was all that I could manage to do. I'd had a hard day in physical therapy, a day when I had expected to see improvement from the countless hours of hard work, but instead had seen only the clearest display of paralysis looking back at me. The weakness and numbness within me seemed to be shouting that it was permanent. That it had grown roots, tightened its grip, and settled within my muscles and limbs with no intention to ever disappear.

When I'd returned home from that session, I went to my bedroom, shut off the lights, and lay down in bed, pulling the covers over my head to create a shield between myself and the outside world. Again, my future had flashed before my eyes, and it wasn't one that I wanted to see.

I had no plan to get back up, and I stayed that way for three long days, silent and unmoving. The sun rose and the sun set and there I was, hoping for a solution to arrive out of thin air. I'd lain there, bargaining and pleading, and desperate for some form of a savior, not yet ready to accept that this savior could only ever be me.

On that fourth day, I heard movement and conversation coming from downstairs. I heard normal activities, maybe someone making breakfast or brewing coffee, accompanied by some easy chatter. Hearing that, from that same position in bed I'd been in for so long, I'd felt simply pathetic. I'd pulled my head out from under my sheets, seeing slivers of sunshine forcing their way through my closed blinds. I sat up. I used my hands to push myself toward the window. About twelve inches of hardwood floor separated my bed from the window's ledge. It seemed an impossible distance, taunting me, daring me to try to cross.

I wasn't sure if I could reach, but I leaned all the way over, holding on firmly to the mattress with one hand, and reaching out with the other. As I extended my fingers as much as I could, and stretched out as much as I dared, my fingertips just barely grazed the bottom edge of the blind. With an act of finality and purpose, I gave one powerful tug, and that window blind flew up toward the ceiling.

The outside light crashed through the window, filling every square inch of the space around me with sunlight. I closed my eyes as I sat at the edge of my bed, hoping that somehow, that light could brighten the darkness within me.

When I was lying underneath my blankets, I could pretend that nothing beautiful existed any longer. I could convince myself that there was no reason to get up again. But that had simply been ignorance. I knew that it was time to find a way to find some happiness again, so when my mom walked in to see me just a few moments later, I said to her the words that no longer felt like a question, but rather felt a necessity.

"I need to get a dog."

I'd found Oliver after a day of looking. It seemed a perfect cliché to have found happiness in the form of a puppy, but the search for him had seemed to renew my energy, and as I looked through each goofy, adorable, and some funny-looking puppy pictures, I felt a smile on my face and a lightness began to nibble away at the darkness.

Oliver's name at the time had been Barnaby, but as I studied his image, I knew that he was meant to be mine. We made lists and held debates and eventually decided on a name. He would officially be, first name: Oliver; middle name: Winston; and nickname: Ollie.

When the trainer who owned him had called me, she asked me a few questions, explaining she always made sure these dogs went to loving homes. She knew of my recent injuries, so she asked me a reasonable question: "Why now?"

I hadn't prepared an answer, but the words just flowed.

"I need a reason," I told her.

I needed a reason to wake up each morning. I needed a reason to get out of bed each day. I needed a reason to get outside, leave the house, make the most of each day. I would take care of myself so that I could care for him. I heard the emotion in her voice, as she nearly choked up replying. Thankfully, she agreed that "needing a reason" was as good a reason as any other to find a dog like Oliver.

We've agreed to meet my stepbrother and his wife in New York. Paul pulls the car into the parking lot of the hotel. He gets my wheelchair out of the trunk and places it beside my open door. I transfer into my chair, and with excitement head toward the door.

We go up to the room that they're already in. The door opens and I hear a slight little puppy bark. "Sitting," I hear them say.

I look in front of me, and there he is, sitting in front of them, looking up for the treat he knows he's earned.

"Hi Oliver," I say, and he turns his head to look at me.

Just as in the image we have at home, his fluffy white ears seem too big for his small head, his eyes are a deep brown, standing out against his nearly pure-white fur, and his head cocks to the side.

Oliver continues to explore this new environment. I watch him as he moves from corner to corner of the small hotel room. Nose close to the floor, he takes in his new surroundings and seems to assess whether he is pleased to be here or not. He's had an adventure today, making the long drive from North Carolina to New York, and now he has one more ride to go.

"Ready to go home?" I ask him.

He barks a few times, chases his tail in a circle once, and sits back down with near perfect posture. Paul picks him up and puts him on my lap. He pushes my chair so that I can keep my arms wrapped around the small dog that feels so delicate, and we go back to the car. I put a blanket across me, place him on my lap, and I watch as he settles into position, propping his chin atop my thigh and closing his eyes. I keep my eyes on Oliver the whole way home. He stays on my lap the entire time, his eyes wavering between drifting closed and peering up to look at me.

I look down at him and a feeling of complete calm takes over. *I'll never feel alone again.*

CHAPTER 20

*I*n front of me, my mom and stepdad hold hands as we make the drive to Massachusetts General Hospital. I'm tired but still can't relax enough to sleep. This week has been a whirlwind of activity. I've made sure to keep busy, not giving myself a quiet moment in which my mind could run wild. It's hard to believe how much happened in only these past few days, but the three-hour drive will give me time to clear my head, time to figure out how I feel.

One week ago, I'd sat in the office of Dr. Smith. As our appointment began, I leaned forward, pressing the pin-lock of my left prosthetic leg. It came off with ease. I stripped off the layers of socks and then the tight silicone liner. Until my leg was bare. I moved on to the right side, and a pit formed in my stomach as I pictured what I might see. I repeated the routine—removing pin-lock, socks, liner—and this is when my face burned red in shame.

I knew it wasn't my fault, but the gruesome site of my limb made my eyes sting and my stomach twist with nerves. I felt that I'd failed him, that I'd failed my family, that I'd even managed to fail myself. I sputtered my apologies, though his focused eyes seemed to hardly notice my embarrassment.

As he leaned back in his chair, my eyes shifted between him and my leg, watching his face for a reaction while studying the pool of blood growing on my knee. Silently, I willed the blood to staying where it was, so that it wouldn't drop to the floor. As he came to some conclusion, he leaned slightly toward me to begin to speak. In this same moment, blood splattered against the white floor. There wasn't much need for discussion after that.

"It's been too long," he decided.

He explained his thinking, reminding me how short my limb was below that knee that caused so much pain and asking if it was worth it to me to save it. He asked me a plain and simple question, one that had an answer that came without thought—one that made the impossible decision easier.

"How sick of this are you?"

I looked down at the blood, so red against that floor.

"I'm so sick of this."

That was that, my surgery for an above-knee amputation was scheduled for one week later.

I still feel sure of our decision. But I still don't know how to feel. I don't know what to expect. I feel like I should be sadder than I am. I feel like I should be more scared than I am. Instead, I sit here, head against the car window, watching the trees pass by, trying to figure out how my life turned out to be this way.

My friends each text me, and it surprises me that they've remembered the day of my surgery. But I don't know what to say to them. I don't know how to explain how I feel, when I don't even know myself. I feel *fine*, and that is unsettling to me, because I know that today of all days, I should not feel fine.

Paul drops us off at the front entrance of Mass General and goes to park the car. I wheel through the familiar automatic doors. I head directly to the elevators, and press the up arrow to head to the third floor. Perioperative care is in the Wang Building, third floor, and we know how to get there. We go in, stop at the desk, get our pager, and sit down to wait. Each step is so routine by now.

I know when to stop eating before surgery. I know when to keep drinking fluids, and when to stop. I know to pack my sleep mask because the machines in the hospital stay lit at night and I won't sleep without it. I wore a light blue matching set of soft pants and long sleeves because I know it will be comfortable in the car and warm enough in the cool hospital waiting room. I know each step of this by now because I've had to do this so many times. Surgery no longer makes me sad—it's the fact that I know all of this, the fact that I have no choice but to know all of this, that makes me sad. But still, I feel fine.

Looking around the waiting room, I wonder what everyone is here for today. Wondering who will leave here today and go back to their lives with ease, and who might have their whole world change after today. I wonder who was hurt playing sports, and who might be dealing with an illness rather than injury. I hope these people in this room are all here to make their lives better in some way. I hope they all leave here today with something fixed, rather than something taken from them.

"I bet no one would look at me and guess that I'm here for an amputation," I say, grinning, and pointing down at both of the legs of my loose pants that hang below where my limbs have already ended.

"I bet no one else is here to get another piece of them chopped off," I continue, now laughing.

"Stop! Why do you have to say everything in such a gross way?" mom asks, but she's shaking with laughter, too.

"I'm just trying to lighten the mood," I say, giving a thumbs-up sign when I look over and see Paul is taking a picture of my mom and me.

The pager buzzes against the arm of my chair, breaking the moment. It's a startling noise. We make our way out of the crowded waiting room, along a long narrow hallway, and into the next room, private and sanitized from the previous occupant. I'm just one patient of many today, moving through this same pattern. This same maze, of one room to the other in an organized, conveyer-belt synchronization. I move on to the next steps, stripping down and changing into the hospital gown, lying down on the gurney and pulling the blankets up to help keep myself covered. More waiting now.

A quiet knock, and then the door opens. My dad has arrived and comes to sit with us. I look at them all sitting beside me in this tiny room. They look sadder than I do.

I've answered the questions from the nurse, and now we wait until someone comes to bring me to the next, and final room, before the operating room. We wait awhile longer, and then the curtain pulls open to another face that I've seen many times before, and I know that the waiting has come to an end. It's time to go. Only one person can come with me now. I love them all, and wish they could all come, but today I need my mom. I say goodbye to Paul, and he gets together my belongings to take with him. My dad comes over with tears in his eyes. I hate seeing my dad cry. He holds on to me tight, not wanting to let go.

"Good luck. I love you. You'll be fine, okay?" he says now.

"Okay," I tell him. "I love you, too."

The locks of the stretcher come free with a sharp-sounding release, and we begin to move. We make our way along another hallway, with tall windows on each side. The bridge, they call it. I keep my head to the side, lying against the pillow and looking around me. Once through the hallway, we get to a set of closed doors. The aide scans his pass and pushes us into the sterile surroundings where everyone wears gowns that match my own. A few anxiously pace, while others use the bathroom before they head into surgery. Another pair of curtains closes, and we're in the final room. My breathing gets a little quicker, and my hands are getting sweaty. But *I'm fine*, I tell myself.

Dr. Smith stops by, quickly drawing a mark on my leg with black Sharpie. A large black arrow, pointing down to signify where the surgery will be, apparently a necessary reminder to ensure they do the correct leg. This step in the process has always made me laugh, as I picture coming out of surgery to see they've done the wrong side. His confidence assures me that I will be okay.

Anesthesia comes in next—my least favorite part. To my relief, my favorite anesthesiologist comes in. Somehow, she has been here for almost every one of my surgeries. I know about her new husband, the new home they just purchased, and the child they now have together.

"I was hoping I'd get to have you today," she says, smiling.

"Do you remember me?" she asks.

"Of course," I tell her. "I was hoping I would have you, too."

It makes me feel better having her here today.

"Can you tell me what you're here for today?" she asks.

It's a strange question they always ask, as if they're ensuring that you know how and why you've ended up here, about to go into an operating room, before they stick an IV in your veins and push you toward confusion and unconsciousness.

"I have to amputate my right knee," I tell her.

I hadn't been expecting it, but my throat lets out a choking noise, as if I've just gagged on the words I've spoken. Tears start to pour down my face, and the sadness I'd been surprised I hadn't felt yet is now in full force, making my chest feel tight. She reaches forward and holds my hand.

"I'm so sorry," she says.

Neither of us speaks for a moment, as I try to gather myself together, feeling as though the air's been sucked out of the room.

She leaves now, but only for a moment. She'll be back soon to place my IV, now that we've gone through all the paperwork and necessary talking points. I decide it's time to say goodbye. Goodbye to my knee. This will be one of the stranger things I've ever done. I sit up straight, look down at my leg, beginning to start the conversation, thinking it will be an easy one to have.

But as I stare at my knee, which still has that oozing sore and is now covered in layers of scars from each time it has healed, I feel an overwhelming sense of loss. There are scars from the skin broken by stiff prosthetic sockets. Scars from all the surgeries, and from the times I pushed myself too hard in therapies and physical activity. Scarred from the day of injury, and from all that it has endured in the aftermath. This knee is such a forgotten body part, often ugly to look at even in the healthiest of humans, but to me, so incredibly valuable. To any amputee, the difference between saving the knee and losing the knee is key; amputations are classified by this one aspect: above-knee and below-knee. Losing a joint and replacing it with a computerized and prosthetic piece is never the preferred option, and will alter everything from your prosthetic options to how you walk and get through each day. I heard someone once explain it perfectly, saying that as a below-knee amputee, it's like walking on stilts 24/7. While being an above-knee amputee is an entirely different ballgame. A piece of you is now computerized and out of your control. Beyond the thoughts of an amputee, to me more personally, it is the part of me that has held on, that has fought to remain, that has been through far more than is fair.

"Okay knee..." I begin, placing my palm against my skin. "Thanks for hanging in there with me, thanks for trying, you really did do your best," I say, my voice getting so thick that the words are hard to form.

Tears threaten, but I push them away. I wrap up my goodbye, unsure how to end. Unsure how to let go. It's the strangest moment—looking at a piece of me that will now cease to exist. Just one more piece of me disappearing.

The curtain opens, and the anesthetist walks back in.

"It's time for your least favorite part. I need to put the IV in," she says.

From past experience, she seems to know I need a distraction and begins telling me a funny story about her little one. Something about how she had found him hiding underneath the sink the other day, but I can only half pay attention.

"Okay I'm going to give you just enough to relax you, and then we'll head into the OR, okay?"

"Okay."

When she tells me it's time to leave again, I reach over to hug my mom, but as soon as I touch her arms, I can no longer hold back the tears. Hugging my mom, I feel like a scared little girl. I don't feel strong. I don't feel ready. I never wanted to have to do this! My mind is screaming at me to tell them to stop moving the bed, to tell them this was a mistake and to bring me back. I can't amputate my knee, I can't lose more of me, I can't do this! This is a mistake. But the bed keeps moving, and I see the familiar scene in front of me. The crowd of people around the operating table, the lights hanging over where I will lie, and the large screen with my patient information and medical history already on display.

I move over to the operating table, needing a little help now that whatever is in this IV has made me clumsier and weaker. My heart is racing. Everything moves in slow motion, as if I'm watching this happen rather than actually being a part of it. Everything seems funny, but I know there's nothing funny about it. I try to help them when I see them placing the monitors on my chest and arms, but I'm moving too slowly and only getting in the way. The familiar faces above me help me feel calm. They're all very kind.

The plastic piece goes over my mouth, and I take deep breaths. In and out. Once, twice. Then the room goes black.

My eyes open, and begin flickering from side to side, taking in my surroundings, and seeing that they are the same. I feel groggy and confused, frantic but slow, and I'm surprised to see I've woken back up while still in the operating room. This doesn't usually happen. Usually, I'm already in the recovery room when my eyes open. At least I think that's how it goes. I can't be sure. Each of these days is so clear in the moment, yet in a few days I know it will all be a blur again, as if each of these dreadful surgery days is manageable only because soon my brain will sort them into the same category that dreams go into. A category you don't often have to remember, in fact, you can't remember clearly, even if you try. It's as if this is a strange gift from your brain, allowing you to forget these unbearable moments, allowing you to live through them only once and not have to relive them over and over again.

A nurse stands beside me, but other than us, the room is empty. The surgery is done. I look down. My limb is wrapped in thick, tan-colored, ACE wrap, but that it is not what I am looking at. It is so short. So agonizingly, terrifyingly different from what I went into this room with, most likely just a few hours ago.

It's not what I had pictured, not what I had expected. My eyes grow wide, and I feel tears sliding down my cheeks. My chest feels tight, as if someone has just placed a weight on me. I don't know who this nurse is, but I turn to her anyways.

"It's too short!" I frantically explain to her through my tears.

"No honey, it's perfect, the surgery went beautifully," she reassures me as she helps me on to the stretcher, so that I can get out of this horrible room.

I lie in the recovery room now. Crying again. My dad walks in, looking tearful as he notices the tears on my face.

"It's so short. It's so ugly," I say to him, my voice cracking.

I can feel my heart breaking into pieces. He leans over the railing of the hospital bed and hugs me tightly. I hear him speaking; I know he's comforting me, but I can't listen. My mom and Paul are here now, too. I might have talked to them, but again, the memories are already becoming dream-like. As if my brain has known that I have already had enough. Knows that I am ready for these memories to disappear. I close my eyes. The fog of medications feels thick and I sink into sleep.

~~~

Recovering from any surgery is far more horrific than the surgery itself. During the procedure, you, as the patient, are given the gift of ignorance. Ignorance of what is going on in that operating room, and ignorance of what your body is enduring. Surgery is gruesome. It goes against all human instinct to allow someone to cut into your body, the body you have spent your days caring for and protecting against all physical harm. Yet in another way, surgery is beautiful. I imagine it to be as complex as a symphony of instruments playing harmoniously together. Each member of the surgical team perfecting his or her skill and working in tune with one another until the piece is completed without error. Their surgical skills are precise, their minds sharp, and they are masters of this craft.

The recovery is when the veil of ignorance is lifted, and only the horrors remain. I am now conscious and aware, in yet another unfamiliar hospital room. I study the remnants of my body. I pull against the thick layers of bandage, trying to give my flesh some air to breathe. The layers around my limb are painfully tight. I try to ignore it, never wanting to complain, but the pain is intense and convinces my mind that something must be wrong.

Panicking, I call the nurse, begging for it to be loosened. She unwraps the layers, and I stare at my flesh in front of me. Blisters have formed above the surgical sight. A long red cut burns against my skin from being twisted within the layers of bandage. My limb is so swollen that it no longer has any shape and hardly resembles a portion of a human leg at all. There are hardly any areas of unscarred skin that remain, or at least that's how it looks, with my rectangular scars stretched wide with swelling. I watch as she rewraps the layers, covering the evidence of this most recent trauma. The pain is great, the incision is large, held together by long rows of surgical staples, and my body is suffering.

The days surrounding this latest surgery will always remain hazy in my mind. The two small white pain pills I take every few hours keep my head floating just slightly above the rest of me, the room remains somewhat out of focus, and my days dream-like. Despite all of this, I know that there will forever be one hazy memory that will stay with me. The memory of a tall man, my nurse for less than a full day, who somehow touched my life forever. His gentleness and kind words opened my eyes to the changes within myself that I hadn't yet noticed. Without knowing the significance of his words, he pointed to unnoticed changes from the timid young girl I had once been to the stronger young woman I am becoming.

He walked into my room with a strange look in his eyes. I could tell without asking that he had just heard my story, heard of the events that made me his patient that day. I have seen this same look in many nurses' and doctors' eyes before: a combination of horror, sympathy, and disbelief. Perhaps even a slight touch of confusion. Each time I watch their eyes skim the pages of my medical records, now downloaded and computerized, I sit silently until they look back at me, always with that same look in their eyes. I've come to expect it.

He asked me to explain this story to him in greater detail, pressing for information as I remember I once had myself. His eyes softened. He continued to work beside my bed as he listened. In an instant, he was no longer simply my nurse, but someone I had known for many years. I usually hold back, giving simple answers, pretending to be far more okay than I truly am. I didn't give him any of those standard answers. I spoke with him, his presence was comforting, and my vulnerability in this post-surgery moment allowed me to do what I never have before— open up, show emotion, and speak of both the good and the bad.

He continued with questions, asking about my life now, how I was doing, what my plans for my life were, and what my dreams and goals had come to be. I had no precise answers. I explained that I didn't know where life would take me. All I dreamed of was making sense of this senseless event. I wanted to make that one horrific day somehow mean something greater than what it has stolen from me.

"You are going to change lives, my dear," he said to me. "I can tell that you are strong and courageous, and you brighten this world. Promise me you'll write a book one day, sharing this story, and I'll be in the first lines to get my own copy," he said.

I smiled and told him I would but doubted this would be something I could ever manage to do.

I have heard words similar to those he spoke before, but I have never felt the warmth in my chest as I did then. I'll never be sure if it was the kindness in his voice or if it was because this recognition came from a stranger, a man who had never known me before, that made them feel different this time. Perhaps it was the fact that his words came at a time when I was suffering, recovering from another setback, that made them feel different. Or perhaps, it was simply the medications and the fuzziness in my brain that made everything feel sweeter. I'll never know. I only know that he changed my life in some small way in our brief time together.

There's a slight smile on my face as I think about those memories from just a few hours ago. I wonder if he knows what his words have done for me, and I'm hoping that someday I have a chance to see this man once again. Though I have already forgotten his name.

My small backpack had been filled with the essentials to get by for several days, and I'd arrived expecting to spend at least three to four days in that hospital. Yet we are already on our way home, only one day later.

"You only lost 50 cc of blood in surgery," Dr. Smith had explained last night. "You have a greater chance of infection here in the hospital, so you'll stay the night, and then in the morning you'll head home. Sound good?"

Eagerly, I'd nodded my head. The thought of recovering in the comfort of home seemed too sweet to be true.

The three-hour drive has come and gone, and we're already home. As I struggle to get out of the car, mom and Paul gently help me inch my way backwards and into my chair. The echoing sound of Oliver's barks wakes me back up, and I smile at the sound.

Ollie's still a rambunctious puppy. Whenever I leave the house, even if for just a moment, he greets me with such excitement it's as though I've been gone for years. An entire night away, and I know he will be wildly thrilled to see us once again. His greetings always consist of a hug, where he runs to my wheelchair and wraps both front paws around my shoulders, tucking his head behind my neck. It's adorable. The plan today is to place him in the mudroom before he has time to reach me and my still stapled together limb.

As we get close to the door, and I catch my first glimpse of him and his excitement, everything within me wants to rush toward him. My tired body protests and a silent reminder tells me to keep a slight distance. As the door slides open and we each enter the house, Paul reaches for a leash to put on his collar, hoping to lead him away to another room. Ollie sneaks a peak at me from behind his legs, as Paul stands in a position to block his path.

We should've known he'd be quicker than we are. He sprints his way around Paul, darting toward me, his nails making the familiar slight scraping sound against the floor as he moves with such sporadic motions that he seems to fight to stay balanced. I hear my family begin to shout, and my body cringes instinctively, feeling pain that hasn't even happened yet.

But suddenly he stops. Coming to a halt right before me, he sits and begins sniffing gently at my leg. His tail wags frantically behind him, a windshield wiper against the floor, but his paws stay planted.

As I pet the top of his soft face, he peeks his eyes up to look at me. "Hi boy, I missed you," I say to him softly.

I'm too tired to stay downstairs, and begin pushing myself toward the stairs. He quietly follows. He waits while I transfer over to the stair lift, watching over me carefully. As the lift climbs each stair, Ollie follows, always just one stair behind. Once in my room, I lie at the top of my bed. Oliver takes up the bottom half, lying close to me, but just barely below my limbs. The air conditioner comes on, and the cool air soothes my skin. As my eyes drift closed, Ollie's eyes close at the same time.

In the days to come, Ollie will refuse to leave my side. In a time when all I feel is pain, and could have felt so alone, I can reach down and brush my fingers against his soft fur, and all in the world feels okay once more.

It's now been nearly two weeks since my surgery. The first few days were each a blur of pain. I could hardly move, hardly breathe; all I could do was sleep. Visiting nurses came and helped me to change my bandages, but they also need to be changed while the nurses are not around. I used to be nauseated by just the thought of blood. These days, that's had to change. As I peel away the bandage, I stare at a gruesome sight, intensely aware of what I have just allowed to be done to my body. Dipping the sterile gauze wrappings into the small bottles of Saline water, I gently press the damp cloth against the stapled area. As I press the staples, the sensation travels through my limb, as if I've just sent a current of electricity throughout my tissue.

Today is the first day since surgery that I've gotten dressed, done my hair, and put a light amount of makeup on. It's my very first "Alive Day"—June 30. A date that I will never forget. One year ago on this day, my life changed forever. As I open my eyes to the day, I feel my mind ringing with silent reminders. In each hour that passes, I think to where I was one year ago. I see the time that marks the moment I rolled over in that small bed and the Bahamian sunshine warmed my skin. I see the time that marks the moment we left our rental home, excited as can be for the day to come. I know when we arrived in that parking lot. I know when it was that I was taking my very last steps, feeling the ground beneath my feet for the last time. I know when it all began. I feel sort of sick.

Part of me still feels as though I'm there. As if I've remained trapped on that island. With an absolute certainty, I tell my family what I must have always known, but hadn't realized until today.

"Sometime in the future, I need to go back to Exuma," I say to them, thinking they'll be surprised by these words.

"We know," they respond quite simply.

On every vacation, every trip away from home, you fly away, going through security and checking belongings, and looking forward to the days ahead. Then, when it's all done, you make your way home again. You sit on another crowded plane, with your skin tanned, your body exhausted, and your mind full of memories. You rest, you talk, you gossip, and you reminisce. You pick up your suitcases, you throw them in the car and complain about your fatigue, and then you drive home to realize how unexpectedly thankful you are to have made it back to your familiar comforts. I never got that second moment. I never really left. My body was picked up and shipped back home, and it's simply not the same.

I need to see it all again. I need to dig my hands in the sand and remember how it felt. I need to place my prosthetic feet on the very last ground that I walked upon, even if I collapse with emotion as I do. I need to say goodbye. I need to sit on an airplane and remember making my way home. I need closure.

But today isn't about that. Today, I will settle for the knowledge that my plans are out in the open, and I will wait for the day that I get to return. I'm still healing, but my friends will be arriving soon. I can wear only my left prosthetic leg underneath the comfortable cloth pants that I've paired with a loose plain white tee, but I'm comfortable, and I feel good.

My roommates, whom I was able to have for only that one short week, are both already here. More of my high school friends have come together. My new friends walk in on their prosthetic legs, and my physical therapist and her family have come to join, as well.

The hours fly by as we talk and laugh, and it's not until hallway through the day that I realize something—the subject of my injuries hasn't been the center of attention. Not once have I felt different from these people around me, even as I sit in my wheelchair at the table beside them with only one fake leg.

As the sun begins to slip behind the mountains, more people, friends of my mom's now, begin to arrive. My friends have each packed up their cars and driven away, and the fatigue I was possibly ignoring all day sets in. I had been animated and chatty and full of laughter before, and now I'm so tired I wonder how I'll make it upstairs. Finding my mom, I let her know.

"I'm exhausted. I have to go to sleep. I'm just going to say bye quick," I tell her.

As she heads outside, she leaves the sliding door cracked open. I yell my goodbye, apologize for needing to leave, and hear their rushed confirmations that they understand as I wheel myself toward the stairs.

I'm asleep as soon as my head hits the pillow.

A deep chill wakes me from my sleep, and I wonder if someone's cranked my AC. The sensation travels through each bit of me, extending through my fingertips and my skull. I realize now, *Something's wrong.* Reaching over to my bedside table, I rummage through the messy drawer until I find the small thermometer. Placing it on my head, I wait until it beeps.

Shit.

I call my mom. I haven't been asleep long, so they're all still outside, but she comes up right away. My temperature is 101.5. Not too much to worry about—except that this is the very number written on my discharge sheets to watch for. It's too late to do much about it, so I take Advil, and close my eyes once more.

When I wake up many hours later, this time to the morning sun and a new day, my eyes take in a scene from a horror movie. My white bed sheets have large, circular-shaped patches of blood, all around me. Not one, not two, but countless pools of dried, and some still-drying, ruby-red blood. In a flash, I'm sitting upright, ripping off the bandages to get a look at what's happening to me. The middle of my incision is no longer held together, and is instead large and incredibly swollen. I've burst through the stitches, creating a gaping hole. My mom walks in, and immediately takes two small steps backwards.

Our eyes lock. She gasps.

She has to be somewhere but insists she'll cancel. I ignore her and call my dad. I throw on a T-shirt and gingerly put on a pair of shorts. I make it downstairs just as my dad pulls in, and once again, I'm on my way to another hospital.

When I arrive at the local clinic, they ask if I've had a fever. A hazy, yet painfully clear, memory comes to mind. There was a moment, in the darkest hours of the night, when I'd woken up again. My body shook uncontrollably. I'd put more layers over my arms and pulled the blankets over my head. Using only the light of my phone, I'd checked the thermometer once again. My temperature was 103.

My head rolled back against my pillow, and my eyes drifted closed, until not much later when I woke up again, this time drenched in sweat, as if I'd found my way to a desert. I ripped off my layers and left only my sheet against my skin. My nerves seemed to be on high alert, as even the air against me seemed to sharply grate its way across my skin. I'd checked my temperature once more. It then read in bright red letters: 104.

My leg tests positive for a Staph infection, and they urgently call my surgeon at Mass Gen to get instruction as to what to do. My leg is rewrapped, I'm given antibiotics, and I make my way home.

The whole reason I had this surgery, why I allowed another part of me to be permanently taken, was to prevent any more wounds.

I'd been spending far too much time in wound care clinics and taking far too many rounds of antibiotics for infections that never seemed to stop recurring. I'd become my own nurse, as changing my bandages each morning became as routine as applying mascara had once been. And I'd come to a drastic decision. I had to remove the problem. I'd allowed a surgeon to cut away the part of me where my bone broke through my fine layer of skin, and it should have stopped.

As I swallow the first, large, oval antibiotic, I lean back against my pillow once more, believing this complication will be the last and that it will soon come to an end.

But it would be only the beginning.

CHAPTER 21

*I*t had seemed horrific timing to have to be in this recovery stage during these treasured summer months, before the winter days come to claim this Vermont land. With my limb wrapped in bandages, I'd feared I'd be in pain and trapped within the house, glimpsing the sunshine only from the window beside my bed, instead of outside where I could savor the feeling of it on my skin. But now we have a visitor, here to push those fears aside.

My neighbor has lived with injuries of her own for far longer than I have. It seemed as though life had picked us up and perfectly placed us beside one another. A vehicular accident, many years ago, had left her paralyzed. So as these foreboding questions march through my mind, feeling hopeless and unanswerable, it is this woman who can share her answers. Her fiery spirit and pure love for life inspire me in each moment that I spend near her, and today she's here to teach me something new.

Her black SUV pulls into the driveway as I sit in the kitchen. I turn to see her already knocking at the glass sliding door and rush toward her. For a moment it's tricky, and we're off to a jumbled start. Ollie runs to greet her with his usual enthusiasm, and the two of us, both seated in our wheelchairs, struggle to determine how to get her inside while keeping Oliver from escaping through the open door. Enticing him with a treat that he can't seem to resist, I lure him to where I sit and he plops down on his back legs, staring up at the treat in my hand with patience and perhaps a drop of saliva on his lips.

Unlike me, who fumbles her way around in this awkward configuration of a wheelchair that I can't seem to navigate, she moves into the kitchen with grace. I watch as she grabs my bag and water bottle, while I carry nothing and follow behind her, still moving more slowly than she does. We fly down my ramp and reach her car. As she makes her way to the driver's side door, I open the passenger door and transfer in to sit beside her.

After a brief drive, we pull into a local college with an empty parking lot that leads out to a quiet Vermont road without much traffic. The road travels past local farms, presents spectacular views of Vermont's famous Green Mountains, and meets the rare and hard to meet criteria of having no steep hills throughout the miles to come. As I get back out of the car, two pieces of equipment stare back at me. Two hand cycles sit low to the ground. One bike is bright pink with a lowered back, so low that the rider lies flat on her back while pushing along the road. The other is a ferocious combination of yellow and black, with a seat that sits more upright before the hand pedals. I get to try them both.

I'd used a hand cycle only one time before this. The bike I'd used then had been clumsy and slow, but I'd never been someone who could be considered anything close to an avid bike rider, so I hadn't had much to compare it to. One day after this, this same neighbor had been visiting at our house, as her dog and mine played in the backyard. We sat on the back deck, sipping glasses of wine. I'd told her about how I'd used that bike, and her reaction had been nothing close to what I expected. She *hates* the kind of bike I spoke of. After her injury, it was this same bike that she'd first been given to try. Unlike me, she actually was an avid biker and had lots to compare it to. To her, that bike had been the greatest letdown, as she told me how she found herself asking: *Is this really all there is now?* But she found there is so much more out there in this creative and adaptive world.

I'd told her that I loved that bike, laughing slightly at just how little I seemed to know. But I truly had loved that goofy little bike. I'd felt like a child again, and I'd laughed more freely than ever before, knowing that I looked ridiculous but quite simply not caring at all. My sweatpants had been tied into knots where my legs ended, they'd given me a brightly colored helmet, and the bike seat kept me sitting up so straight that I was at an uncomfortable ninety-degree angle. The bike was slow, and I felt like a toddler on a tricycle.

"I've gotta show you a better bike than that," she'd said to me, with a sparkling hint of adventure in her voice.

This is how we've ended up here today. It's perfect timing. I can't do much of anything at all, but that's only because of one injured limb. The rest of me is alive, and young, and ready to move.

The yellow-and-black bike is my favorite. I move along the paved road with a surprising speed, and it's one that I hadn't known I'd been craving. When I walk with an assistive aide, I move slowly. When I push my wheelchair, I am only slightly faster. Every moment throughout each day is planned and precise and careful, and as a result, it is slow. It's something that goes against the nature and mindset of any young adult who aches to be thriving and healthy and rambunctiously carefree.

When I move on this bike, I'm no longer slow at all. I want to scream through the air with joy, but I remain silent, leaving only a wide grin on my face and an intent focus in my mind. The long green grass beside me flashes by. The flag that stands tall above this low bike flaps in the wind above me, carrying with it every ugly thought in my mind. All thoughts of amputations and paralysis, of surgeries and recovery, of infections and wounds, of stitches and staples and horror, all blows in the wind behind me. I move right past it all, speeding by it, as if it's all some distant memory.

In this moment, I'm not Stefanie the amputee, the paraplegic, or the girl recovering from surgery. Right now, I'm just Stefanie, the girl who's riding a bike.

Back in the passenger seat of her car, having finished a six-mile ride, I sit so quietly on the way back home, thankful for today. As I sit here, wrapped in my thoughts, a list begins to come together in my mind. It's not the list of goals that I keep carefully and constantly tucked within my thoughts. It's not the list of upcoming surgeries and treatments, and things needed to get done, and it's not the list of legal conundrums or excuses that Bahamian island has sent my way. This time, this list is one that takes me by surprise. It's a list of all that I have come to gain, of all the days and moments and experiences that I never would have had if I hadn't endured all that I have.

The speed and the movement that comes along with a ride on these bikes is a high, and like an addict, I can't seem to get enough. I continue to borrow her spare bike, and I push myself across that road. Each time, going further, going faster, and competing against myself, as though I'm in a solo race that I must win.

At the end of each ride, my arms ache in the best way possible, I'm exhausted in the most satisfying way, and my head hits the pillow with a feeling of total content.

～

Today, I'm joining in on my very first bike race. Granted, though it's called a race, in typical Vermont fashion, it's more of an uncompetitive meandering of people. The only way we can describe it to people is to say "It's *very* Vermonty."

The race begins at a small school, and throughout its course is a series of stops at each of the local farms. The riders are greeted by a homemade farm stand, smiling faces and waving hands ushering you in to see all that they have to offer. At each stop, you're given a small treat, anything from maple iced coffee and shortbread cookies to wine slushies at the last stop to celebrate the miles you have come. We arrive today, planning to ride the fifteen-mile course, a ride that is many miles longer than my current highest of only eight miles. But as we pull in, the energy around me lifts me with a confidence that I simply haven't earned, and I decide that I instead want to ride the thirty-mile course.

My mom and stepdad stand beside me, and my aunt and uncle have joined, as well. I suggest this new idea, and they enthusiastically agree. We head to the stand and grab the directions for this 30-mile trek. A flutter of nerves spreads throughout me as we keep up with the crowd of people, all heading out to begin. We reach the start of the road, look once, look twice, and then we begin. Every nerve in my body feels electric. My senses are on high alert, and my spirit freer than ever before.

Unlike that previous road-loop I rode, this route includes many intense uphill climbs. Each time I sit staring up at a hill that seems too impossibly steep to climb, my mind races with reminders that thrust each arm forward, one after the other, beginning to push my way to the top. A slideshow flickers through my mind, and all others around me disappear. This slideshow is created from each and every painful memory that I have lived. I watch, in clear detail, the moments that had felt impossible to survive. Images of the days when I'd felt too depressed to take even one more breath pass by my eyes. The moment I felt death calling my name, and instead listened to my own, is added to this display. I hear the voice reaching my ears, telling me I am paralyzed, and likely losing my chance to walk ever again.

There are so many cruel moments that somehow are now in the past, each gone and each survived. With each rotation of these pedals, I again work through every emotion—the anger, the hatred, the heartbreak, the joy, the grief, and they carry me along, like a strong wind behind me. They've all made me so much stronger, and maybe, even strong enough to make it up this hill. My shoulders push forward, my abs crunch, and my hands push the pedals in one final rotation. I've made it to the top. The climb is behind me. For an instant I look around me, and then my hair is swept by the wind as the wheels of this bike carry me down again, and I soar down this hill. I want to throw my hands out to my sides and lift my face into the air, and I want to sob with joy or laugh out loud, but I stay focused on the road before me, and I feel the return of that enormous grin.

There it is—the finish line. As we come to a stop in the parking lot, my arms instantly drop beside me, now completely useless, drained from these thirty miles.

I look around me, to all the strangers in their taller bikes, smiling down at me and cheering for our successes, to the family I love who have climbed each path beside me, and to my bandaged limbs ending on the edge of this seat, and God am I proud of us all.

In a whirlwind of emotion, I sit atop the high cushion of my wheelchair. I wheel around these standing people beside me and feel proud to be on these four wheels. My mom stands before me, and I throw my arms into the air into a triangular shape above my head as I see her with her camera pointing my way. My short limbs both sit wrapped in their stark-white bandages, my black Spandex shorts end just below my hips, and my tight short-sleeve top reveals my newly muscular shoulders. An enormous smile is on my face, and my mom snaps a picture.

I look at the image before me, and I see one that so recently I would have hated. I would have ordered her to delete the image immediately and never wished to see it again. This time, I respond quite simply.

"I love it," and I hop back into the driver seat of my car to drive us home.

That in itself feels to me like another victory.

CHAPTER 22

*S*hit! I cannot believe what I've gotten myself into. I take a deep breath, focusing only on each rush of air filling my lungs. Staring down at the floor below me I try to relax, but the proof of where I am is everywhere I look. I see my new sandals, a pair of light pink suede shoes with a closed toe, decorative straps crisscrossing over my feet, and an adjustable heel to keep them on tight and secure. Tripping over my shoes today would be an actual nightmare. Above those shoes are my two shiny black prosthetic legs. One leg is brand new, my above-knee prosthesis that I've so recently gotten, and adds a pop of a silvery color on the computerized knee component. One leg is older, but is a treasured and long-awaited guest.

I shouldn't even be wearing both legs today. Underneath my left, below-knee prosthesis is a massive wound. While I was healing from that above-knee amputation, I had grown as impatient as I was fearful. Impatient to get back upright. Fearful that the time without standing and being back to bed rest and wheelchair use alone would cause me to lose all previous progress. The combination of emotions is what brought me to a seemingly sound decision: to wear one prosthetic leg and stand on this alone.

For a few times, I hopped around and stood straight within parallel bars and the frames of walking aides on that lone fake leg. But there was a dilemma I hadn't considered. It's a combination of things. There is the fact that sometimes prosthetic legs don't fit perfectly. These areas that are too tight or imperfect are often called "hot spots" and are fixed by a prosthetist when pointed out by the patient. But I am also a paraplegic, with no sensation in the bottoms of my limbs. So I cannot feel these points of imperfection, and I cannot feel when my limb is growing sore.

After one of those times of hopping and standing and exercising, I took the prosthetic off to find a wound. A wound that I had not felt forming. A wound that was then gushing blood, and unbearably deep, forming an actual hole in my flesh, so deep I was surprised I hadn't seen my bone staring back at me.

It will not heal despite eveything I have tried. Since then, this prosthetic leg has sat resting against my bed, for months now, as I hoped that by today I would be healed and could wear it once again. Well, I haven't fully healed, but again I had grown as impatient as I was fearful. Impatient to be healed and back on two feet. Fearful in believing there is no chance I am surviving today without both legs to stand upon. So, this morning I shoved that carbon fiber socket over a few layers of bandage that made it a rather tight fit, and I am simply hoping for the best.

This dress that I'm wearing is my only source of comfort. It fits so perfectly that when I tried it on, for the first time in a full year, I felt beautiful again. It's a lovely shade of ivory, a perfect neutral for my minimalistic style. The capped short sleeves hug my shoulders with a protective yet still comfortable tightness, and the only decoration or added style comes from one tight band, the same color as the rest, that hugs my upper chest. I look professional. I look prepared. But my heart races, my palms sweat, and my mind berates me for agreeing to this.

I watch as the speaker before me finishes his words. He's funny. He's confident and enthusiastic and makes the crowd roar with laughter. The speaker before him was just as good. Neither of them seemed to look down at the podium, but instead spoke with ease and conviction, as if they could stand up there all day.

Shit! My mind yells at me once more. *What am I doing here? I can't do this!*

I think back to how this all began:

I hear a knock at the door and push my wheelchair forward to greet them. They are each dressed perfectly. They're both wearing neutral colored pantsuits that are somehow simple yet extravagant, and plain yet flattering. They wear strings of pearls and elegant chunky jewelry. My only accessories are my wheelchair and my prosthetic leg. I feel plain and young and childish. They've asked me to be their keynote speaker at the upcoming event held by the local Chamber of Commerce.

The theme of this year is strength and resilience. "You are the perfect example," they tell me. The theme comes from all that our Vermont community has endured and even begun to thrive within. We are faced with massive storms here—snowstorms that knock out power for miles around, a recent flood that wiped away mountainsides and destroyed roads and homes and lives. We have survived poverty and economic stress, and have begun the creation of new jobs, making this area a still-wonderful place to live. Like the rest of the country, our communities have been struck by a pandemic of drug abuse that seems to be a cruel opponent as it relentlessly takes over homes and lives. Yet despite it all, Vermont has faced each storm, each invasion, and each battle, with our typical stoic and tough attitudes, always pushing forward.

My first instinct is to decline politely, to thank them for the offer, but remain in the safety of this home, away from any eyes looking on at me. But a new voice speaks up now, telling me I am strong enough to do this. I hear it reminding me of all the reasons why I should do this.

Many, if not all, of those who have survived, experienced, or witnessed something traumatic know that often the most challenging part is our re-entry into a world that now feels foreign. It's as if we have to fake it. Pretending that the memories don't play in our minds on a constant loop all twenty-four hours of each day. Faking our way through conversations, smiling, agreeing, nodding, and acting as if we have moved on. As if because we are here and we are alive, we are suddenly whole and well once again. But there is always that pain, the ache of the loneliness that is created by the wish for someone to know of all that I have endured in those moments that no one else was witness to. Not wanting to be alone with the memories any longer. I have something to say. I have something to share. I agree to their request.

Oh God, why did I agree to this? It's time for me to make my way toward the stage.

The only times I have spoken in front of anyone before were past college presentations. Those presentations had each made me physically ill. Every single time, I would stare down at the floor, making my way through the narrow aisles formed by desks in perfectly straight lines, and toward the terrifying front of that classroom. The aisles would sway and blur, and I'd walk with my hands awkwardly out to each side, bracing myself in case I forgot how to walk and fell on my journey forward. Then, I'd stutter and blush and fumble my way through.

If I couldn't do public speaking then, when I had two sturdy feet to stand on, how am I supposed to do this now?

I hear the introduction coming to an end. A beautiful video has been created with images of my recovery; of the work and time I have put in, and interviews with those who have helped me along the way. As I stand behind these curtains, hands firmly on my walker, ready to walk forward, these words pick me up and hand me a dose of confidence. The interviews continue to play, and each kind word they share seems to help me stand a little straighter.

I've got this; I tell myself. The music ends. The crowd cheers. I look at Kate once quickly, and then I put my right foot forward, stepping on to the stage. There's no going back now.

I can see them standing. Our local Paramount Theatre is filled with businesspeople in suits, women in dresses, and a few familiar faces. This is the stage I had once danced and leaped my way across as a young dancer, and I now steadily cross it with intense concentration. One foot in front of the other, I push my walker forward, still staring at the floor, feeling the energy around me but not able to look up at them yet. Instead, I'm watching to ensure these rubber feet of mine do as they are told, ensuring I am on the ground that I cannot feel.

What feels like miles later, the podium comes into view. It's time to leap across this stage once more, or at least give a slight lift up into the tall seat that awaits me. Once I'm sitting, Kate pushes my chair toward the wooden podium, carrying me along with it. The chair makes an awful, loud scraping noise against the floor. As she lifts my walker out of the way so that I can get a touch closer, the legs of the walker get stuck between chair and podium. The microphone in front of me picks up the sounds of our struggle.

Shit, my mind repeats one final time.

After a quick burst of friendly laughter from the crowd, and a rare blush covering the always-confident Kate's cheeks, she makes her way off the stage. It's just me up here now.

I exhale slowly. I feel ready. I know the first line of my speech— it's a quick thank-you to my community. I begin without looking down.

"Hi, everyone, and thank you so much for having me here tonight. Before I dive into my story, I want to use this chance to say a couple of things to everyone here tonight. First of all, I simply want to say thank you."

My voice is shaking. It's unsteady and quiet and all too familiar. *Is this really how I'm going to sound all night?*

I try to continue. Pressing on with my thank-you that was meant to sound as heartfelt as I'd hoped it would as I typed the words. Wishing I could convey how much I mean these words, and hating myself for being unable to do so.

A familiar woman walks on to the stage. Confused, I pause. She lowers the microphone, bending it closer to my face. I quietly laugh for a moment, hoping to break the awkward silence. She leaves now. I smile at her quickly, and I begin again.

My voice is brand new. I've never heard this voice before. I continue with confidence, which strangely enough seems to be a package deal with an unexpected sense of excitement. I give an overview of those first wonderful days. I begin describing the beautiful beaches, and hand over the title of the island "Exuma" as if describing the villain in my story. I laugh at the drinks we had by the pool, share the stories of adventures through the ocean waters, and end with a moment of drama.

"The next, and last thing I clearly remember was knowing that all of a sudden, I was dying. The boat had exploded underneath the seat that I had chosen. I was now lying on the floor of the boat, covered by metal that had fallen on top of me, while the rest of the boat burst into flames."

My voice is all that can be heard in this theatre. Not a single word is uttered; no one fidgets or moves about; the focus is all on me. I don't panic. I'm fueled by a newly found confidence. Word by word I feel weight lifting off my shoulders, making it easier to keep speaking, making my voice only grow louder.

Without planning any approach to this speech, I'd stumbled into a theme. As I'm telling them of every one of the countless times, I had said the same words, "I can't do this," I share with them how those words, every time, were followed by an accomplishment that disproved that earlier claim. It all just took some hard work, support, laughter, and some stubbornness, too.

I continue with sharing the details of my time in kidney failure. This is a period that was never covered by news channels or update posts. It's a time that was the hardest to survive, and yet, seemed to be kept in a veil of secrecy. This is my time to let them in on this chapter.

"We checked my numbers often, which meant a constant need for blood work. As well as very large needles being stuck through my back, all the way into my kidneys."

I hear the crowd gasp and groan. I can feel them flinch away, as if they're holding their own backs, trying to imagine what I have just described. I move on to describing dialysis, the five-hour treatments in the basement of that hospital.

"Mentally, I would look around and see these machines that were keeping me alive and I felt like I was lying in that room basically just waiting to die."

My voice cracks and grows a little quieter. These memories make my throat feel tight and my eyes grow red every time. People might assume that it was the moments before surgeries or the moments hearing a new diagnosis that were the hardest of all, but really, it was this solitude of kidney failure. It was the torture that was also the treatment. It was knowing that if it wasn't for machines and medicine, I wouldn't be alive. It was that time on those treatment beds where the voices telling me to give up were the loudest of all.

I look to my left. I see my sister. I see my dad. I look at them for only a second, and pull myself together. Then I continue.

"Physically, my body was being destroyed. I dropped down to less than eighty pounds, and spent the rest of the day, and every day in between, with my head in a bucket," I finish, laughing a little at that image that is so engraved in my mind.

I speak of my depression. Explaining how I felt as if the pieces of me had been picked up and stitched back together. I speak of my brain injury. I speak of my spinal cord injury and its twisted effects. I speak of the psychological damage from limb loss. I'm sharing it all. I'm taking ownership of a tale that is mine, whose first chapters were written by another, but I will be the one to create the final ending. I am taking control of the character they created.

I tell them of the nights I cried myself to sleep. I tell them of the mornings I got back up again. I joke about the bald spot that formed on my head as I'd lost my hair from kidney failure and trauma.

"I'm sure we'd all rather stay in our comfort zones, right? I mean I know that I did, but let's not forget I was also a young woman in her twenties who still worried about things like how cool I was and what my hair looked like. Now, I was a young woman in her twenties with both legs missing and a bald spot on the back of her head. So, saying I was out of my comfort zone was a bit of an understatement."

I speak with emotion that comes unfiltered, somehow feeling totally in my element. The crowd laughs and I laugh with them. I'm comfortable, even enjoying myself. I speak now of facing my new reality. Describing my first prosthetic legs, with the feet that were "chalky white and looked like blocks of concrete." I tell them of the metal hinges and the Velcro straps that came on those legs.

"With time, a lot of hard work, and actual blood, sweat, and tears, the prosthetic legs have gotten smaller, the Velcro braces have been removed, the hinges are gone, and even the feet have gotten much cuter. Before, I thought I couldn't manage this… today… I know that I can."

I can hear the silent period at the end of that sentence. My words carry a power I have never felt in my life.

I choke up once more as I come closer to the end. I'm ending by expressing the grief I have felt. Painting a picture for them, trying to reach their imaginations.

"I cried knowing that I would no longer be able to paint my toes.

"I cried about never being able to put lotion on my legs again.

"I cried for an *extra* long time, knowing that I would never feel the sand between my toes again," my voice shakes slightly. "I would lie in bed, trying to imagine what I remembered it feeling like, digging my feet into the sand. I tried to remember what it was like slipping on a pair of new shoes that fit just right.

"I let each piece of it break my heart, so that when I was done, I could pick up the pieces… and move back on."

One deep breath, in and out, and I continue. Ready to get to the good part.

"Now today, I paint the toes of each new set of feet."

I'm about to go on, but the once silent crowd erupts in response. I hear them cheer. I hear them laugh. I hear someone yell, "You go, girl!" and I laugh. I brush aside my hair, a simple act, but proving to me that I am fine here on this stage. Proving that I can feel their eyes on me, but I don't want to cower and hide. I want to continue; I want to keep going.

"I enjoy the smell of the ocean instead of the feel of the sand in my toes. And I still buy cute shoes, even if it takes a whole lot of effort and lots of time spent with a shoehorn to get them on those feet.

"I let my story break my heart, but I did not let my story end there."

I have so much to say, but will end in just another moment. I share the simple moments that now feel like extraordinary miracles: glasses of wine with friends, laughter with family, and watching my sister grow up. I look at her as I say those words. Hoping she hears the pride in my voice as I say this. Hoping she knows she helped to save me, that it has been her presence that was often my brightest source of light. This moment, this speech, is my thank-you letter to her.

I've always underestimated myself. Always coming to baseless assumptions that no one ever saw me as anything more than a child, anything more than a somewhat pretty face. I told myself I was someone to be seen, but not heard. This ending is one that takes courage that I have never had. Courage I have searched for all my life. The courage that only comes from feeling worthy.

So, to this crowd of well-dressed adults, lawyers, businesspeople, staff, and everyone in between, I offer them advice. *Advice from a twenty-two-year-old, why would they listen to you?* The familiar voice shouts in my head. I continue anyway.

"The very best thing I ever did for myself was change my mindset to one of believing that I can figure out any problem. Something we should all do for ourselves, is this one thing: instead of having your first thoughts go to, What will it feel like IF I fail, have them instead go to, What will it feel like WHEN I succeed. Make that one change, and watch what follows.

"Thank you."

Holy Shit! You did it! my mind screams with joy.

My greatest fear had been that no one would cheer. Or maybe they would politely clap without any real interest. I don't even have to look up to see if this has come true. Stacking my papers back together, I hear the crowd before me—cheers and applause and shouts of praise. I raise my eyes, and they all stand.

After some time of celebration and chatter, I grab my coat and return to my wheelchair, making my way outside. The glass doors swing open; the commotion behind me disappears behind me as they shut, replaced now by the silence of the night. The Vermont winter air is freezing cold, but my body stays warmed. Lifting my face toward the sky, I stare at the beauty of the starry scene. Then close my eyes as my thoughts begin to wander: *What if I had said no to doing this? What if I had stayed home, and missed out on this? I never would have known I could feel like this—I am so thankful to be here, today.*

My family joins me, and we begin to walk away from the theatre. Feeling like we're going home, returning to a familiar world, while also having just transitioned into a brand-new one; stepping into a life of possibility.

CHAPTER 23

I always feel more motivated for the rest of the day once I've finished my physical therapy exercises. Just getting my body moving in these simple therapeutic ways fuels me with confidence and ambition. I've purchased a set of parallel bars, similar to what a gymnast might use, so that I can do the exercises I learn at my physical therapy clinic right in the comfort of home. They sit at the end of my bed, as if they are daring me to get up and get to work each morning.

I feel eager to use them most days, but today is one of the rare days it has taken a slightly longer self-motivational talk to get started. A little bit longer to find the strength to push back my covers and get out of my comfortable bed. But I'm not willing to let this setback push me back further, so I roll over and reach for my prosthetic leg, which rests against the side of my bed. It has now been nearly eight months of only having this one prosthesis when I clearly need two. Eight months of balancing on one prosthetic foot and trying to move across my room as I cling to my walker. Eight months of pain, of frustration, and of wondering when I can get back to as close to normal as is now possible.

I unplug the small charger just underneath the prosthetic socket. This charges the advanced computer inside of the "knee," a medical advancement that made walking possible for those who found themselves living as bilateral above-knee amputees. An advancement without which—given my combination of spinal-cord injury and above-knee amputation—I would not be walking. It's a relatively new innovation, this microprocessor knee, and if I were to have been in this situation before its existence, the limited amount of walking that I can do now would have been reduced to nothing. I likely never would have stood or walked again.

This is the only prosthesis available that will allow me to do these things. I know this. And my prosthetists know this. Yet if I were to think back, to the process of obtaining this leg, there was nothing simple about it. Because my insurance company holds the commonly held stance that any leg with the microprocessor knee component is not medically necessary. The funding was denied.

These life-changing devices are still seen as *luxury* items. As if there's anything luxurious about replacing your natural limb with a computerized part, I'd scoffed. The positive part of this, though, was that my insurance coverage was privately funded by an individual business, and the company had never had a request for a prosthetic like this one. It had never had an employee, or the family member of an employee, need this type of coverage before I did. And so, though the company could do nothing about it this time, it listened. And it changed its policy.

It was a step in the right direction for this business, and I felt pride in knowing that if the request was ever made again, the coverage would be there for the next person. But I wondered, how could this become a commonly held position? How could the time arrive when an amputee feels the crushing psychological pain of losing a limb and knows that at the very least not only are there advanced prosthetics out there, but that they wouldn't be denied them?

Though we knew it would take far too long to wait for the policy to change, far too long to wait for the coverage, we knew it was necessary, and so I went ahead and had this leg created anyway. And in the meantime, immediately began applying for grants from non-profit organizations, hoping one would respond in time. When an email from The Heather Abbot Foundation, a non-profit created by a survivor of the Boston Marathon bombing, arrived in my inbox, I breathed a sigh of relief. They would cover the startling price-tag of my uninsured leg. Leaning over the edge of my bed, I grab the grey silicone liner that sits in a basket underneath my nightstand, and I put the tight layer over my residual limb. Hoisting the leg up and on to my bed, I inch my way toward the parallel bars, carrying the leg with me. It makes a loud "thud" as the foot hits the floor, and I slide my limb into the socket. Grabbing hold of each bar in front of me, I pull myself upwards until I'm in a standing position. Lifting my foot up and down, I check to ensure the socket is on tightly. My left limb is lamely to the side, covered in the bandages that prevent it from being able to wear a prosthesis of its own. A long mirror hangs on my wall at the end of these bars, and my reflection stares back at me, urging me to get to work.

I begin doing exercises that seem so simple that I had once rejected the idea that they would help me at all. Moving my leg from side to side. Kicking my leg backwards, and many others, each equally straightforward. One after the other, rep after rep, I fall into my routine with concentration.

Once I'm finished, I sit back on the edge of my bed, my face flushed, and I start to think of the tasks I should get done next. The rush of energy I get from exercise pushes me to continue, to move on to the next item on the to-do list. Inching back closer to my headboard, I reach for my laptop, which lies closed on my comforter, deciding to first check my email. There's a message from my stepdad, which takes me by surprise. It's the weekend, meaning he's at home, so an email is very unusual.

"I got this last night," it simply announces, with an attachment at the bottom—a letter from my lawyers.

I hate having to be the person who now has lawyers hired to assist her. It's gone against all of my natural instincts. Instincts that had never allowed me to stand up for myself. But then again, I'd never really needed to. Until now. This is different.

This letter today, was sent as a sort of farewell, as we have mutually decided to go our separate ways—them moving on to newer, and perhaps less challenging cases, and us deciding whether to search for another form of representation or accept the defeat. They've sent all the evidence of their work, so that it can be passed along if needed, and it is quite an extensive list, though no progress was made from any of it. Through no fault of their own.

I'll admit, when I lay in that hospital bed, realizing what had happened to me, I had perhaps been naïve enough to believe that the owner of this boat that had burst into flames beneath me, taking my limbs, my health, my life as I'd known it with it, would come running and shouting to where I was. To offer an apology, to ask what he could do, to try to make up for it in some small way, though we both would know this would never be possible.

I'd imagined him at home on that island, distressed over what had been done, pondering daily what he could do to ease the pain. Then, I had expected graciousness. I had desired kindness. I wished for recognition. Now I know that this was wishful thinking; none of this has been how it has gone. It was shocking to me, to realize that there were human beings out there who could ignore what had been done, who could go on with their lives as though nothing had happened.

I have put time and energy and emotion into this cause, pursuing the recognition no one offered, pursuing conversations no one wanted to have, and pursuing information no one wanted to share. My efforts have been met with silence.

My lawyers and I had worked in sync. We've both crafted emails and sent them into the abyss to never see a response. We've waited on hold for hours, after making calls to numbers we'd found through our research. I've been hung up on, and I'd guess those lawyers have been, too. I can recall the times I was laughed at over the phone, and how often I felt disrespected and belittled.

This letter, apart from being a farewell, reminds me now of some of the obstacles they'd encountered. Short, brief, and to-the-point paragraphs explain each one. There are some of the most powerful points, that stab through me and seem to rip my insides into pieces.

My lawyers had once scheduled a meeting with the owner of that boat company and his lawyer. Expecting to begin settlement negotiations, I had anxiously waited at home, while they flew from Florida to that island. Upon their arrival, they heard that he would not be showing up. It was a wasted trip, a waste of time, another stab to the heart and to the pride. Leaving me again feeling belittled, feeling dismissed, feeling despised and unimportant.

This letter reminds me that they haven't been allowed to even inspect that burnt vessel for themselves. None of us even knows its location. The boat burned atop those ocean waters and seems to have been quietly taken away to some undisclosed location. *Have they gotten rid of it?* I'd wondered. *Are they hiding something?* We were never granted the respect to bring a specialist of our own to try to determine the cause of events, to try to come to our own conclusions, or even just to take a look at the evidence of that day. The boat that I nearly died on has not once been shown to me or my legal representatives.

In fact, not only have we not seen the vessel in person, but the original photographs have been denied to us. We can see only the report that is available to the public, but not the original inspection.

There is also the frustrating legal conundrum: we cannot get jurisdiction to bring this case to the courts in the United States. This case can only be pursued in Bahamian courts. In the United States, lawyers commonly work on a contingency basis. That is, they can pursue their work and their efforts and follow any leads without billing for their hours spent. They are only compensated if the case is won. Such an arrangement allows people like me to hire a lawyer of their choosing without going broke, allows people like me to search for justice without emptying their bank accounts. In the Bahamas, lawyers cannot work on this basis. They charge by the hour, with spectacularly high hourly rates.

Another financial obstacle is one that was shocking to me. If someone does not own any assets in the Bahamas and wishes to bring a case to court, there is a fee. That fee can range in price, but to put it plainly, it's a number I would have never guessed.

In this letter are words that stand out to me. Words such as "stonewalling," "avoidance," and "blatant contempt," to describe how it seems my search and my plea for justice have been treated. These come with other terms such as "infuriating," "inhumane," and "insulting," referring to how I feel they have treated me.

I reach down to my large black prosthetic leg. Turning on the white cap that holds the suction system tight enough for the leg to stay in place, I feel the release of air as the cap comes loose. Sliding the heavy leg off, I slip it off my bed so that the rubber foot rests on the floor. I can't look at it.

My other leg is wrapped in a tan fabric-covered shrinking device, preparing the end for next week's surgery and the next prosthetic leg I will wear afterwards. I've lost count of what number surgery next week's will be. How do they not understand that this is what they have done to me? How can they all protect each other and not me? Why won't anyone stand up for me, for what is right?

I imagine all of them, sitting in the island sunshine, and wonder what they might be doing. Are they sitting at a beach bar, sipping their drinks and laughing? Are they socializing with friends or family, having already forgotten about the group of tourists from Vermont who visited their island? Once those flames had gone out and the smoke had cleared, were they able to go back to their lives, while I sit here staring down at both of my too-short legs and thinking about the life-long impacts those moments had on me?

Frozen in place, sitting against my headboard, I see those parallel bars staring back at me. I see them taunting me. As if using them every day is going to change anything at all. My heartbeat races, and I feel as though my palms should be shaking but they're perfectly still. I need an outlet for the emotions this letter has created. I feel like I know what I must do, and so I move across my bed, more quickly than before, until I'm in front of this frame once again. But I don't stand within them, instead, I reach forward.

The pieces of this therapeutic equipment are held together by large screws and knobs. Twisting and turning, and holding the heavy pieces up, I take the parallel bars apart. One metal piece crashes to the floor, and the piece beneath it begins to fall. I grab the next railing quickly, yanking it in a destructive manner, but end up scraping my hand on the metal edge. Muttering a curse beneath my breath, I try to stop the blood from flowing, and then move on.

I'm unbothered by the noise this process creates, as metal poles fall to my floor, screws pop loose, and pieces clash together. I'm sweaty, and that blood continues to drip across the back of my hand and onto the floor.

One piece won't come loose. I pull it rather than twisting as I know I need to. I start pushing it backwards and forwards, yanking on it and fighting it, wishing it would just break. Wanting to destroy everything. Finally, it comes loose and drops to the floor. Those deconstructed parallel bars lay in a pile on my floor.

Exhausted, I lean back, pleased to see the pieces in the mess I created. I sit still for a while longer, looking down at it, expecting to feel satisfaction. But I don't feel it;; I just feel hollow. With the stress released, I sigh, and I know what I must do again. I pick up the first piece from the floor. One-by-one, I slowly put the bars back together, until they stand tall once again.

CHAPTER 24

*I*n life, I have come to see that "it is what it is," and nothing more. It's a response I have given others as they recall pieces of my struggles, and when they take in my words, they think I am being cold, detached, or even possibly depressed. But I do not mean these words in a negative light. I speak them with acceptance. Often in life, we are handed what we are handed, our circumstances are what they are, but the unspoken remainder of that sentence is where I have found my power.

It is what it is, but only I can decide where I will go from there. The circumstances cannot be changed, but the future is unwritten, and so this is where I metaphorically pick up my pen and write the remainder.

This legal battle has been draining, but I am the only one who can choose to make today a day to refresh, to re-set, to clear my mind and move my body.

Every fiber of my being aches to be up and moving. My brain and body seem to remain at odds, one wishing to push me into motion, and the other pulling me backward with a refusal to heal. I'm now throwing myself into any physical activity I can find that doesn't require two legs, or even any at all.

"Are you going to be ready soon?" Mom asks.

"Yeah, just finishing getting dressed and then I'll be ready to leave," I answer, grabbing my new navy-blue Swix lightweight coat to put on over my thermal top.

My Lululemon gray fanny pack has my white headband in it, which I'll wear instead of a hat, and my long hair is pulled back into a high ponytail. I look in the floor-length mirror on my wall and think how ironic it is that my outfit is put together and perfectly matching, as if I know what I'm doing. I'm dressed far more professionally than my movements will prove me to be.

Today will be only my second time skiing, and my first time going outside of a lesson. I'm too afraid to go downhill skiing, despite living in Vermont and just a short drive away from both Killington and Pico—well-known and highly desired skiing locations—so instead we're going cross-country skiing today. These flat groomed trails are much less intimidating than those downward spirals down the steepest of cliffs.

I used to ski those mountains, so when I began aching to get back out in the fresh winter air, I had thought maybe I would go back. But fear had quickly set in. I thought about the steep trails, and trying to make my way down them without any legs.

"I've already broken nearly everything there is to break. I don't need to break anything else again," I'd explained, only half-joking, to everyone who encouraged me to get back out there.

Finding adaptive Nordic, or cross-country, skiing equipment has been challenging. Rather than simply needing skis and poles, I now need a sit ski, which is similar to a bucket propped up on a frame, connecting the skier to a pair of skis attached below you.

We'd driven to an adaptive center in New Hampshire to get fitted for this frame, and have rented it for the next two weeks. Too eager to wait, I'd asked my mom to go with me today.

I pull up next to the door to my car, put the locks on my wheelchair, and reach up to the ceiling. I pull myself up and on to the seat, and we head up to Killington. Past the popular mountain, there's a separate area on the left for snowshoeing and cross-country skiing. This is where we pull in. I sit and wait in the car while my mom goes in and gets her ski rentals, since the building is accessible only by going up a set of stairs. Looking down at my legs, I feel the familiar frustration that comes with waiting, at another place I can't get into.

Transferring back into my wheelchair, I sit outside, ready to get started. It feels freeing to breathe in the fresh mountain air.

Pushing on the arms of my chair, I lift myself up into the air, move toward the sit ski, and sit into the small black frame. I finish tightening the straps on each side until I'm snugly sitting inside, and then I realize that we're about to start, and I have no idea what I'm doing. I pick up my poles, hesitantly push down into the snow, and feel a flutter of surprise when I glide forwards. *I can do this,* I tell myself. We ski out of the parking lot and over to the start of the trail and pause once more. There's a long, steep hill looking at me. The start of the trail, I realize.

"I don't know how to do hills."

"She said to lean forward and put your poles in the snow to slow down, right?" Mom asks.

"I think so, let me try," I say, leaning down.

As my body moves into a tucked position, the position that I think is supposed to slow me down, the shifting movement instead pushes me forward. I'm now tucked over, in a position that seems to be giving me momentum, and I'm flying down the hill. Gathering speed now, I try to sit up and stop myself. Trying to slow myself down, my arms extend to the sides, searching for a brake that I know doesn't exist. Nothing seems to be working, and there's a turn ahead of me. The widest tree stands just an inch from the side of the trail and grows larger as I get closer. I'm going to crash!

Instinct takes over, and I lean to the side. My skis begin to turn, and that tree disappears from view. Then the turn gets too sharp, sending me flying onto my right shoulder, the bucket frame still attached. Lying on my shoulder, the bucket-frame and skis stick up in the air, and I look behind me to my mom who's still up on the top of the hill.

"Well, I've gotten my first fall out of the way!" I shout while laughing.

We quickly realize that skiing in Killington, Vermont, the place that has impressive alpine ski mountains, and where nowhere is actually flat, may not have been the best place to begin cross-country skiing. We go from uphill, to downhill, savoring the brief moments of flat skiing. I sweat as I work my way uphill, digging my poles into the snow, as I use my core and my arms to pull myself up inch-by-inch, wishing I had the leg muscles everyone else uses to ski, as I feel the burn in my arms.

We've been trying to make it to the nearby lake. The lake will be a large, open, flat area. Great for skiing, but it's farther away than we'd thought. I see it now, though, and think we've finally made it. There's only one more hill to go down to get there. Mom takes her skis off, holding on to the sides of my frame, easing me down the beginning part that is the steepest. She lets go, and I speed down the rest of it on my own, feeling like I'm flying.

I've finally figured out how to turn around each curve with only the changing angle of my body and the tapping of ski poles. I hear my mom yell with excitement as she sees I've made it around each turn, and I sit to wait so she can follow down and meet me here.

We've finally made it to the lake. I can finally just ski without worry. Once my mom is at the bottom of the hill with me, I push down once more and start my way across. Mom waits behind, capturing the beauty of our surroundings by taking pictures and videos on my phone. I'm gaining speed and in love with this feeling. The feeling of hard work, pushing myself across the groomed tracks of snow, combined with the excitement that comes with the thrill of this newly found sport.

I'm distracted, looking around at the blue sky, the tall evergreen trees, and the snow-covered lake, until I look back down. There's a trench in front of me, one made of snow that's melted and turned into thick ice. It's just a few inches wide, but it's wide enough for my ski to get caught in. I already know what's going to happen.

In seemingly slow motion, I'm falling over again. I feel it happening, but I can't stop it. I'm laughing at myself before I've even hit the ground. My right shoulder, once again, falls into the snow. I'm not sure why this one is so funny to me. Maybe it's because it's probably my fifth fall already today. The first fall I had thought would be my last, but each time I've gone downhill I gain too much speed, tipping over on to the same side. It's as though this bucket frame of mine has turned this day into an extreme version of sledding, and this cross-country ski trail has instead turned into a crash course.

Maybe it's because I'd been on a flat surface as I fell this time. Maybe it's because I had hit the one icy trench in the whole wide area. *Of course, that would be my luck,* I think. Laughing at everything that's happened to me recently, teaching me that I seem to be the unluckiest person.

But whatever the reason, I laugh harder than I have yet today. Probably harder than I ever have before, and I feel a tear sneak out of the corner of my eye. I lie there staring up at the clear blue sky, not a single cloud in sight, and I close my eyes, saying a quick prayer to whoever might be out there listening. Thanking them for today. Thanking them for me still being alive, able to have experienced today. Joy grabs my soul, bringing me happiness so pure that it has brought tears to my eyes. I'm lying on my back, tight straps stretching across my legs, keeping me inside this sit ski frame, and yet I feel freer than I ever have before.

I never would've tried this if I hadn't been through what I've experienced. Another item is added to that mental list of all that I have gained.

I think back to the self-conscious young girl I'd been before I was injured. The girl who had cared too much about what people thought about her to ever try something new, let alone try something so obviously different from everyone else. Just the idea of getting into a sit ski would have terrified me, let alone letting myself fly down these hills, falling onto the ground, or pushing myself slowly up each climb with all of my strength, as others who could stand went up them with ease.

I think back to the heartbreak I had felt as I'd looked down at the scars stretching tightly over each inch of my body. As I'd looked down at my legs, ending too soon, and how one of the worst parts had been knowing that I would never be the same again. I could never be "normal" in the sense that I could look the same as other girls my age, or wear the same clothes, and blend in with those around me. But lying here, with my arms stretched out beside me, digging into the snow, and a tear on my face from laughing too hard, I wish that I had known then what I know now. That being different would bring me more happiness than I had ever known.

Keeping my eyes on the sky, I wait until my mom gets to where I am so that she can pick me back up to a sitting position, and I can try this once again.

Just as it had been with biking, I felt the hook of this sport finding a firm hold within me right away. Except this sport, I knew already, is by far my favorite. Everyone keeps telling me, *If you like skiing, you've really got to get back up on the mountain. It's such a thrill!* To which I respond that *this* is my thrill.

Perhaps I always would have loved this sport the most, or maybe it's something about finding myself living in a constant battle that's created a stubbornness that feels right at home on these trails. When I met my first coach in this sport, she put it perfectly, saying to me: "It's not a sport that's for everyone. It's a *different* type of person who falls in love with this." She'd said it with a smile.

It was a smile that seemed to suggest a story, a tale of her own stubborn nature and her own determination, as she was one of those "different people" who felt the same high as she dug her poles into these frozen trails, with no decline or gravity to push her forward. Chasing the thrill that arrives not from a moment of extreme speed, but from winning a small victory with each inch you push forward.

That same coach had right away reached out to the Paralympic coaches for the United States Nordic team. She'd looked at me, studying my body, and I nearly laughed as she commented on something that had nothing at all to do with my missing legs or scars or the news of my shattered spine. She told me I looked strong. I'd felt a familiar rush of pride—the type I'd always craved from all my coaches in my life.

"They're going to love you," she'd said to me as she handed me her business card. Within days, my inbox held an introductory email. Then, without delay, a brand-new sit ski, with its very own

"U.S. Paralympic" sticker plastered on the side, arrived on my front door—a rental for the next seasons to come.

Now, it was still quite obvious that I had neither the physical strength, commitment, nor skill of someone who would normally be in contact with a coach of a Paralympic team. I didn't try to kid myself that I had any of those requirements either. But still, quite simply, it was this quiet introduction, the sticker on this equipment, that was the first knock on the door, opening my eyes to all the possibility that still remains in this life. I'd thought I could never regain any of the past pieces of myself, one of which was that I had been an athlete. All this told me that if I want it badly enough, I can again see myself as this athlete once more.

For now, this sport is a simple way to exercise, to feel good, and to laugh and join in with those around me. It's a way to not feel that overhead label of "disabled" and simply be me. It's a way to chase goals and feel that familiar fire of competition.

Today, with this new and quite beautifully shaped bucket-frame and skis, my mom and I make our way up to Burlington to try out some new trails. The difference between today and our last attempt is clear right from the beginning. The equipment is loaded up faster, our layers of clothing on quicker, and I sit in the driver's seat with my mom beside me looking far less stressed today than the last nerve-wracking attempt.

As we pull into this parking lot and begin to get ready, we each take notice of a rare sight around here. Parked to the side of us is another SUV, with a wheelchair left by the door. A moment later, we see the owner of the vehicle, as a man in his own sit ski, glides toward us.

He introduces himself, and within five minutes of talking, I've gotten what seems a much-needed lesson. He pushes his pole into the ice, and with a twist of his core, shows me how to turn my ski frame sharply—something I had clearly not known how to do last time. We wave goodbye, and with a push of my poles, I glide forward into the trails.

These trails are dazzling. The snow glistens against the rays of sun like rows of diamonds beneath me. There are no trees—or much at all—around us, and the white hills seem to expand for miles. In the first stretch, something feels different about today. It's as though, strangely enough, I actually know what I'm doing.

My family skis beside me, and I dip in and out of the grooves, choosing when to keep my skis within the freshly made pathways and when I want to be out in the wide-open space. The hills are long, and send my ski flying forward, but I angle my body and quickly push up and down with my pole, keeping myself from toppling over. Rounding each edge time and time again. I sweat as I climb my way up each incline, the sun beating down on me, and then glide across each stretch of flat land.

As we pull back up to the cars, mom and I look at each other, our eyes sparkling. We did it! Neither of us fell, and she hadn't had to spend the day dragging me up each hill and guiding me down each decline. We'd just skied, and exercised, and laughed, and every moment had been perfect. "What a day," we say to each other.

The view is breathtaking as we make our way out of the wooded trails. We turn the heat on and strip off our extra layers as we sit back inside the car. Not ready to put this day behind us quite yet, we head to my aunt and uncle's house. Inside, we sit around the living room, and she serves us steaming hot homemade soup and a glass of red wine.

It's not until many hours later, the evening sky darkened and the moon on full display, that we sit back in the car, ready to drive home. Dreaming of our beds and soft blankets, ready to rest from the tiring day we've had.

What a day.

CHAPTER 25

I'd gone into surgery for my above-knee amputation prepared for a six-to-eight-week recovery. But as this time was coming to an end, that ugly wound appeared upon my left limb, the opposite leg that was meant to be healing. I went to our local wound-care clinic seemingly every other day. To the point where the staff recognized the sound of my voice over the phone before any introduction, and a day not spent there nearly felt strange.

Every healing agent and every changed bandage hadn't seemed to help at all. I tried everything from pharmaceutical creams to Manuka honey and remedies made of wildflower. Only physical activity had been the closest to a fix that I could find, as exercise seemed to increase blood flow below my spinal injury, rejuvenating my limb, and afterwards, I would see a slightly more hopeful sight. But even so, it was never close to enough.

This is when I'd returned to the familiar office on the orthopedic trauma floor in Massachusetts General Hospital. With my longtime surgeon, whom I trusted now nearly more than anyone else, we created a plan. Step one was to have surgery. Then, step two was to have one more. And then, I had another. From operating table to home, and back again, I seemed to go in the pattern that now ruled my life. I've now had more than 40 surgeries since that day. But the wound was stitched closed, my knee joint cleared of scar tissue, and my thigh severed with a surgical incision.

After that final surgery, as I began to heal once more, I lay in bed in my typical post-surgical fashion—with a tall glass of ice-water beside me, a bandaged limb propped upon the pillows stacked high, my eyes closed, and my mind settled within the clouds of drugged delusion. The days passed by, as they always do. Eventually, my brain came back down from those clouds and returned to reality, and I realized one extraordinary fact: *I'm all done.*

I'm all done, my mind repeated once more. Done with the surgeries, done with this routine that brings so much pain and so many pauses to my life. Done being taken apart and put back together again. My chest cracked wide with the satisfaction of it all. My head fell back until it rested against my headboard. My arms lifted into the air, and then crashed downwards, landing with my palms gripping the sides of my face and covering my eyes. I'm all done. I've made it.

I began to think over these last months and years, since that one day in June that started this all. It has been painful, and it has been chaotic. I've bled more than I knew I could and cried more than I thought I should. But in between those moments, moments of pain and deep-red blood and salty tears, that is where life became worth living once again.

Of course, I will always grieve what could have been, and what I have lost. And this will never change. I will always wonder who I might have become and where I would have gone if that vacation had been only a vacation and nothing more. If I'd left with only a suntan, and nothing else changed. I'll forever imagine that other version of myself, creating an extraordinary life for her, too, and I'll wish she'd had the chance to make these thoughts true. But I will also celebrate the reality. Celebrating the life that is changed, but well-lived. The life that I have, and appreciate now.

Though I believe the grief will never fully disappear, I seem to have grown around it, until it's become smaller in the distance, blocking it from view with moments of joy and mountains of success and pride. It's now a feeling to remember, but not to drown within. A loss to memorialize, but to move on from. To learn from. To grow from. Because in that earlier life and that earlier version of me, I had not been scarred or injured or missing any pieces, but I had been broken all the same. Broken in ways I have healed from now.

I had been quiet and agreeable, dismissive and insecure, forgettable and not nearly as strong. Battling with the inner demons of wanting to be carefree and at ease, but instead skating through life with only silence and a smile. Doing everything possible to blend in, to be the same, and to never be noticed. Then I woke up, to a body that seemed to cage me in, and hold me back, with changes that had been forced upon me. Not yet knowing that it would be these physical limitations that would, at last, allow me to soar free, and it would be these differences that would allow me to stand in my own light, to grow comfortable with my reflection.

The speeches that I now give, to crowds who sit before me, granted me a voice. As if I'd gone back in time and picked up that young, insecure girl, terrified to ever speak in a classroom or to any crowd, and put her right in the front and center of the room. Because that young girl had grown, and speaks now with confidence in who she is, and in who she is becoming. I speak now with the voice I had always been terrified to possess.

Those many hours I've spent biking, on a handcycle with that flag that blows tall in the wind behind me, with the purpose of alerting others to my presence, gave me a new perspective. I remember the first time I'd used that bike. It hadn't been the ride ahead that made me anxious. It hadn't been the miles to come, or the fear of trying something new. It had been that flag—that brightly colored flag—that made my heart race. Because I knew that others would notice me. Others would see me. But as I felt the challenge, and I felt the blisters on my palms and the soreness of my muscles, I felt strength and not weakness. Because I felt strong, I felt worthy to be seen.

And that bike allows me to see a clear view of the ground that passes beneath me. I see the colors of it turning to a blur as my palms work those pedals. Showing me that I am in control. I decide how far I go. How fast I go, when I rest, when I begin again, and which route I pursue. I am in control of my path, my route, my bike ride, my life.

And then, there is all that I have learned from my favorite activity, the sport that brings the days and the moments that have given me the purest joy. When the harshly cold air slaps my face but warms my soul. When I drive to my favorite spot, as thick snowflakes fall to the evergreen trees. The days the sport of cross-country skiing thrills me for hours.

Skiing taught me to fall, to adjust, and how to keep moving forward. With the simple tapping of my poles, the shifting of my body, I round the turn that looms before me. When I tuck myself into a rounded position, I gain speed. When I dig my poles into the frozen ground, I slow until my movements are intentional and careful.

Sometimes I arrive to trails with freshly groomed snow, and my skis fit perfectly in the grooves made that morning. Other times, the terrain is rough, bumpy, icy—challenging. But no matter what the conditions, choppy or smooth; no matter what my energy level, drained or ready for competition; no matter if I am at a part of the trail with an incline, steep decline, sharp turn, or those beloved flat stretches; one movement always remains the same. I always continue forward. And I do so by adjusting to what is before me, by responding to the changes in terrain, and by never giving up or turning back.

Skiing taught me this: sometimes you climb, fall, soar, stumble, adjust—it is all a part of life.

And those moments in the hospital, when I claimed to feel pieces of myself chipping away, I know now that that was instead the painful process of allowing my brokenness to heal me. It was the hard shell of protection that I'd created day-by-day, year-by-year, finally breaking way. It was being left vulnerable, exposed, and raw. But it was through the torn-away modesty and the ripped-away privacy, through the loss of comfort and the loss of the self I had always known, that I was able to step into someplace new, places I had never been before and places I had never known existed. Stepping out of my comfort zone and embracing change. Seeing now, that I must accept myself fully, for the very first time. I had always thought it would be uncomfortable, painful even, to be anything but the same as all those around me. But I know now that true comfort comes only from being your own.

I have been healing. Not only in the physical sense, with the incisions and wounds and infection and damage, but far beyond that alone. Recovery for me came from accepting that it would never only be about how many steps I would one day be able to take and which walking aide I would use to get there, but that it would be about how far I would push myself to go. How much I could love myself, how much I could give back, how much I could experience and learn and see. Recovery meant waking up each morning and smiling at the sun, ignoring the prosthetic legs that sat beneath the window sill, and stepping into the day without a worry in my mind. It has meant learning to live with legs or without them on, with a wheelchair or with crutches, with others beside me or even moments spent alone.

Recovering is growing and changing, and loving each phase.

CHAPTER 26

*I*t's my twenty-fourth birthday today.

It's a strange feeling, celebrating a birthday when in the back of your mind you are counting *each* extra day that you would have never gotten to experience if one day had ended differently. If that fifty-fifty chance of me waking up again had landed on the other side of the coin.

These past two years, my birthdays have been simple. There were no extravagant parties or adventurous plans. They have been filled with quiet moments with family, close friends, and even my medical professionals joining in to simply celebrate a day of life. They have also brought me the most joy, as all I yearn for now is a moment of peace, an untroubled evening.

I started the day with physical therapy. I was the only patient in the building today, and I worked one-on-one with my longtime therapist, Kate. We went from machine to machine, our movements falling into sync with the familiarity of each other and of these routines. She comments on the progress we've made, and how much different today's session is from when we first started working together.

We ended with walking outside, practicing walking on different surfaces, and the sun shone down, in a rare and treasured moment of warmth. It was the perfect way to start the day.

My dad and I head to the local store, and pick up packets of seeds to plant in the raised garden beds my stepdad, Paul, will soon be creating for me, an addition that seems to actually add to the charm of our modern-farmhouse-style home. They will be at a height that I can easily reach as I stand, with handles on each side so I can hold on tight for balance.

Back home again, I take a long shower, rinsing off the sweat from today's work and savor the fresh cleanliness. Music fills the bathroom, and I'm cheerful as I put my hair up into a towel to dry and tie my softest bathrobe around my waist. I wheel myself across the hallway, and back into my bedroom, keeping the music playing. I hear the front door open, I hear the soft, recognizable sound of Mom stepping up each stair, as she comes to sit with me in my room.

Her phone rings. It's an incoming call from a phone number that we recognize. We've attempted to work with two different law firms so far, hoping that eventually someone will have success with our case. The first firm was well-known in Ft. Lauderdale, Florida, the second was a lawyer from New York. Both groups have run into the same roadblocks, the same lack of information, and lack of cooperation. Neither had made any progress. My aunt is an attorney in Boston. She's put us in touch with some of the best firms in the city. We spoke with a man yesterday, sent him all the information to review, and now he's calling back.

"This isn't a case that I would pursue," he simply says.

We'd been expecting that.

"It's a devastating case, and I won't even begin to go into the pain you must be feeling, but there are just too many obstacles here."

I suppose we had known he was probably going to say that, too. The conversation was short, simple, and to the point. We hang up and I feel no surprise at how this conversation has just gone. It had been more of a formality to reach out to him, another box checked off on our long list, allowing us to feel as though we have tried everything we possibly could.

"I found the phone number of the Bahamian Police, the one that they gave us. Why don't we call them and at least check in on the criminal case?" Mom asks me.

The men and women from the Bahamian Police had flown all the way to my hospital in Massachusetts, so perhaps we'll have more luck with them. The phone rings and continues to ring. No one answers. I ask my mom if maybe we misdialed. She double-checks and tries once more. The phone rings, and this time someone answers it. But there is a long silence.

"Hello... this is Stacey Bender, is anyone there?" she asks.

There's no response. But we both have the eerie feeling that someone is there silently listening. We sit tensely on my bed, looking at each other strangely, wondering what is going on.

"Hello," she repeats.

Three deafening sounds play back to us. The sound of someone disconnecting the phone line. The sound of whoever answered our call realizing who we were and choosing to hang up the phone. Choosing to end the conversation before it even began.

"They just hung up on us," we say to each other at the same time, our voices full of disbelief.

I look down at my phone now. Sometime earlier today, probably while I was showering, I'd missed a call from another number that I recognize. It was someone from the United States Embassy in Nassau, Bahamas. I have an email from her, too. I had previously reached out to her, asking for assistance in hopes to get the Bahamian Police to cooperate, to let us see the boat, and to get my medical records. I read my email first.

"Even the United States Embassy can't get a response from them," I tell my mom.

I send back a quick email, trying to convey my disappointment as I inform them that no law firm is able to represent us without any information being given to us. Reminding her that just next month, Bahamian law states that our statute of limitations will come into effect. By this date, any claim we have, any information we may find, will be useless. We won't be able to pursue our case. We had known they might try and stall until this date arrived; I just hadn't thought they would actually be able to succeed. I hadn't thought that in today's modern age something like this could be possible.

After that day, it will feel to me as if everything that I have suffered no longer matters. But I suppose, to them, it has never mattered at all.

I expected to feel rage, and I do feel it simmering quietly behind the wall I have built around my heart. I push it away, not willing to let myself feel that again. Instead, I will focus on the good. That's all I will focus on today. I will focus on one more beautiful day of life and my family all coming together. I'm taken by surprise, as a feeling of peace comes over me. Knowing that in just eight weeks from today, I can stop tiring myself with these thoughts. In eight weeks, the fight will be lost, and though that may be devastating, it is a desired end to this seemingly never-ending war.

I have been trying to take on an entire island, an entire country. I have found allies to fight alongside me, and yet the other side is always greater. Their laws protect them, and I believe they know it. I didn't get hurt in the United States where we are protected and valued. I got hurt in the Bahamas, a place where, I now have found, you do not want to get injured. A place where, no matter what might happen to you, you will be seen as only a tourist, someone who comes and then goes; someone who is forgotten.

Of course, I can't speak for the entire country, or even this whole island of Exuma. Yet, how can I not feel as I do, when so many have acted as they have? I feel as though they got what they needed from us; they got our money from our tourism. I feel as though they saw my family and me as a source of revenue, rather than as human beings. I feel as though they saw us as greedy Americans, who they wanted to disappear so they could forget that day ever happened. It seems to me that they want their lives to be unaffected, their business unaffected, and their tourism unaffected, and they are willing to leave me to figure out my life on my own so that it can remain this way. They are willing to change my life drastically without stepping up to make it the slightest bit easier. They are willing to leave me suffering, without ever even apologizing.

I have to remind myself that I know it is not all of them that have acted in these ways. There have been those on this island who did try to stand up for me, as they made anonymous phone calls to my lawyers. I have been told stories of those who chose not to simply forget what happened, and how they banded together to pray for my healing. I know of those young men who stepped in in my greatest time of need, climbing aboard our damaged boat and finding me beneath that pile. I know all of this. I will choose to focus on this. Again, I push those first, uglier, thoughts away. The fight is over. It's time to surrender.

I head downstairs, dressed in a silky black short-sleeve top and a pair of new jeans. I grab my crutches and walk into the kitchen. My mom stands by the kitchen island, her hair pulled up into a loose clip on the back of her head, framing her petite face. She's dicing fresh mangos to create perfectly refreshing mango margaritas. My beloved Grammy retrieves ingredients from the fridge, and a homemade raspberry pie sits off to the side in celebratory preparation. My dad has just walked in the door from the back deck, a birthday card in hand. Paul greets him and offers him a drink. My sister follows behind me, and now we are all together, in this perfect group. There it is—a moment of ease, a moment of peace.

I'm filled with an overwhelming sensation of joy in its simplest form. Laughter and pleasant conversation fill the walls of our home. Looking at us, at this carefree image of celebrating another birthday, no one would know all that we have endured, all that we survived. That to me is the most beautiful part of life, our ability to move on, to adapt, and to return to a state of peaceful harmony. Our basic human ability to heal. The idea that despite all of the pain and the suffering in this world, our happiness is still contingent upon our efforts and our choices is a wonderful thing.

ABOUT THE AUTHOR

Stefanie Schaffer is a survivor, debut author, public speaker, and ambassador to many organizations including the non-profit of the American Red Cross. With a Bachelor of Science from Castleton University, where she graduated with High Honors and a degree in Health Promotion, Stefanie has prioritized working with and amplifying the efforts of organizations that aim to improve the physical and mental health of communities. As a Vermont native, she has always had a love for the outdoors, and she can often be found on the local bike trails, cross-country ski trails, or on a long stroll with her Golden Retriever companion, Oliver.

SALES PAGE

Facebook: Stefanie Schaffer
Instagram: @stefanieschafferrr
Website: www.stefanieschaffer.com

Giving a Voice to Creativity!

With every donation, a voice will be given to
the creativity that lies within the hearts of
our children living with diverse challenges.

By making this difference, children that may
not have been given the opportunity to have their
Heart Heard will have the freedom to create
beautiful works of art and musical creations.

Donate by visiting

HeartstobeHeard.com

We thank you.

Made in United States
North Haven, CT
05 January 2023

30653969R00171